SPIT AND SAWDUST

The Story of a Dolgarn Pub
formed
Cordon Bleu' Cook
Licencee
and
Entrepreneur

SPIT AND SAWDUST

The Story of a Fighter Pilot
turned
'Cordon Bleu' Cook
Licensee
and
Restaurateur

WING COMMANDER GEORGE (NEDDY) NELSON-EDWARDS
DFC, MA, RAF (Ret'd.)

NEWTON

First Published in Great Britain by
Air Forces Publishing Service (1995)
P.O.Box 236, Swindon, Wiltshire SN3 6QZ

Copyright © George Nelson-Edwards (1995)

ISBN   1 872308 53 8

British Library Catloguing-in-Publication Data. A catalogue record for the book is available from the British Library.

All rights reserved. No part of this publication may be produced, stored in a retrieval system, or transmitted, in any form, or by any means, electronic, mechanical, photocopying, recording or otherwise, without the prior permission of the publishers.

This book is sold subject to the condition that it shall not, by way of trade or otherwise, be lent, re-sold, hired out or otherwise circulated without the publisher's prior consent in any form and without a similar condition, including this condition, being imposed on the subsequent purchaser.

Printed and bound in Great Britain by Bookcraft (Bath) Ltd.

ACKNOWLEDGEMENTS

First and foremost I acknowledge the support and help unstintingly given by Charles and Loulla Dickie, Directors of Boadicea Travel Ltd, and the Travel Club, Paphos, for granting me the full and free use of their Company's premises and office facilities.

My grateful thanks go to Barbara Brown who spent countless laborious hours of her free time at the word processor.

I pay special tribute to photographer Bernard Cox, late of Ivor Fields (Photography) Ltd., Oxford, who went to great lengths entirely without charge to renovate and update many of the illustrations.

My warmest thanks to the following:- (surnames in alphabetical order)
'Jo' Allum
W M Benn, World Ship Society, Exmouth
Michael Charlesworth OBE
Shirley Daniel, The Bookshop, Haverfordwest
George Haile
Rosemary Jones, Books & Book Finding, Llandysul
John G Kearney (USA
Pat Lelliott
Beryl Pinnington
Olive Round MBE
Donald Stones DFC & Bar, Squadron Leader RAF (Retd.)
David Watkins
Frank Wootton

Last but not least I am deeply indebted to my old friend and Oxford University Air Squadron contemporary Air Chief Marshal Sir Christopher Foxley-Norris GCB, DSO, OBE, RAF (Retd.) for jeopardizing his good name by writing the Foreword to this book.

DEDICATION

As the Battle of Trafalgar in 1805 put fresh heart into the British people at the very moment of disaster upon the Continent, so the Battle of Britain in 1940 came at a time when the land mass of Europe was about to be subjugated by the evil genius of Adolf Hitler.

This book is dedicated to all those brave men and women of the Services who were ready to lay down their lives that Freedom should triumph over infamy.

FOREWORD

Air Chief Marshal Sir Christopher Foxley-Norris
GCB, DSO, MA, RAF (Ret'd.)

This book written by George Nelson-Edwards, my good friend for fifty years, is not just another Fighter Pilot's expanded Combat Report. It if were, one might be excused for sighing "Oh no, not another one," because there have been dozens of these which scarcely get the reader out of the cockpit of the Spitfire - or indeed the Messerschmitt.

Rather this is a story of a period, and of a group of individuals participating in it to the full. Hindsight may try to convince us that we joined the University Air Squadrons and the Auxiliary Air Force because we saw the inevitability of war and wanted to be prepared for it. I take leave to doubt this. The real motives were the desire to fly, the excitement and indeed the glamour of piloting an aircraft, the comradeship and pride in being a member of an elite. We joined because it was all great fun; and when the real thing came, well, at least we were partly although still quite inadequately trained to handle it.

Survival was the name of the game, and the odds against it were high, especially through long periods of combat. George Nelson-Edwards survived, often by the skin of his teeth and managed to inflict considerable damage on the enemy. He retained his extrovert, sometimes Rabelaisian joie de vivre throughout his RAF Service and beyond it. His later activities as Chef, Publican and Hotelier make just as interesting reading as his Service career. I am confident that any reader, whether ex-RAF or not, will agree.

C N Foxley-Norris

Tumble Wood
Northend Common
Henley-on-Thames
Oxon
England

PREFACE

It may be helpful to offer a short explanation of my Christian names and how I came by them.

I was christened 'George Hassall'. Until I joined my first Fighter Squadron I was invariably called 'Hal', an unofficial abbreviation of 'Hassall' which was also my father's name. Two 'Hassalls' in one household was one too many so the family settled for 'Hal', yet because of the confusion or maybe to add to the confusion I was frequently called 'Buster' by family and friends alike.

Thus and an early age I could never be quite sure what my real Christian name was. The story of how I came to be called 'Neddy' is told in this book. As if to pile on the agony I discovered when I married in 1941 that I had acquired a brother-in-law called 'Hal' so the family, especially on my wife's side, resorted to 'Hassall'.

The first three or four years of peace found me being called 'Hal', 'Neddy', 'Hassall' and even sometimes 'Buster' whenever I bumped into old childhood acquaintants, not that there were many of them left.

In 1950 I took the bull by the horns and announced that from then on I was to be known as 'George', and easy name to remember for everyone, even the most dimwitted, so 'George' it has been ever since.

Finally I apologise in advance for any inaccuracies arising from references to individuals mentioned in this book. Conducting long-range research and relying on memory whilst living in Cyprus has its drawbacks.

It is sad to relate that George Nelson-Edwards is no longer with us. Whilst he spent many years writing and compiling his book, he passed away after a short illness on 21st September, 1994. It is a pity that he will not be in a position to finally appreciate the result of his work.

P N E.

PROLOGUE

Looking up I saw an arm reaching out towards a small corner cupboard, my vision partly obscured by steam rising up around my head and bare shoulders. I felt stunned as if struck by a blow from the padded glove of a heavyweight boxer.

Where was I? What on earth was I doing in a bath? I tried to lick my parched lips, my tongue tasting like a strip of sandpaper dredged with a block of cooking salt. I had never had a hangover like this before, I thought, it must have been one helluva party.

A hand appeared, fingers clasped round a bottle, other fingers around the neck untwisting a cork. Thank God, I said to myself, here comes the hair of the dog and not before time! I heard the cork pop out but before I could so much as protest the hand tilted the bottle and poured the contents from above and around me into the bath. Brandy fumes merged with the steam, catching my throat as I gasped for breath.

There followed an unbelievable feeling of calm and serenity spreading through my fibres. I lay back totally relaxed, for the first time I was able to take in my surroundings - even the idea of drinking some of the bath water flashed through my mind.

It was starting to come back now. I remember somehow, but don't ask me how, flicking over and falling out of my shattered Hurricane, being jolted in the crutch by the sudden spreading of the parachute canopy, then the abrupt plunge into the sea, down and down endlessly, until at last I popped up like a cork, mouth and lungs filled with sea water. After what seemed like an eternity I remember strong hands pulling me aboard a ship's lifeboat, stripping off my sodden uniform and wrapping me in blankets. It was already dark. A heavy swell was on so they hoisted me aboard the mother ship in a net. I knew now that by some miracle I had been snatched from a watery grave.

As I lay in the bath I even started to ponder on the probability of such an event. My chances must have been less than pulling off a jackpot on the Football Pools. I began to relive the last few minutes before I baled out. I was flying right up the backside of a Heinkel III, pumping bullets into its belly when, to my horror, I spotted out of the corner of my eyes the deadly shadows of two more Heinkels, one on my left, the other on my right, creeping up alongside me no more than a few yards away, each letting fly a devastating crossfire. The Hurricane was hit and holed everywhere as I dived almost vertically downwards, expecting the aircraft to disintegrate at any second. Petrol was streaming from the wing tanks, the engine cowling twisted, the three-bladed propeller jerking back and forth like some bizarre catherine wheel about to fly off its pivot, the cockpit filled with fumes and smoke emitting a sickly smell of petrol and cordite.

Something had struck my left foot and my knee leapt up almost hitting my chin. I gingerly started to ease back on the stick, thank God I felt a positive response and managed to level off in an unsteady glide nearly stalling the aircraft. There was no answer from the ailerons, I could see both were distorted and buckled. Rudder and elevator were still effective, at least for the moment, affording me limited flying control. What should I do next, bale out into nothingness? I was over a vast expanse of ocean and down to less than twelve thousand feet.

I decided I might as well hang on. I headed eastwards knowing that land was way out of my reach, all that I could see through the gathering haze and scattered low cloud was a limitless spread of green-grey sea.

I remember being told by a World War I veteran that at first one seldom felt pain, so I idly thought perhaps without knowing it my foot might have been shot off. I didn't dare look.

So this was the end, I thought, so this is what it is like, a slow lingering death with ample time to ruminate on life, loved ones, and innumerable sins. In a dream I saw a column of dirty brown smoke rising up in front of me like smoke from a country cottage chimney.

Then I dropped out.

CONTENTS

	Page
Acknowledgements	iii
Dedication	iv
Foreword	v
Preface	vi
Prologues	vii
List of Contents	ix
List of Illustrations	x

CHAPTER		
1	Pubs, Dreams and Public School	1
2	First Blood to the British	10
3	The 'Dark Blue Days'	17
4	Summer Camp Scenario	28
5	The 'Stizkrieg'	32
6	The Stiffkey Connection	36
7	'We Never Closed'	46
8	Slotted in at last	51
9	The Luftwaffe stokes it up	60
10	Spitfire Conversion	85
11	Spearhead to North Africa	93
12	Back to Blighty	108
13	Next stop Normandy	118
14	Cornish Intermission	137
15	Another Flying Start	144
16	Landlord in Absentia	160
17	Landlord in Situ	167
18	One for the Road	179
	Postscript	185
	Bibliography	187
	Copy of Extract *from:* 'Men of the Battle of Britain' by Kenneth G WYNN.	188
	Appendix	189

ILLUSTRATIONS

The Author	Top back cover
Pamela Davidson 1936	Facing page 32
Shrewsbury School Soccer 1937	ditto
Oxford University Air Squadron 1939	Facing page 33
Freshmen - Brasenose College, 1937	Facing page 60
RAF Pembrey No. 79 Squadron, 1940	Facing page 61
CFS Students visit to BAC Filton	Facing page 62
CFS RAF Little Rissington, 1947	ditto
GHNE & Pan - Investiture Buckingham Palace, 1946	Facing page 63
George & Pan at dinner dance RAF Club, 1949	ditto
No. 93 (Spitfire) Squadron 1942	Facing page 100
Belgian and Free French pilots conversion, 1941	ditto
F86 'Sabre' Conversion Course RAF Wildenrath, 1956	Facing page 101
Tactical Air Exercise BAOR, 1953	ditto
No. 8 Flying College Course	Facing page 144
Day Fighter Leaders Course March 1953	ditto
No. 26 NATO Transport Support Course, December 1959	Facing page 145
Group of past CO's of Oxford University Air Squadron	Facing page 160
Visit to BAC, Filton, 1956	Facing page 161
CFS Reunion Dinner, 1966	ditto
GHNE at Pantry Restaurant, Newport, 1970	Facing page 178
'Beer & Sandwich' serving competition, 1966	ditto

CHAPTER ONE

PUBS, DREAMS AND PUBLIC SCHOOLS

For some curious reason I have always loved pubs. Nothing unusual about that, I have spent a good third of my life in them. When I was young, perhaps ten or eleven years old, I realised pubs were something quite apart from ordinary houses. People entered them one way and came out different, as if someone had waved a magic wand and cast a spell over them, like the Fairy Godmother used to do in the Christmas Pantomime years ago; so pubs held a deep seated fascination for me.

As far back as I can remember my father used to let me drink the top off his beer out of his silver tankard at our Sunday dinner table. Mother would frown but say nothing. I recall how my father would come out of the pub with a strange look on his face, his breath smelling of that sweet/sour fragrance of hops.

When I was twelve years old I entered my first pub. It was a small thatched ivy-covered house by the side of a road leading into Mid-Wales. My father rented some fishing in Wales; whenever he got the chance he was off with his tackle and a box of his favourite flies. He spent most of his spare time during the winter fly-tying when he wasn't in the pub. He was the Assistant Bank Manager, Lloyds Bank, Worcester.

Anyway, the front door of this pub opened into a passage with a flagstone floor trodden concave by the boots of generations of drinkers. The walls were half-panelled in old worm-eaten tongue-and-groove wooden slats painted a faded chocolate brown. Beyond was a staircase, only the first few treads visible as they cork-screwed up to the left to vanish into the dimness above, accompanied by a worn wooden bannister rail, rubbed dirty grey by the chaffing of many hands. A smell of what seemed like stale watery vegetable soup pervaded the corridor. To the left was one of those half-doors, like a stable door, a cut-glass window framed in the top half, which slid up and down, open and shut, with a harsh grating noise. It lead into the taproom. Wooden barrels rested on a stillage against the side wall; above, shelves almost up to the tobacco stained ceiling, were backed by a long mirror splashed with beer flecks and dried hop leaves. You could just see a blurred reflection in the mirror between bottles, glasses and paper doyleys, engraved with the words 'Best Ales and Stouts'. There was no bar counter; the Landlord sat in front of the barrels on a high four-legged stool from which he scrutinized his customers and the racing form.

I had a ginger-beer shandy and wondered whether I would get a glow on. I didn't. My father and I called at this pub every year. If it was fine we would sit on a bench outside in the sun and eat our sandwiches. If it was wet we would stand in the passageway, because I was not allowed in the taproom, being under age. I would munch a sandwich and make Chinese faces from the chequered pattern of the floor lino while my father drank his beer in the saloon. I had been told about people being barred from pubs, and I used to wonder whether a policeman would appear from nowhere and take me away before my father had finished his pint.

The first time I was allowed in the taproom I was seventeen, although the permitted age was eighteen. The Landlord had come to know us well. It was raining, so we stayed inside the bar eating our sandwiches at a small round marble-topped table with a wrought-iron base which someone had painted green. I suddenly wanted a pee, so I turned left into the dim passageway past the stairs and through a door into the back yard, where I found a urinal with an old evil smell. The entry was so narrow it was difficult not to brush against the dirty brick walls on either side. Only the one wall was for pissing against, because below it was a slimy trough along the skirting for carrying away the slops. The surface had been painted with many layers of thick black tar, as rough as a crocodile's hide.

"You've been a long time" Dad said "What have you been up to?"

"Admiring the decor of the urinal. I have never seen anything like it before in my life."

"You'll see plenty more like that, my boy, before you're through."

How right he was.

I was nearly thirteen years old when I started to have strange terrifying nightmares. I was high above the earth, all around was chaos and confusion. I seemed to be suspended like a bird on a perch, somehow I was able to reach out and touch some object, or victim perhaps? as it hurtled down through space, streaking and screaming earthwards leaving in its wake a long sinister trail of flame and smoke. As I watched, I was suddenly plummeting down in pursuit, only to end by being buried in the brown earth surrounded by a shattered twisted fuselage and queerly misshapen wings. I struggled out of the burning debris and abruptly woke up. This nightmare repeated itself at irregular intervals. I dreaded the thought of it but it always returned when I least expected it. I was too young to understand what it was all about, but in time I became accustomed to it and it began to exert a terrible fascination for me.

I knew nothing about aeroplanes except the fear of them inspired by

PUBS, DREAMS AND PUBLIC SCHOOL

my dreams. In 1932 there was no such thing as this strange aircraft, with a smooth wing on either side and a long sleek cowling in front. Today I am all too familiar with the lines of a modern fighter plane, so you can say I have the benefit of hindsight, yet during those young years I was never so certain about anything as I was about this fighter of mine.

It was about this time that Sir Alan Cobham came to Worcester with his Flying Circus and set it up on a large stretch of grassed common land known as Perdiswell, bordering the perimeter of the City. Here he sold short flights for 5/- each to people young and old alike who queued up to experience this new thrill.

The aircraft Sir Alan used was the Avro 504, one of the best known RAF aircraft to emerge from World War I. My father took my brother Tom and me to see the fun, offering to pay for each of us to have a flip. Tom eagerly accepted, but I was quite convinced that his last hour was at hand, so I resolutely refused to go. Even when Tom climbed from the cockpit, unbelievably in one piece after his short trip, I continued to prevaricate with silly excuses, reluctant to reveal the truth about my dream which as yet I had told to no one.

I had been at prep school now for nearly four years. It was a Dickensian style Establishment called Mill Mead, just on the outskirts of Shrewsbury, under the joint Headmastership of two extraordinary characters, Messrs. Sandford and Bennion. Sandford was a short plump bald little man with a large hooked nose. He was known as Punch, and he had a sister bearing a more than marked resemblance to Judy. Bennion was a very thin man nearly six feet six inches tall, with a pronounced stoop, and prominent front teeth which smelt strongly of decay as he leaned over your shoulder to examine or correct your work. He was never seen without one of those exceptionally high stiff collars, reaching only half way up his long stringy neck, just managing to touch his proboscis-like Adam's Apple which was constantly on the move. The Matron, a dumpy little woman with cross-eyes and a pince-nez, would trip with quick short steps through the dormitories making a 'clippety clop' sound bestowing on her the name 'Tip tip'. She disliked me from the start. She was in cahoots with Judy to whom she passed on everything she saw, both true and false. I was more than happy when I left Mill Mead.

My grandfather had been the Head Surgeon at the Royal Salop Infirmary, Shrewsbury, for over fifteen years prior to the Great War, when he died suddenly from a stroke. The family, including five girls and two boys, lived in a large Georgian mansion in the town, from where my father and his elder brother George went to Shrewsbury School as day boys. My turn for Public School had now arrived and the clear choice was Shrewsbury. However, since 1922 we had been living in Worcestershire, so being a day boy was out of the question. I was accepted as a boarder starting in the Winter Term 1931.

My parents deposited me outside the back entrance of Churchills' House leaving me alone with an embarrassingly new green trunk reinforced with wooden struts, as in the fashion of school trunks in those days, plus a glistening white tuck-box capped at the corners with shiny black metal plates. A tall lean angular man with a wispy brown moustache approached me. He was Mason, the 'Houseman'. He had a kindly face. He pitched my luggage onto a hand trolley and vanished, muttering something about Mr Whitfield wanting to see me later.

Not knowing quite what to do next I wandered through into the washroom where a succession of small frosted windows, high above the unplastered walls, threw a grey cheerless reflection down on to a closely-knit line of hand basins, hanging precariously on the bare bricks. It was cold and damp that late pale September evening. A small fair-haired boy was standing there looking lost.

"Hello" I said "What's your name?"

"Hillary, what's yours?"

"Edwards. You new too?"

"Yes" he replied. "I'm told I shall be the youngest boy in the school. How old are you?"

"Thirteen and a half," I replied.

"I'm not thirteen yet; you see my mother and father live abroad."

"Oh!" I reflected, wondering whether I had missed anything.

"Yes," he continued. "You see, my father works in the Sudan. My parents can only come back about once every two years during the summer. The rest of the time I have to live with my uncle and aunt in Nottinghamshire."

Dick Hillary was rather small for his age, an abundant crop of fair hair falling down over a high forehead, squat nose, close eyebrows and full lips with a pronounced pout, especially when disconcerted.

For the first three or four years Dick and I were good friends. Although we usually shared the same study we were never in the same Form together, because he took Modern Languages whilst I remained on the Classical Side, until my last year when I took History.

Another study mate of ours in Churchills' House was John Keitley, whose father and grandfather were regular Officers in the Manchester

PUBS, DREAMS AND PUBLIC SCHOOL

Regiment. Although Army-orientated, John was an 'aircraft buff' as he would have been called today.

He had a standing order with W H Smith & Sons down in the town for the two aeronautical periodicals 'Aeroplane' and 'Flight', which he read avidly from cover to cover. We used to sit in our study every Sunday afternoon discussing flying and aviation in general. Photographs of German warplanes like the Me109 were appearing, and already prototypes of the Hurricane and Spitfire were being tested. Most of them looked something like the aircraft in my dream.

Dick always adopted a supercilious attitude towards all this activity, professing to be totally against taking up arms, even vowing that he would be a Conscientious Objector in the event of war. He scorned patriotism and ridiculed John for his outmoded Army traditions and for his unquestioning acceptance of becoming cannon fodder. For my part I used to read everything I could lay my hands on about the National Socialist ideology, including Hitler's 'Mein Kampf' and I came to recognise the evils of the Nazi obsession for world domination.

In 1933 we learnt about the Oxford Union debate when the majority voted for the motion 'We will never fight for King and Country'. It was the subject of vigorous discussion amongst ourselves and Dick was the only one to side with the Union majority.

Once or twice a year, usually the Christmas or Easter holidays, Dick would come to stay at my parent's house on the River Severn at Hawford Lock, near Worcester. We enjoyed things schoolboys usually enjoy, walking, riding, bicycling, boating on the river and going to the pictures. As we grew older our tastes became, dare I say it, more sophisticated, yet compared with the youth today we were still in the kindergarten stage.

One Easter weekend we went to stay with some wealthy friends living near Rugeley. They had a beautiful country mansion called Bellamore, and three attractive daughters, Peggy, Sheila and Betty. I had a heavy crush on Sheila, aged about seventeen, but the moment she set eyes on Dick she had no more time for me, yet the strange fact is that Dick displayed only mild interest in her. Nor, for that matter, did he show much interest in Peggy or Betty who used to tease him unmercifully. This infuriated me because I would see Sheila was just wasting her time instead of focusing her attention on me.

After passing my driving test in 1936 (driving tests were now compulsory), Dick's parents invited me down to Gerrards Cross for a few days. It was summertime and they had an attractive house called

SPIT AND SAWDUST

Shirley Cottage. I persuaded my father to let me drive down in his elderly Austin. Mr and Mrs Hillary left us to our own devices because they spent a lot of time in London. We used to drive out to a pub called the Royal Standard at Forty Green, run by Flora MacDonald, the daughter of Ramsay MacDonald, a very popular place with the younger set, abounding with attractive girls. I was always keen to try my luck but once again Dick displayed little enthusiasm, a pose which in my näivety I found difficult to understand.

The next port of call was a smart new road house called the 'Blue Posts' on the High Wycombe road where there was a swimming pool. We would swim there until early evening, then on our way back to Shirley Cottage stop off for a pint at the Saracen's Head in Beaconsfield.

This was the last time I was to stay at Gerrards Cross; I knew somehow that Dick and I were starting to drift apart.

Dick showed little inclination or aptitude for sport but being small he was made to cox. After a couple of years he started to grow and put on weight, so 'Jo' Whitfield, our Housemaster, decided to give him some coaching in the 'tub pair', a rather primitive method of assessing an oarsman's potential. 'Jo' was on old Cambridge rowing type and fancied himself as a Coach, but he was no better at coaching than delivering sermons. He was a 'Reverend', and whenever it was his turn to take the Service in Chapel the rafters reverberated with unhallowed sounds of choking and snoring.

Eventually we tried Dick out in the Churchills' Four which was shaping exceptionally well. 'The Bull', A E Kitchen, the School Coach, decided to take a look at him, finally selecting him for the number two position in the Shrewsbury School second Eight during our last summer term; yet 'The Bull' always felt that Dick was a bit of a misfit with his bolshie attitude towards everything. Our House Four went Head of the River in 1937, a triumph for Churchills', because it was the first time they had gone 'Head' since before World War I. So our last term at Shrewsbury ended on a high note. Even in the hour of success Dick had to spoil things by trying to convince me that to excel at sport was old fashioned and a waste of time.

"The value" he gibed at me "to be derived from sitting up late reading Goethe is far more rewarding than snatching beauty sleep to make yourself a top-class oarsman'"

"You can keep your beloved Goethe, Dick" I countered. "Don't be a hypocrite. I know full well that you have even surprised yourself by sharing in our rowing success, but you are ashamed to admit it."

PUBS, DREAMS AND PUBLIC SCHOOL

At this Dick lost his temper, grappled with me, and we fell to the floor locked in a bitter struggle. I ordered him to bed and he departed disgruntled and unrepentant. From that moment on we seldom fraternised.

Regrettably, Dick Hillary had come increasingly under the influence of a strange master called Frank McEachran, who had joined the staff from a junior appointment at Greshams School, where his salary had been a pittance. It was said that he didn't even own a suit and couldn't afford a haircut, though doubtless this was an affectation. He could have been, if I may coin a phrase, a 'prewar Hippie'. McEachran's political outlook was Liberal, embracing the teachings of Henry George who preached Land Reform. His radical leanings were even mildy shared by one or two of the other masters, but in general there was little or no enthusiasm for his doctrinaire opinions. I am told that H H Hardy, the Headmaster, looked upon him with suspicion. During the summer holidays he went as a volunteer to fight for the Republicans in the Spanish Civil War. Apparently he did no fighting. Frank McEachran, 'Mac' or 'Kek' as he was known, never married and died in 1975. He taught German and later became head of the Modern Languages Faculty. It has been said that he played an important part in the formation of Dick's character. Whatever else it did, it tended to alienate Dick from his friends and exposed a rather less attractive side to his nature than the alluring image later attributed to him would suggest. There's no denying, however, that in writing the 'Last Enemy', a great work by any standard and a 'Best Seller', Dick had made his mark on the world, otherwise he would just have remained among the ranks of those equally courageous pilots, many of whom had suffered wounds at least as dreadful as he had.

Occasionally during the school holidays my mother would pack me off to London to stay for a week or so with Aunt Maud, one of my father's five sisters. Aunt Maud was a spinster and my godmother; she ran a 'Rescue Home', as it was called in those days. It was at No 48 Great Pulteney Street, Soho, within a stone's throw of Piccadilly Circus. It was a typical nineteenth century Victorian house with a large basement and three floors above, excluding the attic. From the outside it presented a gaunt, rather dirty red brick exterior.

There were about twelve bedrooms and a singular lack of washing facilities.

At first I didn't quite understand what 'Rescue Home' meant. Aunt Maud used to be at great pains to explain that she was dedicated to carrying out God's work in a sinful world. Who was sinning, I asked,

SPIT AND SAWDUST

and what were they being rescued from? Eventually the truth started to dawn on me. Every evening, young (and some not so young) girls came to the front door and were ushered through to my Aunt's private study, into which I was never allowed. I used to sit in the parlour pretending to read a book, but through a crack in the door frame I could observe across the front hall the 'comings and goings', which aroused in me a compelling curiosity. I heard snatches of conversation suggesting that somehow my Aunt was trying to restrain the girls from doing something wicked, or from going somewhere disreputable. Now and again I could spy a girl ascend the stairs carrying perhaps a brown paper bag or a tatty basket as she disappeared up into the dim gaslight of the floors above.

After several holidays there with my Aunt I started to cotton on. The girls were given a bed for the night, or maybe several nights, in exchange for mopping, dusting, polishing and cleaning my Aunt's extensive establishment. I could see that she was clearly on to a 'good thing', and I tackled her about it. Her mission in life, she explained, was to keep young girls off the streets, not hardened prostitutes, she hastily added, but young inexperienced girls coming to London looking for work. Her Rescue Home, she explained, was financed by the Church of England. I was old enough to know that 'hardened prostitutes' also took advantage of a free night's accommodation plus breakfast, and I spotted that they never stopped to do mopping or cleaning.

My Aunt always gave me a small room up on the third floor. It was a pokey little room lit by a single gas mantle suspended from the ceiling, where it waved drunkenly in the draught, emitting a snake-like hissing noise occasionally punctuated by an alarming popping sound.

It was here at No 48 Great Pulteney Street that I had my first sexual experience. It was my third or fourth visit; I was about sixteen I think. One morning a young girl knocked on the door, and entered carrying a cup of tea for me. I had seen her around the house and gathered her name was Lottie. She was very pretty with a neat figure. As she placed the cup on my bedside table she proceeded to unfasten the hooks and eyes at the back of her dress, let it fall to the floor, and stood there in her birthday suit. I was so excited I nearly knocked the tea over. In a flash she was in my bed. I hadn't much of a clue but I more or less knew where everything was, and she knew how to fill in the details. Lottie was very persistent and I started to worry about my Aunt, who must have 'smelt a rat', until one day Lottie was no longer there and I guessed that Aunt Maud had turned her out on to the streets, reasoning that Lottie's fate was less accountable than that of her nephew. Very little was said

PUBS, DREAMS AND PUBLIC SCHOOL

about it and I gained the impression that my Aunt derived some sort of sexual satisfaction from the escapade.

By now I was well acquainted with Soho and the surroundings. I used to wander down into Piccadilly to see the lights, the bright illuminated signs advertising the picture shows and the live theatres in Shaftesbury Avenue and St Martins Lane. Occasionally, if I had enough money, I would go to the movies. I have vivid memories of seeing 'Hells Angels' with Richard Bartlemess and Jean Harlow with the beautiful boobs, which had a long run at the Pavilion, Piccadilly Circus. Their life-sized images were displayed in colour, above the main entrance to the foyer, on a huge hoarding spread right across the front of the cinema, Sopwith Camels and Fokker Tri-planes buzzing round the blue sky above their heads, others spinning in flames towards the ground. I bought a ticket and sat enthralled, memories of my dream flooding back. Once more I was transported into a convolution of spiralling, twisting wings and fuselages plunging earthwards. In the midst of this chaos I somehow saw myself ploughing a deep furrow in the ground, from which I emerged unscathed, surrounded by smoking blackened wreckage.

Another version of 'Hells Angels' was made after the war with David Niven and Errol Flynn. It was called 'The Dawn Patrol'.

On one of my visits to No 48 I recall a certain Vicar who frequently visited my Aunt. She would receive him in her drawing room and have one of the girls serve tea, crumpets, and fruitcake dusted with icing sugar. He was a dapper yet somewhat untidy little man with the remnants of cigar ash sprinkled down the front of his vestment. He had close-set eyes, greying hair, a large nose, thick sensuous lips and a broad dimpled chin. He talked endlessly and seemed always to be in a hurry to go somewhere. I was allowed in to have a crumpet. I liked buttered crumpets, and I managed to pick up snatches of their conversation. It seemed to be mostly about girls; apparently the Vicar was also involved in saving them from something worse, and occasionally he and my Aunt would exchange names and addresses which, although meaningless to me, suggested that the Vicar was in some kind of business. Little did I know it then, but by some extraordinary twist of fate I was destined to marry his *'daughter' Pamela, whom I met in a Night Club just after the beginning of the war. In no way did I associate her with the Vicar who had been dead now for some three years, having been killed by a lion in Skegness. His name was the Reverend Harold Davidson, Rector of Stiffkey.

*The Vicar of Stiffkey was my wife's legal father. Her real father was her mother's lover, a Colonel in the Canadian Army during WW1.

CHAPTER TWO

FIRST BLOOD TO THE BRITISH

The year was 1937. The Munich Pact, signed at Berchtesgaden by Hitler and Chamberlain, giving Sudetenland to Germany and the green light to carve up Czechoslovakia, was still more than a year away. I was too involved with my school activities at Shrewsbury to pay much attention to these matters, I merely knew at the back of my mind that all was not well in Europe. I had no further opportunity for visits to No 48 Great Pulteney Street; I was not to see Aunt Maud again until after the war.

I was School Captain of Boats, School Captain of Soccer and Boxing, as well as Head of House. The 'Jo' suggested it was time I thought of University, and persuaded me to enter my name for the Heath Harrison Exhibition to Brasenose College, Oxford, which took into account not only scholastic ability but also exceptional aptitude for sport. I didn't rate my chances very high but agreed it was worth a try. Entries where to be submitted by 31 January.

In the meantime an attractive project came my way, in the shape of a swap of masters. A German teacher called Fritz Kranzlin arrived at Shrewsbury in exchange for Hugh Brooke, a Cambridge Cricket Blue, who went to teach in the Fatherland. Fritz Kranzlin was the very archetype of a dedicated Nazi, keen, patriotic, radiating physical fitness, and aflame with enthusiasm for the new Germany. German policy was one of friendship towards England and it was to foster good relationships that Herr Kranzlin proposed that the School football team should make a tour of five of the new National Political Schools (Nationalsocialistische Schule), which were founded by Adolf Hitler and set up in some ways in imitation of English Public Schools, with the intention of producing leaders for Nazi Germany. The Schools visited were Bensberg, near Cologne, Oranienstein in the Lahn Valley, Schulporta and Naumberg on the River Saale, and Ballenstedt on the fringe of the Harz Mountains. They were established in large country estates or 'Scholosses', doubtless confiscated from the nobility by the Nazis.

Three members of the School team couldn't make the tour (see photograph) so I selected six players from the Second XI. The party consisted of Fritz Kranzlin, Alan Phillips, the School Soccer Master, his wife and fourteen players.

Prior to our departure Kranzlin warned me that the tour would be closely monitored by the authorities in the Wilhelmstrasse, and that Hitler himself would be taking a personal interest in our progress, therefore we must at all costs behave like proper young English gentlemen!

FIRST BLOOD TO THE BRITISH

We set off for the Continent by train and Channel ferry in early March, 1937, for what proved to be an exciting and fascinating fortnight, during which we gained a close insight into the workings and organisation of these new schools.

The schools were highly selective, the majority of entrants being picked from the Hitler Youth Movement. There was a week of testing before admission and keen competition for places. Their structure was almost entirely military, being run on the lines of an élite Academy for young Cadets, whose ages ranged from about ten to fourteen years in the Junior Grade, and fifteen to eighteen in the Senior. The boys had a collection of up to six different uniforms, from working fatigues to elaborate ceremonial dress. I remember at one school being escorted round the locker rooms where I was proudly shown a remarkable array of military gear such as leather belts with holsters for daggers and Lugers, short shiny black leather jackets, riding breeches and jack-boots. Everywhere was the ubiquitous Swastika on uniforms, caps, knife handles, and other paramilitary paraphernalia. Slogans like 'Deutschland Erwache!' (Germany awake!) adorned the walls. None of this was attractive to us, our reaction varying from the incredulous to the derisory; clad in sports jackets, plus fours, trilby hats or tweed caps, we made a marked contrast to our hosts. However, we were warmly greeted everywhere, and everything possible was done to make our stay enjoyable. The address of welcome by the Anstalsleiter Oberregierungsrat Dr.med.Schieffer, SS-Standartenfuhrer, included the following:

"History tells us that for centuries England and Germany, akin by bonds of blood, have been friends. I remind you of the time of Frederick the Great, of the Napoleonic Wars, of Waterloo, which signify more than a word.

"Only one time was there a black day in the history of the white nations when they did not understand each other, and took up arms. Never again! For that reason it is necessary to get together. The result will be understanding. I ask you to rise from your seats in honour of His Majesty the King, Emperor of India, and of our Führer and Reichskanzler, Adolf Hitler."

The band then played 'God save the King', 'Deutschland uber alles', and the Horst Wessel song.

At each school there was an Assembly Hall large enough to seat cadets, staff and visitors. One first entered a foyer from which one passed on into the main chamber. Painted on the back wall of the foyer was a large map of Western Europe, measuring perhaps 8 x 10 feet, the main

SPIT AND SAWDUST

feature being the word 'Versailles' printed in large black letters across the environs of Paris. Pointing diagonally down through the lettering was a dagger, swastika embossed on the handle, the tip painted red, and blood-red droplets spilling down the wall to the skirting. Alongside was the word 'Vergeltung!' ('Revenge!') printed in large red letters. This was the standard decor at every school.

Ceremonial played a large part throughout the tour. At one school we marched through the streets to the football ground, carrying our boots, accompanied by a band. At another the Union Jack and the Swastika were raised while the teams stood to attention, the Germans giving the Nazi salute. During the visit Hitler's birthday was celebrated, another occasion for parades and displays. Everyone was in uniform of some sort and marching in all directions, the whole scene manifesting itself as altogether bizarre yet spellbinding.

Of course, there was much sightseeing and travelling by train, bus and lorry, including a visit early one freezing morning to a Labour Camp up in the Harz Mountains, where the detainees were being given a hard time. About a hundred blond Aryans, stripped to the waist, each with a hefty log set on the ground in front, were being drilled by strutting Nazi PT Instructors with Swastika arm bands, shouting words of command to which they responded by seizing the logs, lifting them up above their heads, then swinging them from side to side in unison.

As to the football itself, we won all five school matches, scoring twenty one goals against eight. The grounds were rather poor with the centre strip often rough and hard. The German boys played with great spirit and good ball control, but we were superior in our positional play and general knowledge of the game. An extra match against some Storm-troopers from Diez was laid on and we drew with them 2 - 2. It was a rough game with much kicking and pushing, but we held our ground, much to the disgust and disappointment of the Sturmahteilung supporters. Before the game we were made to stand to attention while the S A Band played Deutschland uber Alles. We complied with reluctance, shifting our feet about, looking in every direction except to the front, thus infuriating the officials. In the middle of this ceremony a small girl appeared from nowhere and thrust a bunch of flowers into my hand. I had no idea what to do with it, so as the starting whistle blew I dashed back to the changing room and threw the bouquet into the WC of the nearest toilet. I never knew what became of the flowers!

There were two other incidents of note, the one concerning an abortive visit to a Night Club, the other an affair of pictures being turned

FIRST BLOOD TO THE BRITISH

to the wall.

A cousin of mine in the KSLI who had won a DSO and two MC's in World War I suggested that if I got a chance I should visit a certain Night Club in Cologne called 'La Bohéme' where we would be sure of a good evening. Four of us took a taxi, the driver depositing us outside a large wrought-iron door in a narrow cobbled street somewhere behind the Cathedral, 'La Bohéme', blazoned in bright red neon lights over the entrance. A tall forbidding man in a get-up reminiscent of the Russian Imperial Guard stood barring our way. On enquiring the cost of entry we suddenly got cold feet, turned on our heels, and went looking for another taxi to take us back. I received a monumental rocket from Alan Phillips. So much for our essay into Teutonic night life.

The second incident occurred at Ballenstedt, the last school of the tour. We were accommodated in one of the dormitories, the walls of which were as usual embellished with pictures of Hitler, Göring, Goebbels, Hess, etc. Whilst at breakfast, loud and shrill cries were heard from upstairs, followed by the abrupt entry of an officious-looking Nazi Officer demanding to speak with whoever was in authority. I stepped forward and he dragged me by the neck to the Commandant's office. I had no idea what it was all about until I was informed that the cleaners had reported that all the pictures in the dormitory had been turned face to the wall.

"This is a grave insult to the Führer" bawled the Commandant "and to the heroic people of Deutschland. You will be punished."

I vehemently protested our innocence and insisted that the maids must have done it, which infuriated him as he graduated into hysterics. It was a chilling experience.

The upshot of the affair was that the Chancellor's Office in Wilhelmstrasse telephoned to say that we must leave at once. We were ordered to pack up and board a truck which was to take us to the Station. As we left almost the whole School turned out to see us off, hurling insults and shouting:

"You feelthy Eeenglish pigs", etc. We were more than happy to be on our way I can tell you! Although we left under a cloud we all had a jolly good laugh about it on our journey home.

In little more than two years after the tour, England would be at war with Germany and the two sides would be opponents in a different game. We had beaten them on the field; we didn't know then but we were to beat them again in a life and death struggle; at the time we had no conscious feeling that we would ere long be shooting at each other, although the militaristic concentration of the Schools made its impression.

The open encouragement of homosexuality was duly noted. Wasn't Ernst Röhm, one of the leading Nazis, an insatiable pervert, to mention but one among many? Their ostentation, regimentation, blind allegiance to the Führer, and their pledge to die for the Fatherland, tended to leave us cold. It was bad enough to put on our coarse khaki fatigues, puttees, enormous black boots, and then shuffle reluctantly onto the OTC Parade Ground once a week!

The postscript is a sad one. Of our party of fourteen, five were killed in the war. Derek Atkinson flew Hurricanes in 213 Squadron, fought in the Dunkirk evacuation and in the Battle of Britain, was awarded the DFC, and was finally shot down and killed on Sunday 25 August 1940. Lt John Glover, RNVR, died when his ship went down off Dunkirk in 1940. Peter Blagg was killed in Burma serving with the Royal Welsh Fusiliers. Monty Cave, an Officer in the Commandos, was killed on the Anzio beachhead in 1944. It was a high casualty rate for one group of boys; but one speculates that the casualty rate was higher for our opponents. Not many of those whom Hitler specially called to leadership in 1937 can have survived till 1945.

The first week of March brought a communication from Brasenose College, Oxford, summoning me to appear before the Board of Examiners on Tuesday, 27 March 1937, as a candidate for the Heath Harrison Exhibition. Two Exhibitions were awarded annually, a Senior and a Junior, open to all schoolboys over the age of eighteen, prior to the commencement of the next University Michaelmas Term, in October.

On Monday, 26 March, I caught the train from Shrewsbury to Oxford with my sponge bag, pyjamas, my first ever dinner jacket, and with very little idea of what was in store for me. 'Jo' had booked me in for three nights bed and breakfast at the Eastgate Hotel, at the bottom end of the High Street towards Magdalen Bridge. He gave me enough money for a taxi from the Station on Monday and for a taxi back to the station on the following Thursday, plus something for the hotel expenses.

I arrived in my hotel bedroom to find a paper marked 'Brasenose College - Candidates' Programme', which took care of my activities for the next two days. I was to report to the Junior Common Room at 9 am on Tuesday morning to fill in forms etc., and then to sit written examinations from 10 am to 12.30 pm and again, after a light lunch in Hall, from 2.30 to 5 pm, then back to the Eastgate for an early night. On the Wednesday morning we were to sit further examinations from 10 am to 12 noon, and then all candidates were to assemble in the Junior

FIRST BLOOD TO THE BRITISH

Common Room for sherry and snacks to meet some of the senior undergraduates of the College.

There were about thirty candidates in all from a variety of Public Schools ranging at the top from Eton, Harrow, Winchester, Charterhouse, Marlborough, Uppingham and Shrewsbury, down to Kings School Worcester, Bromsgrove, Highgate and so on. Afterwards we were free to do what we liked until 7 pm when we were to assemble in the Senior Common Room suitably dressed in dinner jackets, ready to dine with the Principal, Doctor William Tenlon Swan Stallybrass, more commonly known as 'Sonners'. Also present were to be a number of Senior College Fellows.

I cannot remember what we ate, but I know I was highly impressed by the decor, college silver, and the napery. There was no lack of wine, and of this I had been warned. Apparently it was intended as a trap to loosen young tongues. Sonners and the Fellows were watching carefully to see who succumbed first. Somehow I managed to stay the course, aided no doubt by my being not altogether unused to drinking, but many shuffled unsteadily down to the ablutions, never to be seen again that evening. After dinner the remainder retired to the Senior Common Room where we were seated at a highly polished refectory table, laid at intervals with port glasses, coffee cups and bowls of fruit and nuts.

Whilst the port was being passed round Herbert, the Head Scout, handed us each in turn a large silver snuff box from which we were expected to take a pinch. I hadn't the courage to refuse, but taking some up between thumb and forefinger I craftily dropped it into my coffee. I had no intention of drinking the coffee, I hated the stuff. I then found myself sitting next to the Vice Principal, Maurice Platnauer, an Old Salopian. He talked about A E Houseman and the 'Shropshire Lad'. I had read it once when I was in the School Sanatorium with measles, but I couldn't remember much so I was forced to improvise. Luckily, by this time Maurice, who had consumed what seemed to me to be at least two bottles of vintage port, was now becoming inarticulate. Suddenly everything became dim and confused, things started to spin round. How I got back to the hotel I shall never know, but I awoke next morning in my room with a painful and unfamiliar stabbing sensation in my head. My one thought was that I must have fluffed it. Blurry eyed, with a pain in my head and heart, I caught the train back to Shrewsbury, finally collapsing into my bed in the House dormitory at about midnight.

Ten days later I received a letter post-marked Oxford, with BNC printed on the top left-hand corner of the envelope. Prepared to read the

SPIT AND SAWDUST

worst I hesitatingly slit it open. I couldn't believe my eyes. In black and white it read: 'We are pleased to award the Senior Heath Harrison Exhibition to G H Nelson-Edwards, Shrewsbury School. The Junior Heath Harrison is awarded to Charles Grover, Winchester College'. I went straight into 'Jo's' study, showing the letter as if I had misread it, but he was very pleased and called Megan, his wife, a meek but charming little lady who displayed almost ecstatic pleasure, asking me in for sherry and canapés the following evening. The Headmaster, H H Hardy, know as Adolf because he had a fringe of dark hair over his forehead and a moustache just like Hitler's, was very pleased indeed and invited me to dinner on Sunday evening at Kingsland House, the Headmaster's official Residence. I was regaled with mutton cutlets, which was a regular feature on the menu whenever senior boys were invited to the Headmaster's table for Sunday supper. This special Sunday evening repast was given the name of 'Mutlets'.

CHAPTER THREE

THE 'DARK BLUE' DAYS

When the day came for me to leave Shrewsbury and go to Oxford I went with a glad heart and full of high hopes. The two years that now lay before me were to be the most enjoyable and most treasured I was ever to experience.

In September, about a month before I was due to take up residence at Brasenose, the BNC Captain of Boats wrote inviting me to Henley-on-Thames to join a pre-term training session for the University Coxless Fours, the first rowing event of the coming University Year. We were booked in at the Old White Hart Hotel in Hart Street, the College authorities having obtained a grant to buy a new boat, a set of new oars, and to pay for our fortnight's accommodation on the dicey premise that we would win. I stroked the Four with Con Cherry, the current President of the OUBC, rowing at No 3; Fraser Caddy, a crazy Australian from Geelong, at No 2 and Dick Newell - who had rowed with me in the Shrewsbury First Eight - at Bow as steersman. Undoubtedly we were the strongest College Four on the Isis. On paper we should have won easily but as 'Jo' (J O Whitfield, my old Housemaster) used to say: "Boy, no one rows on paper!" At the last minute Fraser Caddy went down with hepatitis and we were beaten by a splendid Oriel College Four stroked by Christopher Pepys, a direct descendant of the immortal Diarist.

Brasenose College was founded in 1509, although its roots can be traced back to 1262. The corporate designation of the College is: 'The Principal and Scholars of the King's Hall and College of Brasenose in Oxford'. BNC had a tradition of inclining towards sport rather than academics. This tendency was maintained by Doctor Stallybrass who prided himself on having more 'Blues' in Brasenose than in any of the other Colleges. When I first went up we must have had nearly three dozen 'Blues'. For example, the eleven members of the University Soccer Team were all BNC men, which meant I had no chance of a Soccer 'Blue' although I was selected to play in a Trial. I settled for rowing. It was said that BNC was 'the most Cambridge of all Oxford Colleges', Cambridge being regarded as populated by beefy rowing and rugby types and having a very poor record in the scholastic world.

Oxford, city of dreaming spires, green swards, quadrangles, College Staircases and Scouts. As I started to take it all in I slowly began to absorb the atmosphere and to capture the feeling of liberty and freedom

SPIT AND SAWDUST

from restraint, not that I was contemplating a life of total licentiousness.

My tutor was Edgar Stanley Cohn MA, Lecturer in Modern History. After an introductory glass of Amontillado Sherry he presented me with a programme of History lectures for the remainder of the Term.

"Take it or leave it, Hal, the choice is yours. The lectures I recommend I have marked with an asterisk."

I sensed a feeling of importance to know I was free to choose which lectures to attend and which not. Stanley did not appear to care much either way. He was a small squat man with a pallid complexion, a round head and a flat droopy nose, full lips slightly curled up on one side, suggestive of a cynical disposition. His only condition as to my work was that once a week I should present a treatise on what I had garnered the previous seven days. This was to be followed by discussion and criticism. I soon discovered that Stanley Cohn was a most agreeable person with a shrewd penetrating mind, and a true friend. Plans for the future, for a career, did not seem to be of importance. I was reading History, to what end I honestly didn't know. I vaguely thought of being a Schoolmaster - an easy answer (or so I thought) - perhaps at my old School, Shrewsbury, where I could be a rowing Coach too, and enjoy frequent holidays. I was more ignorant of business than an office boy. I had one other vague idea, to try for the Colonial Civil Service, but one had to gain a good second-class Degree and the idea of working really hard just didn't appeal to me at the time. I don't deny that this frame of mind, this casual attitude, was shameful. Perhaps luckily for me, although I didn't know it then, the decision was to be made for me. Whilst we all knew in our hearts that war with Germany was a matter of time, we held people like Hitler, Goebbels and Göring up to ridicule, just as we had turned their pictures to the wall on the soccer tour. Whatever was to befall us we were coldly confident of putting them away. A popular tune at the time was 'Bei Mir Bist du Schoen' played incessantly on the gramophone up in the Restaurant at Ellistons', a rendezvous much favoured by undergraduates for morning coffee. Conversation was about anything but war; it was about opera, communism, poetry, sex and even sport.

My dream came again early in the year, a forceful reminder that maybe the hand of destiny was beckoning me to break the spell I was under and so bow to the inevitable.

I knew that soon all of us would be called upon to offer life and limb in the cause of freedom. What was it to be for me? Was I being warned that to fly would be lethal for me? That I would be plunged to death before I had even started? Or would I find the answer I was seeking by

THE 'DARK BLUE DAYS'

a long impassive look into the nature and purpose of flight?

In the Michaelmas Term, 1938, I was picked to row in the University Trial Eights, to which I shall refer later on. I came to know a great many rowing types, among them Melvyn Young from Trinity, who rowed in the 1939 'Blue' Boat. He eventually lost his life flying with Guy Gibson on the Dambuster Raid. Previous to that, returning from a bombing mission, he was forced to 'pancake' way out in the North Sea. He took to the dinghy and drifted for two or three days, finally picked up near to death; from then on he was nicknamed 'Dinghy Young'.

One evening Con Cherry asked several rowing types round to his digs in Magpie Lane, including Melvyn and myself. Melvyn was already a member of the University Air Squadron. We sat drinking port - the rowing man's beverage - listening to 'Orpheus in the Underworld'. The conversation got round to flying. Melvyn, a heavily built man with clean features, straight dark hair and shoulders like a gorilla, started to talk to me about the University Air Squadron which was regarded as one of the more 'up-market' clubs to belong to. It was a cheap and easy way of learning to fly. The Headquarters were situated in Manor Road, incorporating a popular bar and dining-room, plus the usual offices.

"You must apply to join, Hal, I'll put in a good word for you with the CO." I hesitated, visions of my dream flooding back.

"I don't know, Melvyn, give me time to think about it." "You'll never regret it, Hal, I assure you. A war is coming, it could be the answer for you. You'll have to do something, you know."

Too true, I knew I had to do something. Despite my inhibitions, was I after all destined to fly? Perhaps as Melvyn said, it might be the answer. It was the end of the Michaelmas Term, 1938, so my application to join the Squadron didn't reach Headquarters until the following February.

It was obligatory to obtain one's parents' permission to join the Squadron. My mother was totally against the idea but my father's signature was all I wanted and he gave it willingly. In March I was invited down to Manor Road for an interview with the CO, Wing Commander Hibberd, a World War I fighter pilot. I couldn't help noticing how his hands trembled and his lips twitched as he lit a cigarette. Is that what flying does to you, I asked myself? I need not have bothered. He was no freak. He knew exactly what he was about and, having accepted me, gave a complete run-down on the Squadron's function. I wasn't to know then, of course, but almost exactly fifteen years later I would be sitting in the same office, in the very same chair. I also met Miss Olive Round, MBE, the Squadron Secretary, for the first time, who would also be there when

SPIT AND SAWDUST

I returned to Manor Road as the Commanding Officer.

The OUAS was equipped with about ten Avro Tutors for elementary training and three Hawker Harts for advanced training. The Squadron flew from RAF Abingdon which in those days was a grass airfield. A weekly flying programme was posted in the Lodge of each College and also on the Notice Board in the Squadron Headquarters in Manor Road. With luck, most of us managed to fit in about two trips a week between work (?), lectures and sport - in my case rowing. Transport was provided by means of two magnificent Rolls Royce motor cars on hire to the Squadron from a firm called Humphries, long since extinct. These two Rolls Royce cars were nicknamed Castor and Pollux, presumably by some bright Greek scholar, after the two sons of Zeus each of whom, the legend says, lived every other day! Each Rolls was used on alternative days and they were almost identical, so it was very difficult to distinguish which was Pollux and which was Castor. We used to take bets on it with the driver. These limousines created a favourable impression amongst our fellow undergraduates. We felt very grand and superior to be seen riding in luxury, clutching a black leather flying helmet and wearing the Squadron blazer with gold RAF buttons. Daily the 'duty' Rolls would call at each College Lodge where members were waiting to be picked up for the short ride to Abingdon, and then to be returned to College after flying.

"I had better help you put that on. I'm Bill Bailey, incidentally, and you are coming up with me next." "Thanks" I said, struggling with the straps of a parachute. He showed me how the quick release box worked. I vaguely wondered if the parachute itself would work, what it would be like to drop from the sky knowing that it had failed to open.

"Hell, hurry up! Don't start thinking of your next lecture, here's the kite, hop in the front."

I climbed into the Avro Tutor in a daze. I was going to fly, I thought, and I was going to be taught by a type called Bill Bailey. I wasn't sure why, but somehow, this seemed very odd and I nearly burst into hysterical laughter. For me the trip was successful, though I wouldn't know what Bill thought. He never said much. I was just kicking myself with joy, because from the moment we left the ground, I suddenly knew that to fly was what I had wanted to do all the time. That first trip was the answer to the fear of my dream. In seconds my mind was clear. I knew it was OK now. I decided I was going to apply for a Permanent Commission - 'stuff' Schoolmastering and the Colonial Civil Service.

I hadn't seen much of John Keitley since I had been at Oxford. He had passed through Sandhurst and was a Second Lieutenant in the

THE 'DARK BLUE DAYS'

Manchesters. I was able to get away for a few days towards the end of the Summer term and arranged to meet him at Aldershot. I was full of my new flying experiences.

"I think you knew all the time you were going to fly, Hal."

"Well, maybe," I rejoined.

"But do you remember when we used to talk about the Hurricane and the Spitfire? I'll never forget it, I used to sit riveted to their pictures so much I was almost flying them. Now I am a humble Lieutenant in His Majesty's Army. I wonder if my father would be upset if I tried to transfer to the RAF."

I thought this was a great idea and tried to talk him into it.

"Let's face it," John continued "the country will soon be at war, we all know that now. Soldiers, as well as Airmen, will be needed and there aren't many of them either. I guess I will have to stay put." Then, as if talking to himself "If all goes well, I promise I will be flying with you within a couple of years."

"Fair enough, John, I just can't wait for the day."

Driving back to Oxford the following evening with the talk of war ringing in my ears, I thought of John's words and wondered whether, after all, he would find himself irreversibly committed to the Service he had chosen. I knew John would make a fine soldier whichever service he joined, the Royal Air Force, Army or the Royal Navy. I was not so certain about myself, but I was sure of one thing now. I wanted to be able to fly if there was going to be a war. I couldn't visualise myself doing anything else.

In those carefree prewar days, London was irresistible if one had money. A favourite haunt for pleasure-seeking undergraduates was the Cavendish Hotel in Jermyn Street, run by a well known lady called Rosa Lewis. She was reputed to be the illegitimate daughter of King Edward VII. Where the name Lewis came from I never knew.

She encouraged young débutantes and moneyed ladies to patronize the Cavendish, and engineered illicit unions between them and approved Oxford and Cambridge undergraduates. Dick Hillary was one of Rosa's favourites and the Cavendish Hotel was where he used to foregather with his friends, among them a young wealthy Armenian called Noel Agazarian and Stephen Rochford, whose father owned Quaglino's, a famous West End restaurant.

As for my own financial state my father, who was now Manager of a branch of Lloyds Bank in Great Bridge, Staffs., afforded me a small allowance of about £20 per term. My principal income, however, derived from three other sources. First, the Heath Harrison Exhibition worth £75 per annum, Second, a County Major Grant (Worcester County Council) worth £50 per annum. Third, a private grant of £25 per term from a very wealthy gentleman named H N Spalding, a benefactor of Brasenose College. So in all I had £260 per annum to survive on, including the cost of my College Battels, tuition fees and vacations.

There was no way I could raise the ante to join the Cavendish set, but I did manage a trip to London about once a term with a cheap day return ticket to Paddington. Two BNC friends usually came with me, Ian, an old Wykehamist, who rowed in the College Eight, and Peter, who was educated in France. We were after girls, good food and gambling, in that order. We were never very successful with girls, but we managed to cover our expenses now and again by gambling.

Gifford Rossi, a wealthy American BNC undergraduate, once introduced us to a fascinating high class Spanish prostitute called Carmelita, and she entertained us each in turn, I being the last. Afterwards, Carmelita invited me to a club in Curzon Street where she gave me food and drink, then she took me back to her luxury flat in Brook Street, and allowed me another session without charge. Afterwards I rejoined the others at Paddington just in time to catch the 'Flying Fornicator', the midnight train back to Oxford.

Doctor P C Mallam, known as 'Pat', an Oxford Blue, Olympic oarsman and rowing coach, took charge of the Oxford University Trial Eights in 1938, together with Gully Nickalls, also an Olympic oarsman, and John Garton who had succeeded Con Cherry as the OUBC President. These trials were the run-up to the 1938 Oxford and Cambridge Boat Race which, as fate would have it, was to be the last Boat Race until after World War II. Dick Hillary and I both rowed in the Trial Eights and were elected to Membership of the Leander Club.

The Trial Eights Race was rowed from Marsh Lock to Hambledon Lock, Henley-on-Thames, on Saturday 26 November 1938, resulting in a win for 'A' Crew by one and a quarter lengths. I rowed at No 4 in 'A' Crew, Dick was No 2 in 'B' Crew. According to the Times Rowing Correspondent, the standard of both crews was well above the average. 'B' Crew was stroked by Ian Esplin, an Australian from Sydney, who joined the RAF as a pilot during the war, and stayed on in the Service to retire some years later in the rank of Air Vice Marshal. During the early stages of training for the Boat Race, John Garton decided to stand down due to other commitments, so I was lucky enough to be put in the 'Blue Boat' at bow. I held this position for several weeks, until shortly before

THE 'DARK BLUE DAYS'

we moved to the Tideway, when John decided to row himself after all, so I lost my place. Although I missed getting a 'Blue' by a whisker I bore no grudge, John was the more experienced oarsman. I accepted his decision without question. As it turned out neither Dick Hillary nor I gained a 'Blue', the war disrupted our lives, so we were never granted another chance to try again. For good measure we each won a place in the Isis Crew, the University Second Eight.

Pat Mallam and I became good friends. He had a practice in Oxford, his surgery being in a large house in Holywell, where he also lived. Pat was very fond of his drink. He frequently asked me out to dine together with an Irishman called Hilary Crawfurd from Hertford College, a University Rugby Trial Cap. It was always a problem to escape Pat's hospitality in time to rush the BNC Lodge gates before they closed at midnight; consequently I often had to stay the night. Peggy, Pat's wife, was a superb cook and I think this was when I first became interested in cooking, although my mother was also a cook of some distinction; she was occasionally asked to broadcast recipes on the BBC from the old Savoy Hill Studios in the late twenties; perhaps cooking was in the blood.

Sometime in late October 1938 Pat, a boxing enthusiast, asked me if I would like to go up to London to see the World Light-Heavyweight championship fight at Harringay between Larry Gains, a coloured boxer, and an up and coming boxer called Len Harvey.

Pat booked a table for dinner after the fight at a Soho Restaurant called Pinolis, I don't think it exists now, it was probably bombed in the Blitz. We first went to Scotts for a couple of sherries. I don't remember much of the fight except that I believe Len Harvey won the title. Afterwards we took a taxi to Pinolis where we had what I thought was the most exotic and exciting meal I had ever eaten.

The decor was old fashioned, walls covered with dark oak panelling hung with signed pictures of society, sport, and stage celebrities, who had dined there over the years. As an hors d'oeuvre I chose a dozen oysters with slices of delicious fresh buttered brown bread. I had been told that oysters must be swallowed whole. I tried this but choked over the first two or three, so I decided to chew them with a dash of Tabasco and bite of the brown bread. I experienced an indescribably rich flavour, far surpassing anything I had ever tasted before. I was hooked on oysters, and have been ever since. We had a bottle of Puligny Montrachet 1929 with the oysters and a Chateau Margaux 1931 with the tournedos. We talked lightheadedly about the boxing match until we got round to rowing and the Trial Eights.

SPIT AND SAWDUST

"Hal, what's your opinion of Dick Hillary?" Pat asked suddenly. "You were at Shrewsbury with him, you must know him pretty well."

"I should say so! We were in the same House together, once upon a time we were good friends."

"I've noticed you don't seem very matey, on or off the river. Why's that?"

"I'm not sure, Pat, maybe its because he once swiped my girl friend."

"Tell me more."

"Well" I said "He was once staying with us on summer holidays, when I introduced him to some very wealthy friends of my parents. I was mad keen on one of the daughters, but as soon as she saw him she didn't want to know me any more."

"You can't blame Dick for that, you know" Pat countered "but I can see that he's a very conceited young man."

Of course I knew there was more to it than just youthful rancour.

Motoring back to Oxford late that night in Pat Mallam's car, along the Western Avenue through Beaconsfield, High Wycombe and Stokenchurch, I pondered on this evident anomaly of having an old friend who suddenly disowns me, yet we still share the same friends in our small world of rowing and training for the Boat Race. My thoughts rambled on and I began to feel resentful at Dick's self-assured egocentric attitude. The tragedy is that his life was cut short before the final reckoning.

In retrospect, I realise that I attributed to him faults which I now know I shared with him - lust, envy, jealousy and covetousness. In other words, in our heedless materialistic young lives there was little to chose between either of us, and the war which was about to erupt around us was to change everything.

Pat always kept a crate of bottled beers in the boot of his car as a stand-by for when the pubs shut. One evening he called on a lady patient at a house in Dorchester, while Hilary Crawfurd and I waited outside in the car. Suddenly he came out from the house, seized an empty bottle from the crate in the boot and carried it indoors, muttering something about taking a sample. We thought no more about it and when he returned to the car he replaced the bottle in the crate. A few evenings later we were going out on a pub crawl ending up at the Beetle and Wedge on the Thames near Crays Pond, Goring. On the way home to Oxford we stopped off at Shillingford Bridge, hoping the pubs would still be open, but they weren't, so we each grabbed a bottle from the crate in the boot and unscrewed the stoppers. There were no crown corks in those days.

THE 'DARK BLUE DAYS'

Pat had forgotten about the lady's sample, and as luck would have it I had taken a swallow before I realised, to my horror and loathing, that mine was the bottle containing the sample. I was sick all the way back to Holywell.

Prior to the 1938 Michaelmas term I again spent two weeks at Henley-on-Thames on a pre- term training session for the College Fours, to be rowed early in November, a repeat of the 1937 effort. Our Four comprised Dick Newell, at bow, Michael McNabb (an old Bryanstonian) at No 2, Ted Baillieu (an old Wykehamist) at No 3, and myself at stroke. Tony Tisdall (an old Carthusian) was spare man. We stayed at the Little White Hart, next door to the Henley Town Rowing Club bang opposite the Leander Club across the river. We kept our boat in the Leander Boat House.

After a very expensive Summer vacation we were naturally all skint, so we had to survive on bed and breakfast only, plus an occasional snack during the daytime, whenever we could scrape up a few shillings between us. The BNC Boat Club funds were low and the Treasurer would agree only to the cost of housing the boat, and a tip for the Leander Boatman as a parting gesture. Fortunately for us, half way through the fortnight, Ted Baillieu's father came to see us and stayed for two or three days. He was good for a few free hot dinners, but I suppose he could afford it because he ran a very expensive Rolls Royce. In the event we were beaten this time by a good New College Four, so all our pains and sacrifices were in vain.

I missed celebrating my twenty-first birthday, which was on 8 March, due to my rowing commitments, but I made up for it by throwing a sherry party in BNC on Saturday, 7 May. My own room being far too small, I borrowed two rooms adjoining one another in the Old Quad, one occupied by Alan Goodfellow, the other by Ian Tetley of Tetley's Brewery, which together could accommodate about thirty to forty thirsty young men. My father produced a dozen cases of splendid Amontillado from the Wine Society, and Ian Tetley produced two cases of Pol Roger. The College Chef provided canapés and my scout, the worthy Bert King, scrounged near enough one hundred glasses from the cellar. Needless to say we all got sloshed.

I had laid on a late buffet supper afterwards for about fifteen of us at the Wheatley Bridge Hotel, on the main road to High Wycombe, where we managed to assemble in one piece at about 9 pm. We arrived in an assortment of motor cars, including Ian Tetley's Lancia Lambda which we called 'The Flying bed Pan', Peter Whalley's De La Haye given to him

SPIT AND SAWDUST

by a wealthy aunt living in Paris, and Ted Baillieu's Lancia Aprilia. After eating, we spent some time on the lawn alongside the river below the bridge drinking beer, when we heard a horrific crash, jerking us out of our stupor. Followed by the others, I dashed on to the bridge to find a crumpled motorcycle smashed against the parapet but no sign of the rider. As I turned back in the direction of the pub, I saw a stationary car about two hundred yards down the road; on approaching it I heard the most ghastly noises coming from underneath. It was the motorcyclist, pinned under the car at the point of impact on the bridge, and dragged along from there underneath the car until it came to a stop within a few feet of the hotel car park. By now we had all sobered up. We had to lift the car up bodily before we could free the victim, whom we carried into the hotel lounge and laid on a sofa. Although still alive he was horribly injured and uttering the most blood curdling sounds. He died just as an ambulance arrived. We all returned to Oxford sober and brought down to earth by what we had seen. It was indeed a sad end to my party, and it gave me much food for thought.

In the Trinity term, 1938, an Australian from Melbourne, R H Leonard, coxed the BNC First Eight. He was a thin emaciated little man with a large head perched on the top of a long thin stringy neck, his cranium protruding backwards in a curve, like a globe artichoke wavering on its slender stalk. He was only just five feet tall, very ugly, droopy eyelids, hooked nose and protruding teeth. He had a rasping accent and a sharp tongue. He must have been the runt of the litter, and he weighed a mere seven and a half stone. He had the utmost difficulty in directing the process of turning an eight-oared boat round one hundred and eighty degrees on the river, because he was usually drunk, consequently the College Boat Club Fund was slowly dissipated by the cost of repairs to bows, rudder and stern, touched off by frequent contacts with the stony banks of the Isis. Salters Boat Yard was the beneficiary. The Boat Club tried to get rid of him, but there was no one else in the College willing to take on the responsibility of Cox. He was nicknamed 'Dopey' after the character in Snow White and the Seven Dwarfs, which was having a long run at the Super Cinema opposite the Martyrs Memorial in Magdelen Street.

Dopey occupied a room on the first floor on No 1 Staircase in the Old Quad. As you ascend the ancient steep wooden stairs, loud creaking noises follow you up. Upon reaching the landing, Dopey's room was on the left; opposite was the room of the Vice Principal, Maurice Platnauer. Henry Drew was the Scout on Staircase No 1, and he was the oldest and

THE 'DARK BLUE DAYS'

most senior scout in the College. He was small, wizened, balding, with a dried up appearance; in fact, without much imagination, he could almost be mistaken for Dopey himself at a casual glance.

Maurice and Dopey kept Henry busy every day removing the empties and struggling back up the creaking stairs with liquid replenishments, although surprisingly Maurice and Dopey were not drinking partners. Neither seemed to be aware of the other's presence nor drinking habits, because almost always they sported their woods. Dopey was reading law, and he would work throughout the night after drinking all day, apart from coxing the college eight during the afternoons. For his size he must have had a strong constitution, because he seldom took to his bed. Henry for his part, maintained a kind of resigned countenance towards the goings on up Staircase No 1. He was not easily given to conversation and, such as it was, was brusque. On being questioned how or where Mr Leonard might be, Henry would reply with a shrug of the shoulders and an eloquent hoist of his eyebrows.

Dopey's tutor was Humphrey Waldock, who made a name for himself five years later as one of the principal advocates in the Nuremberg War Crimes Trials. For some reason Dopey dubbed him 'The Insignificant Humph'.

Dopey's father, amongst other things, owned the Melbourne Race Course plus all the trappings, and by any standard he must have been a very rich man. This was borne out by the fact that his wife, in 1935, had purchased a villa in Le Touquet, and rented a three-bedroomed apartment in Boulevard Berthier, Paris VII'ième, where she spent six months in every year. I had met Mrs Leonard on the only one occasion she had ever visited her son in Oxford, and for some strange reason she had taken to me.

CHAPTER FOUR

SUMMER CAMP SCENARIO

I remember one morning some years ago at school rushing to make the classroom in time for the 7.45 am lesson which was before breakfast and was immediately followed by morning chapel. I nearly knocked over a boy by the corner of the entrance to the School House. I pulled up just in time and noticed at once that he looked ghastly white.

"You know Harris?" he gasped.

"Of course, what's making you look so groggy?"

He clutched his books. "He's just fallen out of the dormitory window. Killed. Hit the concrete yard at the back."

I felt sick and all turned round inside.

Harris dead? I asked myself. It couldn't be. It was only yesterday I saw him playing cricket. It all seemed so unreal , and yet it was true because at morning chapel the Headmaster made a solemn announcement to the whole school.

So when I saw Percy Burton climbing down from his aircraft and walking towards me as I stood outside the mess tent at Lympne, the first thing I noticed was from how far away I could see his face, because it was deadly white, like that boy in School House who told me about Harris. I thought perhaps Percy had cricked his neck or something.

"What's up Percy?" I called to him. He was groping into his pocket for a match, a cigarette trembling between his lips.

"I've just seen something pretty ghastly, I think it was a collision in midair but it happened so quickly I couldn't take it all in."

My God, I thought, suddenly remembering that someone had said David Lewis was a few minutes overdue. David was one of the most experienced pilots in the Squadron, there should be no need to start worrying about him yet.

"I saw a large yellow panel," Percy continued, "Gyrating down like an enormous sheet of cardboard. Then I saw other pieces falling past my port wing tip, though I couldn't see anything recognisable."

As Percy spoke, several members came out of the mess tent. Suddenly 'Crackers', Squadron Leader Cracroft the Chief Flying Instructor appeared, demanding to hear more details. With that he dashed into the tent and grabbed the phone looking pretty ghastly, I thought. Things started to swim before my eyes and I felt an acute twist in the pit of my stomach. Quite a crowd had gathered now, the atmosphere was tense. It seemed like an eternity until 'Crackers' appeared again and looked at us. There was silence.

SUMMER CAMP SCENARIO

"It now seems certain," he said, "that David Lewis has had a midair collision. Two planes are reported to have crashed about half an hour ago near Canterbury. There is no trace of David having landed anywhere, and he certainly wouldn't have had any gas left by now."

He gave us a sidelong glance and turned away muttering under was breath.

Although, like myself, David was an Old Salopian, we were acquaintances rather than friends. I came to know him better at Oxford, especially after I had joined the OUAS where we often met in the Squadron Bar at Manor Road.

Within minutes it was known throughout the Camp that David had collided with a plane flown by an instructor and pupil of the Civil Air Guard. All three were killed. It suddenly dawned on me that I was probably the last person to see and talk to David. I remember I spoke to him just before he climbed into the cockpit of his 'Hart' - I had picked up his goggles which he had accidentally dropped; they were expensive ones and he was very proud of them. It struck me at the time that I could use a pair of goggles like that.

So for one evening death was near us all, perhaps a timely reminder that the younger generation was not at liberty to fly planes indiscriminately around the sky without a single thought for anyone or anything. We were to learn all too soon how fatal accidents made pilots feel churned up inside like when passing a nasty pile-up on the Brighton Road on a Bank Holiday.

After a spirited game of tennis and hoisting a few beers aboard in Folkestone that evening, we all felt better. The David Lewis incident faded from memory but he was not forgotten; we knew we had learned another lesson albeit at the cost of his life. This and countless other lessons we learned at Lympne that Summer.

It was not long before Percy and I were introduced to formation flying with Bill Jenna and Bill Bailey, our two flying instructors. We used to take off in the Avro Tutors at about 6 am in the morning, well before anyone surfaced, and rendezvous over the sands at Hythe winging it down the beach in tight formation towards Folkestone pier, a good ninety five mph on the clock! We seemed so close we could almost reach out and touch one another and as I looked across at Percy, I felt the thrill of formation flying and yearned for the day when I could take control and do it myself.

I went solo on my second day at Lympne and was learning something new every day. This was not so difficult because our instructors were hand picked.

I fully realised the demands made on them, the boredom, the irritation and the repetition. I was conscious all the time of trying my best to avoid making the same old mistakes over and over again, so that by the end of the day the instructors' nerves became ragged and frayed, but if this was so Bill Jenna never showed it. He had a habit of whistling down the Gosport speaking tube, and once he stopped in the middle of a flat rendering of 'Sweet Fanny Adams' to shout

"You must never think you know everything! Right now you know nothing, but your attitude towards flying is good. Avoid over confidence; pilots who accept this will not only be good pilots but stand a good chance of survival."

I feverishly went on doing turns, nose following the horizon and 'Holding Off Bank' with grim determination. Later when I was flying fighters during the war I would occasionally remind myself how much I owed to Bill Jenna.

I had borrowed my Father's Morris 8, a somewhat dilapidated Tourer with a canvas hood and shabby perspex side-screens, for the Summer Camp stint. Not many of us had cars at Lympne, so my Morris, which I called Ronald, came in very handy and was in constant demand. It could often be seen of an evening coasting into Folkestone crammed with about six bodies making for the White Cliffs Ballroom. Harry Bandinell, whose mother was French and lived in Bordeaux, had borrowed her smart Peugeot open two-seater with a folding dickey seat at the back, which took a further three or four bodies.   When the Camp ended in August, Tony Disdall invited me to stay with him at his Mother's flat in Hendon. With a few passengers we drove up to London in convoy with Harry Bandinell bringing up the rear in his Peugeot. That evening Harry took us to a Club in Sloane Street frequented mainly by members of the French Embassy, where his favourite girlfriend, also French and very delectable, introduced us to some equally voluptuous females.

The war situation was now hotting up and already plans for evacuating families from Dockland and the East End were being put into effect. Daily bulletins detailing the call-up of sundry Reservists were being broadcast over the BBC.

Tony and I decided it was time to make tracks for Oxford to report to Squadron Headquarters, taking in Maidenhead en route. Whilst rowing in the BNC Eight during Henley Regatta the previous June we had met two attractive sisters, Joan and Beri Stutchberry, who lived at Maidenhead, so we phoned them to say we would be calling, whereupon

SUMMER CAMP SCENARIO

they invited us to stay a couple of nights. We arrived midst incessant talk of war and the evacuation of London.

The idea of going to war seemed almost exciting, we both felt elated because we knew we were now set to be pilots. We took Joan and Beri to Maidenhead Station where we helped their mother to sort out the bewildered be-labelled children and mothers arriving train after train from the East End. A Reception Centre had been set up in the local Council School. We went there again the following day to try to comfort the mothers and kids with pop and cups of tea.

There was a large wireless set in the School Hall. At precisely 11.15 am on 3 September 1939, we stopped to listen to Neville Chamberlain announcing to the world that we were now at war with Germany. It seemed uncanny to be standing around taking a breather and hearing someone calmly announcing that England was at war. I glanced out of the window to see clusters of children in the playground. They seemed lost and confused, whilst the women spoke about strange places which were soon to be their homes for goodness knows how long. Who could say if it would be a long or short war, I thought, as I idly watched a small boy climb up on to an old field gun, a relic from some past campaign?

CHAPTER FIVE

THE 'SITZKRIEG'

I was now expecting my commission in the RAFVR to come through at any minute. To while away the time for the next four weeks, I alternated between my home in Regal and Oxford whilst trying to keep myself busy. At Oxford I stayed with Pat Mallam. Every morning after breakfast I would rush down to the Squadron Headquarters at Manor Road hoping for news. War or peace, my commission must surely come before the end of September, because all Squadron members were automatically commissioned in the VR provided they had the necessary recommendation. Be it acceptable or not this was a prerogative granted to members of the OUAS, a privilege of which I was all too ready to avail myself.

My generation took for granted the distinction between those who were born to be leaders by virtue of hereditary descent, unlimited money, or a public school education, and those of more humble origins who enjoyed no such privileges and opportunities, so were obliged willy nilly to work their way up through the ranks. We were soon to learn that some of the greatest leaders of the RAF in World War II came from the latter sort.

I was still taken with the idea of applying for a permanent commission. I approached the Squadron Adjutant for details, only to be told that there would be no more permanent commissions granted until after the war.

It was therefore with some surprise, on bumping into Leonard Cheshire one morning in Holywell, that he told me his permanent commission had just come through, in fact he said he must have been granted the 'Last PC' of the peace. He was very excited about it. After lunch in the Squadron Mess we went off together to his house at Boar's Hill and played tennis for the rest of the afternoon, joined by his brother Christopher.

I was beginning to think I would never hear anything. I motored home one day to Regal feeling miserable and forgotten. Many Squadron friends were already wearing uniform and departing to training units. However, one morning in late September, when I had long given up hope, an official looking letter arrived for me at the door. It was my VR Commission granted with effect from 26 September. As I went to break the news to my mother she waved a hand and said,

"It's alright, dear, don't tell me, I know already what that is."

Suddenly I realised that this was not to her liking and I almost

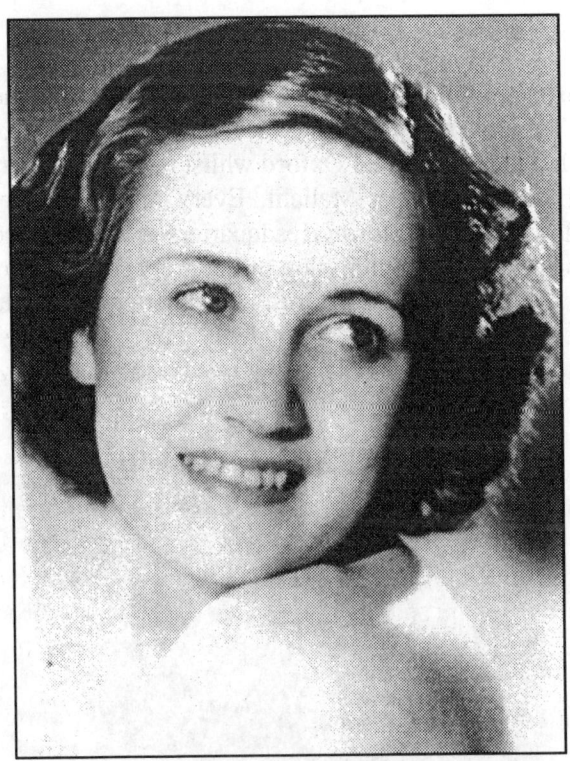

Pamela Nelson-Edwards, neé Davidson, taken in 1936 when Head Girl at the Windmill Theatre

Shrewsbury School Soccer Tour — Germany. Visit to Hitler Youth Camp in the Hartz Mountains (circa 1937)

Shrewsbury School — Churchill's Four which went 'Head of the River', 1937. GHNE at Stroke, Richard Hillary at No.2

Oxford University Air Squadron at Summer Camp, Lympne, 1939

THE 'SITZKRIEG

apologised for being selfish.

My instructions were to report at once to Downing College, Cambridge, in uniform. I already had my uniform which I had bought from Burberry's in the Haymarket. Michael Burberry was a member of the OUAS so it seemed the natural thing to get my new rig-out there.

Early the next morning my father ran me to Snowhill Station, Birmingham, where I boarded a train for Cambridge dressed up like a dog's dinner, wearing my round peak hat and a glossy pale blue greatcoat with shiny brass buttons, reaching nearly down to my ankles. I had an hour to wait at Northampton for a connection to Cambridge, and I remember feeling infuriated with some small boys loafing about the platform making pointed remarks at me from a safe distance. They rudely asked me what was on at the pictures that night. I realised that I must have looked a real twit, something like a wax model in Montague Burtons' showroom. I had barely started to fly and yet there I stood in RAF Officer's uniform providing entertainment for some wretched little ruffians.

When I arrived at Downing College that evening, things started to look up. I found most of my old Oxford friends there, just as if we were congregating again for another summer camp. We were all in it now, all in uniform, all looking like glorified Cinema Attendants, so my spirits revived. I went with some friends to eat steaks and drink beer at the Fountain. I remember feeling highly pleased with myself for no special reason. I didn't know it then but I was to have little reason to feel pleased during the following long months of the phoney war.

One of the first signs of the change in my life came with my acquiring the cigarette habit. It was at Cambridge that I first started to smoke. I will throw aside all this super fitness nonsense, I thought, in the face of death who knows how long there is to live? I decided I would probably never row again so I might as well learn to enjoy the pleasures of tobacco while there was yet time.

The accommodation at Downing was spartan to say the least, not the sort of thing spoilt young undergraduates should be expected to endure. We each slept on a narrow wooden platform raised about three inches from the floor, laid with a thin palliasse. There were about twelve to a room spaced out with not more than a foot between each palliasse. It was a problem to find one's own particular billet, especially when returning in the blackout, so a small pocket torch was essential to avoid treading on somnolent bodies.

The ITW at Cambridge was a kind of holding unit for ab initio pilots

SPIT AND SAWDUST

prior to being fed into the flying training sausage machine. In those days flying Training Schools, or FTS's as they were known, were comparatively few and, despite the desperate need for fully trained pilots, there was a limit to intake capacity so hundreds of aspirants from the RAFO (Reserve of RAF Officers) the RAFVR and Civil Air Guard were held in limbo for months waiting for a slot on the conveyor belt. In mid-November most of us were transferred from Cambridge to another ITW at Hastings in Sussex, which was an improvement because we were billeted out in local hotels and boarding houses, where we had proper beds to sleep on.

I found myself in a private hotel called the Wellington in Warrior Square, St Leonard's-on-Sea. The ITW was commanded by 'Acting' Air Commodore Critchley who in peacetime had been the head of an organisation known as the Greyhound Racing Association (GRA). His headquarters were housed in a large modern building on the sea front named Marine Court. The majority of the Staff Officers originated from the GRA so they were more used to training greyhounds than an unruly body of recalcitrant undergraduates and the like. The RAF had requisitioned a very large underground car park beneath the promenade where we were made to march in threes up and down, morning and afternoon.

At roll call every morning there would always be a few of us missing, mostly in London. We developed an almost foolproof system of answering for the absentees. The authorities were either unable or too disinterested to do much about it, consequently we enjoyed more than a little freedom of action.

The Warrant Officer in charge of Drill Instruction was a Mr Hoy, whose favourite and frequent expression was "Nothing in it, like my front room!" For some inexplicable reason this would trigger us off into uncontrollable paroxysms of laughter which gave him enormous pleasure. He turned a blind eye to our comings and goings, he had to, he had little choice in the matter!

Apart from the foot slogging, the GRA made an effort to keep us physically fit. To this end two internationally known professional boxers, Len Harvey and Eddy Phillips, were drafted into the RAF as Physical Training Instructors and posted to Marine Court. They conducted evening keep fit classes which we were supposed to attend, and for which we displayed a singular lack of enthusiasm, so Len Harvey thought up the diabolical idea of making us draw lots for two rounds in the ring with either one or the other. I was drawn against Len Harvey. Having been

THE 'SITZKRIEG

School Captain of Boxing at Shrewsbury I felt honour bound to put up some sort of show. I lasted out the two rounds at the expense of a bloody nose and a bruised ear. I don't think I touched any part of Len's anatomy except his arms whilst trying to avoid his gloves. When we shook hands afterwards he said, because I had been so game, he would recommend me for a bout with Eddy Phillips. I said,

"Thank you very much, I have no intention to taking him on."

"Oh yes you will," Len said, "but I'll fix it so that he will let you hit him like he was a punch-bag."

Several evenings later I had two rounds with Eddy and really enjoyed myself. They were both great guys.

In December we were told we could have Christmas leave and to report to the Marine Court Headquarters. They were looking forward to being rid of us for a few weeks so leave was readily granted from 14 December until 4 January 1940, subject to immediate recall in an emergency. God knows what we would have been asked to do if recalled, perhaps to swell the ranks of the St Leonard's-on-Sea Home Guard.

I caught a train to Waterloo and booked in at the Regent Palace for two nights. Two friends also came with me, Peter Barlow and Roddy Knocker. We decided we wanted to see the new Flanaghan and Allen Show, 'Run Rabbit Run' at the Palladium, featuring Roma Beaumont and the hit song 'My Heart belongs to Daddy'. After the show we decided on a night club crawl. A taxi driver dropped the three of us off at a club called the Blue Lagoon in Carlisle Street. I was very taken with an attractive girl in sheer black stockings and a short ballet type skirt selling cigarettes, chocolates and expensive dolls. Much to the annoyance of the Management I danced with her the rest of the night, and we made a date to meet the next morning outside the Pavilion Cinema, Piccadilly Circus. I learned that her name was Pamela Davidson.

CHAPTER SIX

THE STIFFKEY CONNECTION

Pamela and I spent the following day together. She took me to meet her mother, Mrs Moyra Davidson, who was living in The Boltons. I gave them lunch at a very pleasant pub off the Brompton Road called the Ennismore Arms. It was here that I first learned the full story of Moyra's husband, the late Reverend Harold Davidson, Rector of Stiffkey, the eccentric Vicar who provoked a nationwide scandal in the early thirties through his alleged relationships with London prostitutes. He was tried by an Ecclesiastical Court at Church House, Westminster, for immoral conduct and found guilty, being later unfrocked at a Ceremony held in the side-Chapel of Norwich Cathedral in October 1932.

I was shocked when I realised that this Harold Davidson was none other than the Vicar who used to visit my Aunt at her 'Rescue Home' in Soho, and that Pamela (known in the family as Pan and later to become my wife) was his daughter. Subsequently Moyra confessed that Pan was not in truth the Rector's daughter, but the result of an illicit union with a Colonel in the Canadian Army during World War I. We talked for hours on end and I heard the whole spellbinding story.

The Revered Davidson was born on 14 July 1875 in a small village called Sholing near Southampton. At the age of nineteen he sat for a scholarship to University where his father had hoped he would study for Holy Orders but he failed. Instead he took to the stage. For four years he was a struggling actor playing in provincial Theatres and Working Men's Clubs. Then he tried his luck in London, and scored a notable success as 'Charley's Aunt' which kept him almost solvent, until finally he was accepted for Exeter College, Oxford in the Michaelmas Term 1898. His father was unable to finance him so he was obliged to continue with his acting in order to pay his way, necessitating frequent interruptions to his academic studies, with the result that it took him five years to gain a BA. He was lucky to have influential friends because otherwise he would surely have been sent down by the College Rector. One thing he did learn was that at the threshold of the twentieth century there was little future for a budding actor without private means, so reluctantly he abandoned the stage for the Cloth, which he took in 1904 to become a Junior Curate. He spent quite some time in London's Dockland Settlement sponsored by the Toynbee Family. In 1905 he was appointed Assistant Curate at St Martins-in-the-Fields where he married Moyra in October 1906, an event presided over by the Bishop of London. It was said that whenever a virgin was married there the lions roared in Trafalgar Square. Just prior to the

THE STIFFKEY CONNECTION

wedding Harold had been appointed the Rector of Stiffkey and Morston where he and his new wife took up residence after a honeymoon in Italy. They now settled down to the humdrum life of a sleepy pastoral vicarage.

Whenever Harold proposed intercourse, which was not often, he would first kneel beside the marital bed and offer up a prayer to God beseeching Him to forgive the sin he was about to commit, whilst Moyra languished between the cold sheets until she went completely off the boil. Thus the sexual side of their married life, although it produced four children, was lukewarm and passionless.

When the war came Harold, inspired rather by the prospect of freedom from his family than by patriotism, volunteered for the Navy and was accepted as a Chaplain assigned to a Cruiser Squadron in the Shetlands. In 1917 he was transferred to Middle East waters where he remained until the end of the war in Europe. He spent much of his time in Cairo and soon became ensnared by the lure of the Orient. A friend of his, Lieutenant Locking RN, said that to drag Harold away from a Cairo whorehouse was like trying to extract iron ore from a gold mine. He was fascinated by the belly-dancers and the scantily dressed girls.

By the time he was demobbed in 1919 he had been parted from Moyra and the lonely Rectory in Norfolk for nearly four years. In the meantime an old school friend of Harold's from the Southampton days had arrived on the scene, the Canadian Colonel. He was in the trenches in France and spent several leaves at Stiffkey. He and Moyra fell in love, but he returned to Canada in November 1918, and the following March Harold came home to find his wife pregnant. Although Harold knew he could in no way be responsible for her conception he agreed to sign Pan's Birth Certificate, which was registered in the sub- district of St Clement, Oxford, on 23 July 1919, thus legitimising the birth. She was christened Pamela Cushla Le Poer.

It became increasingly clear that the Rector had a growing conviction that he was divinely appointed to convert prostitutes from sin to salvation. He now made this aspiration his mission in life. During the twenties he spent less and less time with his flock and more and more time in the West End of London. After taking Evensong in Stiffkey Church on a Sunday evening, he would take a taxi to Wells-on-Sea to catch the last train to London, arriving at Kings Cross at about 10.30 pm, or sometimes he would bicycle to the station. The cycle ride took about thirty minutes longer than the taxi but, as always, he never allowed himself enough time, arriving at the station just as the train was pulling in with screeching brakes, enveloped in billowing white smoke, the Stationmaster shouting

SPIT AND SAWDUST

"Wells-on-Sea! Wells-on-Sea!" Flinging the bicycle to the ground he would dive past the ticket office onto the platform and hurl himself at a carriage door just as the train was moving off, hanging on to his Homburg hat with one hand and the door handle with the other, whilst the Stationmaster would hesitate between blowing the whistle and waving the red flag to stop the train. A similar procedure took place in reverse the following Saturday evening. It was a familiar sight to see him tearing down the platform at Kings Cross in a desperate attempt to catch the last train back to Wells-on-Sea. It seems he was never on time for anything, yet somehow he was seldom too late.

On arriving back at the Rectory he would retire to his study and smoke endless cheap sixpenny cigars sitting in an old worn leather arm chair. He never went to bed but continued like this through the night. There was always a family row when he pressed Moyra for a loan towards his London expenses the following week.

Around the time of the General Strike in 1926 almost everyone was short of ready cash and the Davidson family was no exception. Yet the Rector somehow managed to raise money from somewhere. He had extraordinary powers of persuasion combined with an audacity and cheek which knew no bounds. He pestered people and his victims would pay up in order that he might go away.

His one and only appearance with the family was at breakfast on Sunday morning. Entering the dining room he would make straight for the breadboard, seizing the bread knife and cutting up the loaf into small pieces about the size of Oxo cubes. Moyra would shout,

"Why should I provide for your parishioners at Holy Communion out of my housekeeping? You owe me for that."

The Rector's reply was to sweep the croutons into a brown paper bag and, clutching it under his arm, triumphantly beat a hasty retreat out of the house into the vestry, just in time to don his robes and kneel in front of the alter rail mumbling,

"The body of our Lord Jesus Christ," etc., etc., simultaneously pinching morsels of the pilfered breakfast loaf between thumb and forefinger, passing hurriedly from one supplicant to the next like a ticket collector on a London bus, the brown paper bag still clutched under his arm. Not one of the congregation would have missed this performance for the world. Such eccentric behaviour encouraged regular attendance, for there was always keen speculation on what he would do next.

In the early days there were house guests frequently staying at the Rectory, at least during the time when Moyra had money to spare. After

THE STIFFKEY CONNECTION

dinner, for the more distinguished guests such as Bishops and so on, there were usually a half Stilton, Bath Olivers, coffee, cigars and a decanter of port.

A certain Bishop was once invited to the Rectory for lunch. It was a fine day, the east wind, which normally beats into the Norfolk flats, had eased. The sky was blue with a haze over the horizon, a light breeze wafting from the southwest. After lunch the Rector and the Bishop retired to the study for coffee, port and cigars. The Bishop was a large paunchy man, about six feet tall, white hair and balding, shiny fat pink cheeks and full red sensuous lips. Pan, who was then about four years old, was playing in the garden and, seeing that the French windows of the study were open, ran in and was greeted by the Bishop who was alone, the Rector having gone to fetch more coffee.

The Bishop started to stroke Pan's hand with one smooth podgy white hand and with the other felt her small bottom, then bending over to kiss her he stuck his wet tongue deep into her mouth. Pan was terrified. Although she didn't understand, she sensed that something was very wrong. She fled crying from the study into the arms of her mother in the drawing room.

"What on earth's the matter with you child?"

"Mummy I'm frightened!"

"Frightened of what, dear?" Moyra replied.

"I don't know" whined Pan.

"Don't know? Come on child, don't be so silly."

But Pan would say no more despite attempts at cajoling and persuasions by Moyra and Lady Townsend.

"You had better go to your room then," Moyra said in a stern voice.

So Pan ran up the stairs and waited there until the Bishop had gone. From that day on Pan told no one, she didn't even confide in Nugent her favourite brother, but it left an ineradicable impression on her mind.

As the years rolled on Moyra had luckily retained some private money for school fees, just enough to finish off the education of the two boys, who went to Public School, and the two girls who went to the Ursuline Convent in Cheltenham. Pan also attended the convent but by 1933, when she was barely in her teens, the money was running out due to the high costs of the Rector's case. Through no fault of her own she could not go back.

The family now had to move out of the Rectory and they rented a house in Norland Square, Holland Park, where Pan at the tender age of fourteen became a reluctant domestic help, so she longed for a real job.

SPIT AND SAWDUST

Like so many young girls of her age she was attracted to the romantic world of stage and screen.

The Rector's case was still fresh in everyone's mind and hardly a day passed without a call from some newspaper reporter trying to ferret out new titbits with which to titillate their readers, or from some individual trying to cash in on the family's misfortune.

One day Pan sat drinking a cup of tea in the Express Dairy Cafeteria in Charing Cross Road near Cambridge Circus. She only had 6d left and she was reading the 'Jobs Vacant' column in the 'Stage', a weekly paper, when a strange female came up behind and looked over her shoulder. She was a faded blonde in about her late thirties; her figure, though still passable, had seen better days.

"'Scuse me ducks, you lookin' for a job? P'raps I can help."

"Could you really? I do so want very much to be an actress."

"Well dearie, I can't exactly promise you a stage job, but I am looking for a girl with a flair for acrobatics and trapeze work."

"I'm afraid I have never had experience of that sort of thing, and anyway its not really what I'm looking for."

"You want money dearie?"

"Yes, of course."

"Well then, when you are starting from scratch you can't be too choosy, you ought to know that."

"Perhaps you are right" agreed Pan unhappily.

"Look duckie, I run an Agency for girl troupes on the Music Halls, my hubbie has an office across the road in Newport Place, why not hop over with me and have a chat?"

With that the blonde lady paid for the cup of tea and before she knew what was happening Pan was taken by the arm and propelled across the road into Newport Place and into a grotty little newsagents shop. There were dailies and periodicals displayed in profusion at the front, and behind were literary paraphernalia consisting mostly of pornographic magazines and photographs mixed up with sweets and chocolates.

"What's your name?"

"Pan Davidson."

"This is Johnny Schofield, my old man, and my name's Renée."

After that they sat down in the back parlour and Renée started to explain that she was looking for girls to join a new troupe she was getting up for a company running a circus, which was due to open in Bristol in a week's time. The money was good, 15/- per week plus board and lodging. She would have to share a bed, of course, with one of the girls.

THE STIFFKEY CONNECTION

Pan was now fifteen, miserably unhappy at home, education neglected and no money apart from what she could occasionally scrounge from her brothers, or from an odd job she managed to get from time to time. The idea of running away to join a circus suddenly appealed to her, so there and then she accepted. Renée gave her a few shillings to go home and pack, with instructions that she was to be back in two days time at Newport Place, where there would be a truck waiting to take the troupe to Bristol.

Pan could hardly contain her excitement. With difficulty she refrained from telling her mother. She slipped out of the house early one February morning with a small suitcase containing her meagre belongings.

She caught the tube from Notting Hill Gate to Leicester Square and a few minutes walk found her in Newport Place, where already there were about six young girls waiting in the newsagents' shop. Renée introduced her to them one by one, Doris, Pat, Annie, Gladys, Madge and Donna. Renée didn't seem to be such a bad sort after all. She fussed the girls like a mother hen, took them next door for a sandwich and a cup of coffee while they were waiting. Pan could not help wondering what Renée and Johnny Schofield were getting out of it, a fortune no doubt. Even at her age she already knew that young girls were a valuable commodity, but she had the blinkers on and she could see no further than the vision of crisp £1 notes coming her way. But of course it was not to be like that.

"My name's Donna."

Pan could not remember the girls names within seconds of being introduced. A tall dark girl was talking to her.

"Have you ever been on the stage?"

"No, worse luck, have you?"

"I once went for an audition for an interval act at the Cricklewood Empire but I wasn't even called."

"I had a job as an usherette," Pan replied "which is about as near to the stage as I will ever get, I suppose."

"Never mind, this circus thing could perhaps lead to something. How about sharing a bed with me?"

"I don't mind, Renée says we must all share so why not?"

The transport arrived at the Shaftesbury Avenue end of Newport Place and the girls piled in. They parked their cases on one or two boxes which were lying around. There were no seats, so with them hanging on by their eye lashes, the truck weaved its way down the Great West Road, through Reading, Newbury, Hungerford and Bath, until they reached the circus compound on the outskirts of Bristol, bruised, bewildered and

SPIT AND SAWDUST

exhausted.

It was too late to find their digs so they had to kip down in an empty caravan normally used for transporting ponies. The floor was covered in straw and smelled strongly of horse shit. Everyone was very kind, even the marquee boys rallied round and produced hot tea and Cornish pasties; one of them had a squeeze box and they all sat round singing songs until the generator ran out of gas, and all the lights went out. This was on a Saturday, the show being due to open the next Monday evening.

Renée Schofield had given them the address of their digs, so on Sunday morning the girls, carrying their bags and cases, had to walk about two miles to find the boarding house, which was in a poor quarter on the outskirts of the city. Pan and Donna selected quite a nice room for themselves with a very large double bed. There was a toilet at the end of a long passageway, the only washing facilities being a china bowl and jug on a wash stand in the bedroom. They had to go down to the basement to fetch water.

Monday morning came and they had to take a tram to the circus location. None of the girls knew what they were supposed to do. Someone grabbed Pan and started to teach her to tumble, she seemed to be good at this, and before long she even tumbled with a team of clowns. She was told that in between acts she was to scrape up dung with a large dustpan and brush. Everyone was very kind and the clowns dressed Pan up in the proper garb so she proceeded to tumble. She enjoyed it immensely, and she was not really bothered at all by occasionally having to follow the horses and elephants with the tools of the trade. She was even applauded by the crowd, and this gave her the first taste of audience participation, which she soon came to recognise as the food and drink of the professional.

About Wednesday, after a very exhausting day of matinée and late evening performances, Donna and Pan flung themselves into their double bed and talked for a while before putting the light out. Suddenly there was a movement at the bottom of the bed and Pan, terrified, felt something grab at her toes. Alarmed she turned screaming to Donna.

"What on earth's that, what's at the bottom of the bed?"

"Oh God! Don't tell me its Blini, I told him to stay away" she gasped, as she reached out and switched the light on.

"For God's sake what are you talking about?"

At that moment a face appeared from under the cover at the bottom of the bed, and an extraordinary little dwarf less than three feet tall stood up reaching across for Donna. Pan jumped out of the bed in alarm and

THE STIFFKEY CONNECTION

horror. It was Blini, the Hungarian dwarf. He had fallen in love with Donna and she with him. There he was attempting to make love to Donna before Pan's very eyes and Donna wanting it. This was too much, and Pan rushed out of the room looking for space in another bedroom with the other girls.

Much to Pan's relief, the next day Donna booked a room in a cheap hotel off Park Street where she and Blini could make their strange love uninterrupted, except that Donna had to smuggle Blini in and out of the hotel undetected by the management. Discovery of the dwarf would have meant expulsion.

Pan now shared her bed with Madge. It seemed that Blini had plenty of money and he took all the girls out to a road house one evening where they had a hilarious time.

The girls had about eight weeks with the circus, but Pan started to get homesick, and sent a postcard to her mother to say she was coming back home. When she was paid off she had only just enough money for a ticket to Paddington, and a Chinese meal at Ley Ons in Wardour Street, before arriving bedraggled, tired out and penniless at Norland Square on Sunday evening. Moyra gave her a thorough scrub in the bath and put her to bed.

The following year, 1934, Pan stayed at home most of the time except for odd jobs and a month in Blackpool at the Rector's bidding. She help her mother move from Norland Square to South Kensington where Nugent was negotiated the purchase of a maisonette in The Boltons near Earl's Court, three bedrooms and all 'mod cons' for about £3,000. There was just enough money left, hidden from the Rector, to pay for it outright. Nugent had married Lorraine Sandow, with two children from her previous marriage to Douglas Brown of African Browns, Manchester. They now had a daughter, Valerie, and Pan used to baby sit for them at their flat nearby in Onslow Gardens. Lorrie was the granddaughter of Sandow, reputed to be the illegitimate son of Kaiser Wilhelm II. He was in his day deemed the strongest man in the world.

It was about this time that the Rector bribed Pan to go to Blackpool with the promise of £100 for staying with him in a stall on the seafront. Luke Gannon, Harold's impresario, provided the money, because he was persuaded that if the vicar could be seen lying in a bed beside an attractive young girl, the money collected from admissions would more than treble. Inside the booth two beds were installed side by side in a large box made to look life a coffin, the top of the 'coffin' almost completely covered by a sheet of plate glass. At the rear of the 'coffin' was a trap door wide

SPIT AND SAWDUST

enough for the Rector or Pan to slip out at night for a breath of fresh air. The entrance to the booth was from the pavement on the sea front, just like many similar side shows up and down the promenade; the public being admitted through a turnstile at one side, filing around the coffin to peer down through the glass, and out again on the pavement on the other side. Under each bed was a chamber pot, the use of which was possible if and when the turnstile was stopped, to allow time for either one of them to restore their personal comfort. The idea of this was to delude the public into thinking that they were viewing a vicar and a young female lying in bed together, thereby titillating their imagination.

An additional feature of this display was the Rector's public declaration that he and his lady friend would fast for forty days and forty nights. For the first twelve hours or so Pan only just managed to survive without food, but very soon she was slipping out after dark through the trap door in search of sausages and chips. As curious viewers passed slowly round the coffin the Rector, irrepressible and voluable as always, talked continuously and persuasively to those willing to listen, in order to justify his flagrant and perhaps outrageous way of condemning the Church which, as he explained, had so unjustly unfrocked him.

One day a young man passed shouting a string of invectives accusing the Rector of blasphemy, profanity and desecration.

"What's more," he shouted "you may like to know that my father was a Colonel."

The Rector, looking up from his gruesome resting place, replied in a flash:

"My boy, how very ashamed your father must have been of you."

Pan managed to keep up the pretence for about three weeks, but finally succumbed and bade her father goodbye, taking with her what was left of the £100, which she rightly felt she had more than earned considering the macabre circumstances.

On her return to The Boltons, having bought herself some new clothes from '5th Avenue', a cheap gown shop in Regent Street, Pan set out to find another job. She bought the 'Stage' every week, and soon spotted an 'ad' for girls to attend an audition at an address in Palm Tree Court, just off Holborn Circus. She was one of about sixty girls and it looked pretty hopeless. Whilst waiting to go in for the audition, she filled in time by wandering down into the basement, where she met a man busy with a lot of packing cases. She got into conversation and straight away he asked her if she was looking for a job.

"What's involved?"

THE STIFFKEY CONNECTION

"Oh, just putting these packs into cardboard cartons for insertion into slot machines. They're in most ladies toilets in the West End."

"What on earth are they?" Pan asked.

"My dear, you should know, you're old enough, they're sanitary towels. Ten towels to a pack, safety pins with each towel."

"Yes, I see that now, but what do you pay?"

"Well" the man said "I think that 10/- for twenty four cartons would be fair. Your job would be to fold them up so, and fit them ten to a carton, that's about five or six hours work, depends on you of course."

"OK, I'll give it a try."

"Right, see you here tomorrow morning at about ten."

With that Pan dropped the idea of the audition, there were still crowds of girls in the queue, so she caught the tube home. She was thinking that if she could manage more than twenty four cartons per day, in six days she could perhaps clear £3, plus enough money for her tube tickets and the weekly 'Stage'. She became quite excited about it, and when she got home she told her mother that with luck she could pay her 5/- per week for her keep, so long as the job lasted.

CHAPTER SEVEN

'WE NEVER CLOSED'

Every week as usual Pan meticulously went through the ads in the 'Stage'. She was confident that sooner or later she would see what she was looking for. Sure enough, in about her third week of folding up sanitary towels plus safety pins, she read ...'attractive young girls wanted for chorus line in new show opening soon at a West End Theatre. Apply in the first instance to: V Van Damm 105 Windmill Street W1.'

She was just taking a lunch break. Without another thought she dropped everything, and caught the tube to Piccadilly Circus and found herself outside the Windmill Theatre. She waved the 'Stage' ad in front on an important looking gentleman in the foyer, who somehow got the message, and beckoned her to come with him into a small office where he produced a form for her to fill in. It was the usual thing, name, address, telephone number, if any, stage and dancing experience, etc., and name and address of a referee. It was with some trepidation that under the heading 'experience' she put 'Circus Tumbler'. She could not think of a suitable referee. She almost wrote down the Rector's name, then realised that this would not do her much good, so she finally plumped for her newly acquired brother-in-law, who was the Deputy Chief Chemist at Bass' Brewery in Burton-on-Trent, recently married to her sister Sheilagh. She vaguely wondered whether V Van Damm was a teetotaller.

"If Mr Van Damm decides he wants to interview you we will be in touch," said 'Fatty', for that was his name.

"Oh God, how long will it be?"

"I can't say luv, we have ten times the number of applicants we need. Run along now, you'll hear from us if you're on the short list."

That night Pan couldn't sleep; she knew it was the start she was looking for, had the thought of Fatty's indifference depressed her, and with every hour of darkness she grew more despondent. At breakfast she unburdened herself to her mother, who told her not to be so silly and to put it out of her mind. If she even heard anything, which was unlikely, it would be a bonus. So Pan went back to her sanitary towels with a heavy heart.

The following morning the postman came to the door with a letter for her. She was summoned to an audition at the Windmill Theatre at 10 am Tuesday morning. No acknowledgement was required. She was elated beyond belief, and for the next twenty-four hours she lived in a dream; she could not concentrate on the sanitary towels any more, so she decided to pack the job in.

'WE NEVER CLOSED'

Tuesday morning came and, dressing herself in her best suit, one of her recent purchases from '5th Avenue,' she arrived at the Windmill Theatre to find herself with about twenty-five girls who had already beaten her to it. Other girls continued to turn up until their numbers swelled to over fifty. Fatty directed them up the back stairs to the rehearsal room above the theatre, a barn of a place with a piano, a few stools, and a rough wooden floor pock-marked by the tap shoes of multitudinous dancers.

Although obviously inexperienced, Pan had carefully worked out her routine, based on the dancing lessons at the Irving Academy in Cheltenham, which she once attended for a term or so until there was no money left to pay the fees.

Each girl in turn was put through her paces. A man whom she assumed was the elusive VD, together with an imperious but attractive looking woman of indeterminate age, plus a few assistants, were sorting out the wheat from the chaff. It seemed endless, going on all day. Finally, to her amazement and incredulity, Pan found herself named with the last twelve girls who were to form the chorus in the new show. It was opening at the Piccadilly Theatre in Shaftesbury Avenue in less than three weeks time, so it meant non-stop rehearsals for the next fortnight. Pan was thrilled beyond belief and sang all the way back to The Boltons.

From then on things started to happen. Two months later Van Damm suddenly lost two girls from his Company at the Windmill Theatre at very short notice, so he decided to replace them from the chorus line at the Piccadilly. He selected Pan and an attractive vivacious girl called Lorna Tarr, with whom she had become friendly, they were both around the tender age of sixteen years. It was difficult to comprehend that, all at once, they found themselves permanent members of the Windmill Company, soon to become world famous as 'The Theatre that never closed'. Shortly afterwards another girl joined the Company, Jean Carr, an attractive auburn haired girl, with a good figure and an arresting speaking voice. Later, when she left the Windmill, she changed her name to Jean Kent and became a successful film actress.

The pay at the Windmill was not fantastic, about £2 a week, but VD looked after the girls as if they were his own. He could not do too much for them, whether it be to help with medical expenses, or to pay a taxi fare to get a girl back home if she missed the last tube. However, he was a stickler for discipline, especially punctuality. If a girl arrived late for work, even by only one or two minutes, he would dock her pay and if it happened a third time he would sack her on the spot. Jobs were hard to

SPIT AND SAWDUST

come by, so in this way VD ran an efficient and happy Company.

Later on, in 1936, VD was looking for a new Head Girl to replace an attractive blonde called Bobby Cooper. To her astonishment he selected Pan. At first she just could not take it all in. This meant an automatic rise in her wages, which would now amount to the handsome sum of £4 a week plus a few privileges.

During Pan's two years at the Windmill, much to her annoyance, the Rector often called at the Stage Door to see her. He still frequented the Soho area in between his Blackpool exploits. The Windmill was a handy place to stop and have a chat with his 'daughter'. In the beginning she thought these calls with purely social. Occasionally he would try to borrow money from her, needless to say without much success. On the other side of the stage door, there was a small room with a staircase at the far end, up and down which girls passed on their way to and from the back of the stage. Pan noticed the Rector always stood at a vantage point from where he could see up the stairs, and back the other way to the wings. The girls were usually in too much of a hurry to be concerned about their obviously scanty clothes, and would pass back and forth showing everything. One evening, on his second or third visit, the Rector stood there as a shapely show girl came down the stairs wearing only a flimsy chiffon scarf, leaving nothing to the imagination. Pan noticed the Rector's eyes nearly popping out of his head, thus confirming her suspicions that these visits were just an excuse for him to feast his gaze on naked girls. Although she did not know the meaning of the word 'voyeur', she realised the Rector clearly derived sexual gratification from the spectacle of female nudity. Pan did her best to discourage him, because these visits were an acute embarrassment to her. She refused to see him any more, but even then he persisted in calling, until VD learned about it and ordered Ben, the stage doorman, to throw him out.

Like all youngsters, Pan was on the look out for new experiences, and although perhaps not wholly motivated by the prospect of more money, she was beginning to feel that after two years at the Windmill she was getting into a rut. One Wednesday morning around October 1937, her old friend Donna from the circus days called at the stage door. Together they popped across to Jose's for a salt beef sandwich and cup of coffee.

"Pan, how would you like to go to Germany?"

"Can't say I'd object, tell me more."

"Well, you've heard of Harry Jackson's Dance Troupe, you know, something like the Tiller Girls."

Pan took a long drag on a cigarette.

'WE NEVER CLOSED'

"Well, Harry's been to Germany, and has signed up for his troupe to join a fabulous new stage show in Cologne called 'Sonne Für Alle'. I'm in it, but we are short of one girl, and I told Harry about you. He said that's OK by him if you are free."

Donna filled Pan in with the details. The show comprised a large company of artistes of many nationalities, musicians, dancers, conjurers, comedians, trapeze acrobats and so on, in fact a glorified circus.

"We will be the chorus girls" Donna continued. "And the pay is good. Harry's contract is for two years. How about it?"

"How long have I got to decide?"

"Not long darling, we will be leaving for Dover a week on Friday."

"Christ Donna, I need time to think, besides I have to ask my mother, apart from giving notice to VD."

"Well, make it soon love, Harry wants to know this coming Saturday at the latest."

"Alright," Pan replied, "Meet me here 7 pm Friday and I am pretty sure the answer will be yes."

Moyra of course did not approve, and when Pan went to tell VD about it, he gave her a lecture on the dangerous and sinister goings on in Nazi Germany under the Hitler Regime. It was no place for a young girl he said.

At the same time, although he was loathe to lose his Head Girl, he would not stand in her way if she was determined to go. They parted good friends.

Pan borrowed some money from Nugent and Paddy to buy a large suitcase and a travelling costume, and met Donna and Harry Jackson with the other girls at Victoria Station early the following Friday morning. They set off on the journey by boat and train, eventually finding themselves at the German border at Aachen. They were interrogated by some very aggressive Customs officials who gave them a difficult time. They took a dislike to Harry, insisting he must empty all his cases, many of which contained the costumes and trappings for his troupe which greatly intrigued them. They took everything out, and found numerous other items, apparently contraband or something like that, so Harry was taken away for interrogation. By this time the train was due to leave for Cologne, but the girls were not allowed to return to their carriage, so it steamed away without them. They were all very frightened and apprehensive, until an official in a Nazi uniform appeared, and with a bow and a friendly smile escorted them to a large Gasthaus near the station, where they were treated to an enormous meal of Sausages, Sauerkraut,

SPIT AND SAWDUST

Katoffel, ice cream and cakes, apparently all on the Nazi party. They were then given rooms for the night and told they would be allowed to catch the next train to Cologne in the morning.

Meanwhile, Harry turned up none the worse for his experiences, by which time officials from the Customs House and the local Nazi Detachment also joined the party. The troupe proceeded to give them an impromptu performance and everyone had an hilarious time singing, dancing, and swilling down litres of Dortmünder. They managed to catch the train next day and slept all the way to Cologne.

'Sonne Für Alle' was a great success. It played to packed houses in Cologne for over nine months, and toured all the major cities of the Reich prior to Berlin, which was the target for their final triumph. Towards the end of 1938 the show was playing in Dresden. Late one evening after the last performance, the girls went down to a well known Bier Keller where they were singled out by a party of obviously senior Nazi Officers, who sent messages to join them. One of them was a small, ugly, misshapen man with a club foot who was clearly the boss, and persisted in forcing his attentions on Pan. He was spending money like water, ordering dozens of bottles of Champagne for everyone. He would dance only with Pan, and despite his infirmity he danced quite well. He tried everything to persuade her to stay the night with him, but she resolutely refused, and managed to escape to her hotel room in the general chaos. The following morning two men in Nazi uniform forced their way into her bedroom, pulled off the bed clothes, made her dress, and marched her off to the Gestapo Headquarters, shouting, "Juden! Juden! Evil daughter of David!"

Stricken with terror, Pan was thrown into a prison cell, where she was interrogated by a vicious arrogant type with angry red scars down the side of his face. Pan's surname being Davidson meant only one thing to the Nazis, she was a Jewess. She thought the end had come, when suddenly a man appeared with an enormous bunch of red roses to which was attached a card inscribed 'To my charming danseuse, my humble apologies. Josef Goebbels.'

That was the end of it for Pan. Christmas was coming up, and many of the Company were looking forward to a break. Their contract took them through to September, 1939, but Harry agreed to pay expenses for Christmas at home so long as they returned in January.

Pan never went back, she had learned her lesson.

CHAPTER EIGHT

SLOTTED IN AT LAST

I spent Christmas with my parents at Rugeley and returned to Hastings in January to resume the old routine. On about 6 January a blizzard struck, and for two or three weeks we were snowed up, which didn't stop the daily drill in the underground car park, but seriously curtailed our quick dashes up to Town. The roads were impassable and train services cut. Poker and bridge became our main recreation and I fell in with a hard school in Warrior Square, amongst them Roddy Knocker.

Roddy was a short but well built young man, clean features and the splitting image of a film star called John Clements. He boasted that he was continually pestered by girls for his autograph. He was a great friend of Sabu, the young Indian actor, who made his name in the film 'Elephant Boy'. Roddy invited Sabu down to stay at his parents' house in Sevenoaks. We decided to organise a 'Curry Contest' in London as soon as weather conditions improved. London was the only place we knew we could find an Indian Restaurant. Nowadays there are Indian and Chinese restaurants in most towns throughout the UK, but I am sure they were a rarity prior to World War II, except possibly in a few large cities like Glasgow, Manchester and Liverpool.

Little did I know it then, but after retiring voluntarily from the RAF in 1960 I was to establish, with my wife, four restaurants of our own over a period of twenty six years, coupled with two pubs.

By mid-February train services were back to normal, so Roddy laid on a day trip to London. Sabu booked a table for eight at Veershwameys Indian Restaurant in Swallow Street, W1, where we were to decide who could eat the hottest curry. We all met first for a pre-prandial drink at Scotts, in Rupert Street. Out of the total of eight participants, apart from Sabu and Roddy, I could only remember two, Flying Officer Derek Whittingham (RAFO), a married man, who could not pronounce his 'r's', and Percy Burton. Sabu won the contest of course, Roddy being a close second. As for myself I don't think I ingested any food for nearly two days after, apart from gallons of lime juice and soda.

Within a couple of weeks, about 1 March, I was summoned to Marine Court to be informed that I was posted to the RAF College, Cranwell, on No 2 War Course for flying training, with effect from 6 March 1940. I just couldn't believe it; what I had been waiting for all these tiresome months suddenly became a reality. My mood was jubilant to say the least. I went about the business of Clearance Certificates, Railway Warrant, etc., with a light heart. I succeeded in getting through on the phone to my parents in Rugeley, to tell them that I was on the move. They sounded worried and apprehensive.

Early on the morning of the 4th I took a taxi to Hastings Station, which I shared with Percy Burton and Derek Whittingham. Also on the train with us were Roddy Knocker, Harry Bandinell and Frank Waldron, an Old Salopian and Oxford Rowing Blue, plus a few more whose names I have long since forgotten. We arrived at Sleaford, the station for Cranwell, in the late afternoon. RAF transport, in the form of a 15 cwt Bedford truck, was waiting to pick us up and deposit us and our baggage at the side entrance of the imposing looking Officers' Mess. We were allotted to our sleeping quarters, two to a room, and I shared with Percy Burton.

Cranwell College was the RAF equivalent of Sandhurst, the cradle for hand-picked cadets subjected to a three year curriculum, in which academic studies were as much a part of their training as flying. These cadets were to be the 'career' officers from whom future leaders of the service would be selected.

The war had now changed all this, and the College was converted to the role of the conventional Flying Training School. The new curriculum was an intensive three months course, culminating in the award of RAF Wings. The school was divided into two Training Squadrons, the Intermediate and the Advanced, with the accent on flying, interspersed with an abridged ground training programme. Pre- war second and third year cadets were still in residence, but they were now being phased into a shortened accelerated scheme, separated from the new war courses. To date I had flown only about twenty six hours on Avro Tutors with the OUAS. Now I was to start straight away on Hawker Harts, which in those days was considered quite a step forward. The Hart, although obsolete, was still designated a 'service type', and I was awestruck by the thought of what was in store.

I need not have worried; our instructors were hand picked like those in the OUAS. My Flight Commander was Garth Slater, an individualist, a forceful personality who instilled into us the vital importance of flying discipline, or 'airmanship' as it is called. It was not good enough to be a fearless split-arse pilot, if you couldn't observe the rules of the air, thereby endangering your own life, the lives of others, and causing damage or destruction to valuable aircraft and property.

Garth was a showman, at all times he wore a non-regulation white pigskin helmet, and round his neck a red scarf with white spots. We all knew he was a split-arse pilot naturally! His one ambition was to get on

SLOTTED IN AT LAST

to Ops, but he was much too valuable as an instructor. As far as I know he never made it.

Much has been written about learning to fly, the hopes, the despair, the depression, the elation. To add to it now offers nothing new, but perhaps I may be forgiven for relating a few personal experiences. Sitting at a table one morning in the crew room, I was in the middle of a four-handed bridge game, when an orderly appeared to inform me that Garth Slater was to take me up for a dual check. There was nothing unusual about this but it always put one into a flap. I was holding a good hand, and with spades as trumps I was about to finesse the queen through dummy, which meant I would have made five tricks although I had only called four. Sergeant Nottage, my instructor, appeared:

"Wake up, Edwards," he shouted, "you're wanted for the Flight Commander's final check. You're for the high jump."

At that moment my finesse failed.

"Get cracking, Hal," shouted Roddy Knocker, "Garth only wants to satisfy himself how bloody awful you are before kicking you off the course" then he hid his face behind his cards.

"OK, take it easy," declared Nottage, "It's just the usual routine. Make sure you don't hold off too high, and fly the machine as if you had a purpose, Edwards. Use your loaf, Slater likes that."

"Some hope," Roddy interjected, "How does he know he's got a loaf?"

I knocked Roddy off his chair and made a beeline for my parachute.

I climbed into the front seat, fastened the straps and slotted in my Gosport speaking tube. Garth was already there in the back seat, with his white buck skin helmet on, his red scarf with the white spots flapping in the breeze. I would have made a much better start, I thought, if I had already been there waiting, map in hand and everything on the top line. Nothing was said as I taxied out and headed into wind for take off. I heard a cough through the Gosport Tube, more eloquent than any word, shoved the throttle forward to full revs, held the stick steady to the moment the wheels stopped bouncing, then eased back until the Hart parted company with the grass, and we started to gain height to about five hundred feet when, without warning, the throttle lever was wrenched back. Another cough.

"Your engine's cut, Edwards. Show me an emergency landing."

I was almost stricken with paralysis. I knew the golden rule, never to turn back, but what did the future hold for me? Just a head-on plunge into a row of trees, a hump backed bridge across a river, and then some

SPIT AND SAWDUST

greenhouses.

In desperation I clutched the joy-stick to adopt a kind of gliding attitude as I had been taught. The temptation to cover more ground by pulling back on the stick, thereby inducing a stall, was almost irresistible. Suddenly I spotted a gap between the trees to the left, and a green patch beyond. I gingerly banked to port and pointed the aircraft towards the gap, my air speed dropping dangerously low. It looked as if I had almost made it when, with a powerful forward thrust on the throttle lever, Garth shouted,

"OK Edwards, I've got her," and the engine roared to full revs as we started to climb away.

"Edwards, most likely you would have made it."

I breathed a sigh of happy relief.

"We are going to do some aerobatics now," Garth shouted.

Well, he made that Hart sit up and beg; I had never experienced such flying.

"OK, now it's your turn, do a slow roll to the right."

Not forgetting to keep a good look out, I eased the stick forward to gain speed then, at full throttle, I gently pulled the nose above the horizon, banked hard right, simultaneously applying top rudder. Then slowly throttling back, I levelled the wings with the horizon in the upside down position, at the same time trying to keep straight with the rudder, and stick forward to hold the nose up. The engine cut. With a struggle I rolled out on to the other side, losing about three thousand feet in the process.

"Not a bad effort, try another one to the left."

I did one or two more and began to gain confidence. Suddenly without warning the throttle was cut again.

"Right, you are out of fuel, land in that field," Garth shouted, pointing down to a large meadow with a spinney on one side. We were at about two thousand feet.

I had plenty of time, and planned my glide path to bring me to the threshold of the field into wind with enough height left to clear the hedge and side-slip in. Beads of sweat were running down my face, partly prevented from swamping my eyes by the seal round my goggles. My chinstrap was wet and cloggy. The wheels touched the grass like a feather duster. I throttled back and the Hart came to rest, prop still turning.

"If you keep that up Edwards, I can assess you as exceptional."

The prop was still idling, there was almost no engine noise. I could not believe my ears. It must be beginners' luck.

SLOTTED IN AT LAST

"Always remember to re-cap your faults immediately, when you start thinking you haven't any. Recognise your shortcomings, and above all do not get over confident. Do that and with good luck you may survive."

"Thank you, Sir," I stammered.

"OK, take her home Edwards."

Garth never touched the controls again, but sat in silence behind me all the way back. I was happy and full of gratitude. I then made one of the worst landings I had ever done. Shamefacedly I taxied back to the flight and parked the aircraft, whereupon Garth climbed out and walked away without so much as a word. That was 25 April. On 26 April I was due for the CFI's test, marking the end of the 'Intermediate Stage'.

The CFI was Squadron Leader A J 'Speedy' Holmes, a well known County and England Cricketer. He had been awarded two bars to his AFC, which must almost have been a record in those days. This time I was strapped in, all geared up waiting for 'Speedy' to appear. His conversation was monosyllabic. I took off, went through the same exercises as I had previously done with Garth Slater, and there was hardly a word spoken throughout the trip. On landing all he said was:

"All right Edwards, see you at the Course Party."

On 12 May, after I had already passed on to the Advanced Training Squadron, my Log Book was returned to me with an assessment, under the heading: 'Proficiency as a Pilot on type.' Is Average! I was dumbfounded, I had expected to be assessed at least as 'Above Average'. This quickly cut me down to size.

There is a tale about Speedy involving a pupil on a subsequent course named Jimmy Baraldi, whom I later met in North Africa when he told me the story. I think it is true to say that most pupils on flying training at this time were determined at all costs to become Fighter Pilots. Despite all his efforts to be recommended for fighters, they told Jimmy he was earmarked for bombers. In desperation he requested an interview with Speedy Holmes. Speedy habitually spoke slowly, pausing to add weight to each word. He took pains to explain why Jimmy must go on to bombers.

"By the way, where were you at school?" Speedy suddenly asked.

"Harrow" replied Jimmy.

"Did you play any games?"

"Yes Sir, cricket. I played cricket for Harrow for three years" lied Jimmy.

"My God!" shouted Speedy jumping to his feet "The man's a Cricketer! You must be a Fighter Pilot, it will be fixed immediately."

SPIT AND SAWDUST

Within a few weeks Jimmy was flying Spitfires.

On graduating to the Advanced Training Squadron we soon reached the night flying stage. This was carried out at a satellite airfield called Harlaxton, alongside the A1, just south of Grantham. The Hart was not the easiest plane to land in a perfect three- pointer at any time, but at night, with a few goose neck flares to mark the direction of take off and landing, holding off just prior to putting the aircraft down was like a nightmare. One's impression was of an endless blackness upwards, sideways and downwards, the naked flames of the flares merely producing a weird fiendish effect, without giving any true indication of height, speed or direction.

My night flying instructor was a small, tough New Zealander, called Flying Officer Laud. If he ever had any grey hairs I gave them all to him. On my first dual trip with him, I came whistling down far too fast and too high, trying to aim at touchdown near the second or third flare. I heard a hoarse rasping sound through the speaking tube.

"Jeezus Cherist!"

Without another word he grabbed the throttle and joy-stick, and flew up into the outer darkness.

After some more night dual I began to think I was at last catching on. The final decision to send me off alone was made by Slater, who commented that at least I would only kill myself if I crashed, thus saving Laud's life, for which I ought to get a medal posthumously.

Speedy Holmes came down to the flare path to see me go solo, and I felt like a gladiator about to be bumped off in the arena, not my idea of entertainment, I thought, as I opened the throttle. The paraffin flares sped past my port wing tip until they were behind and below me. As I turned left I looked down into a vast expanse of blackness. I felt lonely and frightened; there was no visible sign to indicate that the earth was just below me, so I continued to turn left, and then left again like an automaton, until suddenly I found myself across wind. I picked out the line of flares. I banked towards them, reducing my speed as I started my approach. Quicker than I expected the flares loomed up large and bright on my port side, and I knew then I was too high. I dreaded the thought of going round again so in an act of foolish bravado I slammed the throttle shut, pulled the stick back into my stomach and prayed. I dealt the third flare a glancing blow, checked the rudder just in time, simultaneously hitting the ground with the front wheels so hard I sat waiting for the undercarriage to crumple.

Instead, the aircraft bounced three or four times, before tearing along

SLOTTED IN AT LAST

at an alarming rate into the blackout, well past the last flare. Slowly it lurched to a halt. As I gingerly turned the aircraft round, I glimpsed the flare path way behind me flickering like the harbour lights at Dover when seen at night from the Cross Channel Ferry, en route to Calais. I took my time taxying back, and to my intense relief found that Speedy and Garth had already left in disgust. I thankfully piled into the Bedford truck with the rest of the detail, and we were on our way back to the Mess and bed.

The stark reality that death lurked round the corner came to us one night when a pupil pilot named, I think, Pilot Officer Cramer, was doing circuits and landings in an Oxford, the standard RAF twin engined Trainer, when an engine cut on the approach. He was too low and too slow for the other engine to save him, he crashed just short of the airfield, and went up in flames. Once more I was given something to think about.

One of us who failed to make the grade was Frankie Waldron, the Oxford Rowing Blue. Through no fault on his own he could not overcome airsickness, so he was transferred to the Army and joined the Guards. However, before the arrangements were finalised, he succeeded in taking some leave in the South of France, much to everyone's envy and disgust!

Another Oxford Blue on our course - Rugger in this case - was Joe Coles, who gained for himself a certain reputation as a 'Navigator'. It was easy enough for the best of us to get that utterly lost feeling on a solo cross country, but he got more than his fair share of it. On almost every flight he ended up landing at a strange airfield to enquire his whereabouts. It became a standard joke among the instructors, who used to gather on the tarmac to watch him disappear into the far blue yonder, then toss up to decide who should take off in the next hour or so, to find him and fetch him back.

As the course was drawing to a close, I had a letter one day from my father, to say that I could have his Morris 8 Tourer, which was lying unused in the garage at home in Rugeley. Speedy Holmes gave me permission to take twenty-four hours off to fetch it. Lee Pyman, a CUAS member on our course, came with me.

It was a fine clear night on our way back, and within a few miles of Cranwell we saw the glow of the flare path, and above it the navigation lights of several aircraft circling the airfield as they queued up to land. On reaching the Guardroom we suddenly became aware of complete darkness everywhere. What had happened to the flare path? Where were the aircraft? Had we had too much to drink? Admittedly, we had stopped off at Newark for a pint, but we were perfectly sober.

Suddenly I heard a shrill whistling noise uncomfortably close, then

SPIT AND SAWDUST

a terrible rending splitting crash, followed by a hot searing shock wave. We flung ourselves out of the car, and plunged blindly towards where I knew there was an air raid shelter, when there was a second ghastly ripping explosion, and I found myself flat on my face, clutching and biting at the grass like some hungry-mad demented bullock. Simultaneously my right knee was torn on a wicked barbed wire entanglement, which I remembered from air raid practises, surrounded the shelter, leaving only a small gap giving access to the entrance. The significance of always using the same route to and from the shelter could not at this moment have struck me more forcibly. The right leg of my trousers was torn clean off, and my knee cap was ripped open.

After the raid was over, I managed to stagger to Sick Bay where I had fifteen stitches in my knee. Apart from shock, I was none the worse for having suffered my first war wound. Lee Pyman without a scratch followed up in the Morris, and drove me back to the Mess.

About the middle of May I received a very sad letter which momentarily stunned me. It was from Jennifer Keitley, John's sister, with the shattering news that John was reported 'missing believed killed' during the retreat from the Franco-Belgian Border. His battalion had been wiped out somewhere near Charleroi, and there was little hope of survivors. Only three weeks ago I had had a letter from him post-marked 'Somewhere in France'. He said his application for his transfer to the RAF had been accepted, and he was looking forward to joining me in a Spitfire Squadron some time in 1941. Shattered dreams.

Following that brief Christmas Leave in London, which now seems so long ago, when I met Pamela Davidson in the Blue Lagoon Night Club and heard her amazing story, rightly or wrongly I had since indulged in a few sexual adventures, from which I derived small enough pleasure, with one exception, when I met a singularly beautiful ATS girl in the Black Boy in Nottingham called Yvonne.

She was tall, blonde and curvaceous, so even in her shapeless khaki uniform there was no mistaking the sensual symmetry of her body. Now and again I managed to snatch a few hours from Cranwell to drive to Nottingham to see her. My little Morris was too small for comfort, so I applied the 'blanket on the ground' technique, which worked well enough to our mutual satisfaction, so long as it didn't rain.

Yvonne's parents kept a pub on the outskirts of the City, in a pleasant residential area, where we would return for a drink and a bar snack, before my drive back through the night to another week of flogging Harts and Hinds round the Lincolnshire skies. Her father had recently

SLOTTED IN AT LAST

purchased a radiogram, very much an upmarket piece of equipment in those days, which he installed in the Lounge Bar, where we would listen to my records, which I had loaned to the family because they did not have many of their own. Amongst them were hit numbers of Glenn Miller, Bob Crosby, Lew Stone and many others, which had caught on in a big way with the Armed Forces.

I knew that our infrequent yet evocative intimacy must end sooner rather than later, and when it came to our final parting of the ways, I completely forget about my records. I have often wondered what Yvonne did with them. Perhaps she has them to this day, if so they would be worth a few bob, I daresay.

The Cranwell Course ended on 20 June, exactly ten days after Mussolini declared war on the Allies. We were all clamouring to go onto Fighters. I was relieved and delighted to be told I was posted, together with many of my friends, to a Fighter Operational Training Unit, No 6 OTU, at RAF Sutton Bridge, on the Wash near Kings Lynn.

There was just room for Percy Burton and myself, plus luggage, to squeeze into the Morris. On 22 June we set course for the Wash in high spirits, totally oblivious to what fate was cooking up for us, our conversation and thoughts centred solely on the enthralling prospect of flying Hurricanes.

Among others to join us at Sutton Bridge were Derek Whittingham, Roddy Knocker, Lee Pyman, Chris Andreae, an Old Salopian who had been with me in Churchills', and Harry Bandinell. Out of the six of us from our Flight at Cranwell, four were to give their lives before the end of the Battle of Britain in October.

CHAPTER NINE

THE LUFTWAFFE STOKES IT UP

We were now listening to hourly broadcasts on the evacuation of Dunkirk, about the heroism of the skippers of the 'little boats' dashing back and forth across the Channel, rescuing our troops beleaguered on the Dunkirk Beaches. Interspersed with these bulletins were the propaganda rantings of Lord Haw Haw, William Joyce, claiming that the BEF was being annihilated and that it had been abandoned to its fate by RAF Fighter Command. We happily poured scorn on it all. Our morale remained high and unimpaired.

Sutton Bridge was a small RAF Station, with a hutted camp on the northwest border of the airfield, plus one or two hangars for aircraft maintenance and storage. The OTU was divided into two Flights, 'A' and 'B', located round the south side of the field, instructors and ground personnel being mostly in tented accommodation, the aircraft dispersed around the perimeter. These consisted of about four Harvard Trainers and eight Hurricanes per flight, plus a few of each type on repairs and inspections.

Percy and I again shared a room together, this time in a slatted wooden hut, in contrast to the luxury peacetime brick-built Officers' Mess at Cranwell College. There were four or five similar wooden huts in parallel, with accommodation for about eighty Officers, two to a room, plus ablutions at the end of each hut. These huts were connected by a long narrow corridor to the lounge, dining room and main entrance. In front was a parking area for Officers' cars.

The next morning Percy and I reported to 'A' Flight, and were introduced to Ian Scoular, the Flight Commander, and some of the instructors. Most of them had just been posted from Fighter Squadrons operating in France, prior to the Dunkirk evacuation. They looked exhausted, drained, their nerve ends shredded. We viewed them with awe and reverence, for these pilots had been baptised in fire, and now their job was to teach us the facts and realities of aerial combat. In our youthful innocence and ignorance, we associated the idea of being fighter pilots with visions of Knights of the Round Table, pitting their skills with lance and sword, like brave horsemen riding singly into battle to down the foe.

I think this was the picture in the minds of most young men striving to become pilots when war broke out. The unhappy thought is that the majority were to lose their lives as bomber pilots, never to know the thrill of flying single seat fighters in a duel to the death.

I was allotted to Flying Officer Lewis, a Canadian pilot, later killed

Freshmen Photo — Brasenose College, 1937

L–R, Front Row: Newell, J; Nelson-Edwards, GH; Vickery, BC; Warshaw, AC; Fraser, PM; Sparks, EJ; Nicholas, JKBM; Giles, FTR; Millar,* K; Rothery-Jones, HF; Burness, AD; Stein, KH.
Second Row: Adamson, DFD; Greenwood, JN; Pershke,* J; Goodfellow, A; Tetley, RID; Tucker, PAD; Henriques,* JDQ; Radice,* J; Allsebrooke, PW; Whalley, PF; Rossi, GV; Wellman,* HR.
Third Row: Woodruff, SA; Church, DG; Simpson, DA; Clayden,* AR; Leonard, RH; Armstrong, RA; Penna, EC; Binch, JH; Allan, AM; Burrow, JCN; Tisdall,* A; Davoud, JG; Power, G.
Back Row: Duffie, WDC; Long, AEFC; Fryzer, JF; Harding, T; Graham, GEL; Ghashghaie, MM; Charbit, SI; Taylor, JIC; Pasic, N; Hodgkinson, JFN; Gray, FH
* Deceased

RAF Pembrey, 1940. 79 Squadron Dispersal. Left to Right: Flt Lt Trevor Bryant-Fenn DFC, Flt Lt Dicke Dennison (Canadian) killed in action, Flt Lt 'Peggy' Hugh O'Neill DFC, GHNE

RAF Pembrey, 1940, 79 Squadron. GHNE and Flt Lt Douglas Cliff (now retired and living in Tenby, Prmbrokeshire)

THE LUFTWAFFE STOKES IT UP

whilst in No 1 Squadron at Northolt. He showed me the 'taps' on the Harvard and told me to jump into the front cockpit, he sat in the back. The Harvard was a single-engined two seat tandem monoplane with retractable undercarriage.

Typically American, it had comfortable bucket seats to accommodate the parachute pack, and the safety harness left plenty of room for directional movement of the body. Unlike the Hawker Hart, which only had a brake handle, the brakes on the Harvard were two angled metal foot plates, hinged at the base, to give the required braking effect by depressing the pedals forward, something like a car foot brake, except that by pushing the left or right foot the aircraft would turn left or right. By pushing both feet simultaneously the aircraft, with luck, would stop. The radial engine was started by an electrically operated inertia fly wheel which, when engaged, produced a high pitched ear-splitting, metallic rending noise until ignition. The metal propeller also gave forth a frightful high pitched blue note as the aircraft passed overhead, a noise by now all too familiar to the locals.

Of the other instructors in 'A' Flight, I particularly remember Flying Officer De Mancha, who was later killed in 43 Squadron, and Pilot Officer Peter Ayerst, whose daughter Jane I was destined to know some thirty years later, when she was married to an RAF Lightning Pilot. They were both customers of ours in our 'Spit and Sawdust' Mark 3 at Little Haven, Pembrokeshire.

After two short trips with Flying Officer Lewis on the Harvard, I went solo. The next morning, 25 June, I was sent off for my first flight on the Hurricane. I can only say that I was petrified as I left the ground, and forgot to raise my undercarriage, until I realised my air speed was little more than stalling speed. Having locked the wheelsup, I then started to worry about getting them down again for landing. Soon I forgot about the Hawker Hart biplane with its fixed undercarriage, for my first few flights on the Hurricane opened up a new world. If I could stay alive, I thought, I would soon be a fighter pilot. It looked like a piece of cake.

After a few days I received a message from the Station Adjutant to remove my car from the airfield. Apparently a New Routine Order had been issued that private cars were no longer allowed to be kept on the Station. I had befriended a technical Sergeant in 'A' Flight called 'Spud' Crisp, who suggested I should have my Morris painted in official camouflage, with the help of a Flight Sergeant friend of his in the maintenance hangar. It badly needed a respray so I agreed, and my Morris 8 emerged looking like a mini bren-gun carrier. Believe it or not, its

SPIT AND SAWDUST

presence on the Station was never queried from that moment on. Several of us, including 'Spud', went to the Globe at King's Lynn one evening to celebrate the transformation.

There was a radiogram in the Officer's Mess anteroom with a pile of records in the cabinet. The most popular record of all was Glenn Miller's 'In the Mood.' For some reason I cannot explain, it became an inspiration for me, a morale booster if you like; it sent vibrations down my spine, instilling in me a heady desire to fight and destroy enemy aircraft, of which at this stage I was totally incapable, because after only three and a half weeks at Sutton Bridge, I had not even fired the eight Browning Machine Guns, the Hurricane's standard armament. Without a doubt 'In the Mood' motivated me.

Almost as exciting was a record by Benny Goodman with Gene Krupa on drums called 'Roll 'em', which we also played incessantly. The sounds of either of these two records, even today, arouse in me painful yet thrilling memories, conjuring up all the traumatic and deadly experiences of those incredible days.

The Hurricane Conversion Course ended on 19 July, and I was to join 79 (F) Squadron at RAF Acklington in Northumberland. Percy Burton was posted to 249 Squadron and Lee Pyman to 65 Squadron.

It was the parting of the ways. This time I set course northwards, alone in my Morris 8, with just my kit for company. Acklington was on the northeast coast beyond Newcastle. I had no idea what it was like up there, except I was told it was pretty bleak. I felt deeply disappointed I was not going south with the others where the action was, but I sensed that perhaps my turn was to come.

Just before leaving, a letter came for me which had been forwarded on from my home address in Rugeley. It was from Pamela Davidson, the girl I had met in the Blue Lagoon Night Club the previous December. I had often thought about her, and wondered whether I would ever see her again, but had thought it unlikely having lost her address.

The unexpected letter from Pamela Davidson cheered me up, and I promised myself that as soon, if ever, I got a spot of leave I would go to London to re-establish contact. I forgot all about Yvonne. Memories of Pamela and the few hours we had spent together in London came flooding back, and I recalled with a shock what she had told me about her father, long since dead - killed by a lion in Skegness - the notorious Rector of Stiffkey, whom my Aunt Maud once knew whilst running her Rescue Home in Soho. I vaguely wondered what my parents would think if they knew I was running around with the Rector's daughter, but I couldn't care

CFS Students on visit to Bristol Aeroplane Company, Filton — The Brabazon

CFS RAF Little Rissington. No.100 (All Purpose) Flying Instructor's Course, April-August, 1947

GHNE and Pan after an Investiture at Buckingham Palace (circa 1946)

George and Pan Nelson-Edwards at a dinner-dance at the RAF Club, 128 Piccadilly (circa 1949)

THE LUFTWAFFE STOKES IT UP

less, life was too short!

My instructions were to report to the Station Adjutant, RAF Acklington, by midday 20 July. I made good time, and arrived at SHQ to be told that the Adjutant had already left for the Officers' Mess, and that I was expected to report there. A Flight Sergeant and two elderly corporals were in the Orderly Room, and for some strange reason they were exchanging ill-concealed grimaces and glances in my direction. For the second time in my short RAF career I thought I was about to be asked what was on at the local Cinema. In front of these old timers I was made to feel like a Commissionaire, and it upset me.

I drove the Morris round to the front of the Officers' Mess, to find a group of about twenty Officers waiting outside the main entrance. Not connecting this with my arrival, I parked the Morris in a discreet slot and walked casually across in the hope of bypassing the gaggle without being noticed. Suddenly, from somewhere, a gramophone gave forth the strains of Nelson Eddy and Jeanette MacDonald singing 'Rosemarie, I Love You,' from the popular Musical. I still did not associate the outburst with myself, and attempted to barge through, but I was stopped by someone shouting "Three cheers for Nelson Eddy", at the same time thrusting a piece of paper in front of my face as they all sang 'For He's a Jolly Good Fellow.' I nervously glanced down at the paper, I could see it was a written order of some sort, then the penny dropped. I read the words 'PO Nelson Eddy posted to 79 Squadron etc.' displayed in bold print. So they thought they had a film star on the Squadron! It was rumoured that one or two American film stars were enjoying some publicity by coming to Britain to join the Forces. The misprint on my Posting Notice must have led everyone to jump to the conclusion that I was none other than Nelson Eddy, the famous singer. The realisation that I was just another 'sprog' replacement temporarily created confusion and embarrassment, and it took a while to live it down. Needless to say, within hours I became known as 'Neddy'. This name stuck with me throughout the War.

Prior to 1938 No 79 (Madras Presidency) Squadron, together with 32 Squadron, was based at RAF Biggin Hill. During the RAF prewar buildup the Biggin Squadrons, plus others, were busy re-equipping with the new single-seat Merlin engined monoplane fighter types - the Hurricane and the Spitfire. 79 Squadron was formed from 'B' Flight, 32 Squadron, first briefly on Gladiators and then re-equipped with Hurricanes in 1938. 79 Squadron History is not part of this book but, for the record, 79 scored Biggin's first victory of the war on 21 November 1939.

In May 1940 the Squadron was despatched to France for Fighter

SPIT AND SAWDUST

Operations with the BEF where it chalked up twenty-five victories, and after the Dunkirk evacuation it returned to Biggin to fight the convoy battles in early July. The Squadron suffered some losses both in pilots and aircraft, including Squadron Leader Joslyn, a first class Commanding Officer, who was shot down in the Channel on 7 July 1940, allegedly by Spitfires. The end of July found the Squadron at RAF Acklington, in Northumberland.

Together with about twelve 'sprog' pilots (including myself) the new CO, Squadron Leader Harvey Heyworth, set about the task of recreating the Squadron as an operational fighting unit, backed by a handful of very experienced veterans of the prewar 79, including David Haysom, a South African, Rupert Clerke, an Old Etonian, Teddy Morris, also a South African, Dimsie Stones DFC, John Parker, Trevor Bryant-Fenn, and two stalwart Sergeant Pilots, Whitby and Parr.

Harvey Heyworth was the Chief Test Pilot for Rolls Royce, Derby, and a member of No. 504 (County of Nottingham) Squadron, Royal Auxiliary Air Force, based at Hucknall. Prior to World War II his job was to sell the Merlin engine to the world via the medium of the Hurricane and Spitfire airframes. To do this he performed miracles of flying and aerobatics skills, almost akin to those of Jeffrey Quill and Alex Henshaw, who were the acknowledged masters of precise and sophisticated handling techniques. He had had little or no previous combat experience, so he was thrown in at the deep end. He had an ebullient, outgoing personality and although, to put it crudely, he didn't know his arse from his elbow, it took him only eight days of intensive squadron training to get us declared 'Operational'. Harvey proved himself to be a brave and inspired leader.

By the 2 August we were maintaining 'Readiness' states, which meant sitting in the Crewroom at dispersal waiting for the phone to ring, drinking endless cups of tea and playing poker. Sadly the Luftwaffe ignored our Sector, except for an occasional lone intruder to break the monotony. It was 9 August when I first fired my guns in anger. With Rupert Clerke and Sergeant Wright we shot down a Heinkell III into the sea just off Sunderland, thus claiming a third each. It all seemed so easy.

15 August was a different matter. It was when the Luftwaffe flew the maximum number of individual sorties against Fighter Command, on any day during the Battle, a total of one thousand seven hundred and eighty six. That morning I was lounging in the Mess when, at about 1200 hours, an order came over the tannoy ordering all pilots of 72 and 79 Squadrons to take off immediately. Our truck was outside so we piled in. What was

THE LUFTWAFFE STOKES IT UP

it all about? Was it the real thing at last?

Whatever it was we were clearly ill-prepared. A large number of hostile aircraft was plotted approaching the East Coast; they were still about fifty or sixty miles off. We had to throw ourselves into the air, yet as luck would have it, we reached about fifteen thousand feet before spotting the first wave. There were about one hundred HeIII's escorted by Me110 long-range fighters. The confusion which ensued was indescribable.

79 Squadron with Harvey in the lead bored into the bomber stream. By this time it was every man for himself. 72 Squadron followed suit. We succeeded in breaking up the formations, so that the sky was now filled with aircraft turning and weaving in all directions, I found myself squirting .303 bullets everywhere at various enemy aircraft, without any visible results when, to my horror, I spotted an Me110 coming at me head-on from about two thousand yards. As I thumbed the gun-button the Me110 exploded in a flash of flame in front of my eyes, bits and pieces flying past me on either side, oil splashing my windscreen. I did a steep turn and saw the twin tail plane assembly gently twisting round, like the paper darts we used to make at school, until it slowly descended into the sea in a shallow graceful glide. Suddenly the sky appeared totally devoid of any sign of aircraft, whereas only seconds before I had been in a twisting vortex of friend and foe. I felt isolated and lonely in my efforts to re-orientate myself. It is a very strange phenomenon, which I think will be borne out by many fighter pilots, that one second you are in a frantic melée of aircraft twisting and turning, guns blazing, and the next second you are in total emptiness.

After landing back at base, I was interrogated by Bill Edwards, the Squadron Intelligence Officer. I told him about the Me110 blowing up. It transpired that some other pilots had also seen the aircraft explode, and assumed I had shot it down. I knew I had not had time to press the gun button at that precise moment, and in all conscience I couldn't claim it as my kill. Just how näive can one get? If I had kept my big mouth shut I would have been given my first confirmed victory.

On 16 August several of us were granted a 'long weekend' leave, which could amount to about four days with a spot of manipulation. I decided on a dash to London to try to contact Pamela Davidson. There was a fast train service from Newcastle. I caught the morning express leaving at 0630, arriving at Kings Cross at about 1100. I booked in at the St Regis, Cork Street, a block of small self-contained apartments let on a day-to-day basis. Later in the year it was flattened by a German bomb.

SPIT AND SAWDUST

I took the tube to Earls Court, and went to her address in The Boltons, only to find that Pamela was up in Birmingham, where apparently she had got herself engaged to an Army Padre. She had been up there making bomb doors for Wellingtons at the Hercules Bicycle Factory, now turned over entirely to war production. I had written to say I was coming, and sure enough she turned up at The Boltons the same evening. We went to dinner and met again the next day. To cut a long story short, I talked her out of marrying the Padre on the strength of her unhappy relationship with the Rector of Stiffkey, prior to his death in 1937. I persuaded her that another 'God Botherer' in the family was one too many.

The next day was warm and sunny, so we caught a train to Maidenhead where we hired a punt and took a picnic lunch. We ended up having dinner at Skindles. This was when I first learnt how Pamela came to be called 'Pan'.

We just caught the last train back to Paddington, and for old time's sake decided to go down to the Blue Lagoon. Pan bought a bottle of Haig at half price because of her old association with the Club, so we spent the rest of the night drinking and dancing until six in the morning. It left me with just a few minutes to spare to collect my things from the St Regis, and catch the train to Newcastle. The Army Padre had been 'ousted'.

I reported back to the Squadron to be informed that I had overstayed my leave by twelve hours. For the next twenty-four hours I was taken off flying, and given the job of Station Duty Officer as a penance. Within the week both 72 and 79 Squadrons were ordered south to 11 Group. We arrived at Biggin Hill on 27 August.

We were soon in action; on 28 I claimed a Heinkel III 'probably destroyed', and in the late afternoon I had a half-share in the destruction of an He59 Float Plane with Flying Officer Brian Noble, who was later shot down in combat with Me109's on 1 September and badly burnt. I am obliged to admit that I didn't feel especially proud of downing the He59; it was an obsolete plane and used for Air Sea Rescue. Its maximum speed was only about one hundred and thirty knots, its sole armament a machine gun in the nose. However, HQ 11 Group had instructed pilots to attack these float planes, because they were used for the recovery of German aircrew and for reconnaissance, whilst falsely displaying the Red Cross, so they were legitimate targets.

The Luftwaffe assault on airfields was now under way. Biggin Hill took a packet, the worst being on Friday 30 August. Taking off and landing became extremely hazardous due to the sate of the airfield - craters everywhere, not to mention unexploded bombs. That day I flew

THE LUFTWAFFE STOKES IT UP

three sorties, but I made no claims. Early on Saturday morning we were scrambled to intercept a raid heading our way, but it was too late, bombs started falling before the Squadron had taken off, the sky above alive with low flying Me109's. Dodging the hazards some of us managed to get airborne. Locking my wheels up I 'pulled the tit' and went full bore to get away from the circuit, to build up my airspeed and gain some height.

At about two thousand feet, with two hundred knots on the clock, I was at the critical split second moment when the Hurricane, magnificent fighting machine though it was, was a sitting target for the Me109 when making its 'bounce' out of the sun, with the advantage of height and speed, as I learned to my cost. There was a loud shattering bang and an Me109, with a bright yellow spinner, flashed past within a few feet of my starboard wing tip and vanished. In seconds my temperature gauge went off the clock, and there was a strong smell of overheating pistons and cordite. Then the engine seized up. I couldn't make it back to the airfield, so I pointed straight ahead hoping there were no more Me109's around, feverishly trying to work out my next move.

Having switched everything off, and by now down below one thousand feet, too low to bale out, I headed for a green patch beyond some trees to my right. It seemed miles away but my only hope. I slid the hood back as I just scraped over the last of the trees, and with wheels and flaps still retracted I belly-landed, slithering along the grass until all but crashing into a twelve foot high brick garden wall. I hit my left eye and head on something very hard indeed and went out cold.

On coming to I was amazed to see the bright green head and back beak of a large parrot peering into my face across the open cockpit. For a second or two I couldn't think for the life of me where I was. Was the 'other world' one glorious aviary populated by exotically coloured birds? Was I destined for ever more to be in the company of the feathered variety? Then a hand appeared, proffering a large rummer full of a golden liquid which I gratefully received, pouring the lot down my throat in about two gulps. As the owner of the hand turned away for a moment, I could see it belonged to a man wearing a Harris Tweed jacket stitched with a leather shoulder patch which extended full length down the right-hand side of his back. It was stained from top to bottom with thick white and yellow streaks of bird droppings, some quite fresh. I couldn't help wondering whether my underpants were still clean. I suppose shock and hallucination played their part, for I kept thinking what an ingenious way to prevent Harris Tweed from being fouled up.

Standing on the main spar, he reached across to help me release myself from the safety straps and parachute harness. Fumes from the hot engine were accompanied by an ominous hissing noise, like gas escaping. Sudden realisation that the aircraft might catch fire shook me out of my torpor, and I struggled free. The man helped me down and I staggered away, half expecting to hear an explosion as the Hurricane burst into flames. Nothing happened. Next, a lady appeared and helped me through a gate in the garden wall towards a large house with French windows which opened into a pleasant room where there was a table laid up for breakfast.

She dabbed the cut on my head with disinfectant and put a dressing on it. Worse was my eye, which by now had become so swollen it had completely closed. I was lucky, such minor cuts and bruises were as nothing compared with the grievous injuries suffered by so many fighter pilots, worst of all the horrific burns to face and hands, as if attacked with a giant blowlamp. I thanked the Almighty for having so far granted me escape from this torture.

It was a splendid breakfast, hot coffee, fresh cream, kidneys, tomatoes, sausages, bacon, eggs and fried bread, croissants and real butter. The effects of the brandy, plus the delicious smell of frying, quickly restored my appetite. I was famished. My host telephoned Biggin Hill to report the crash and soon a WAAF, driving a Hillman Minx Staff Car, came to fetch me back. A Civilian guard from the Oxted Police Reserve was stationed to guard the aircraft. One of the guards was a Sergeant Withers, who by sheer chance I was to meet again in Oxted forty years later, by which time he was over ninety years old.

It also happened that my host was a wealthy German who had escaped from the Nazis in 1936, bringing his parrot with him. His wife was English and it seems he was exempt from internment. He kept a large white cob in the stable which he rode to Oxted on shopping expeditions. Apparently he vanished after the war. Nobody knew where he went, but people to this day remember him riding through the streets of Oxted, and tethering the white cob outside the grocer's shop. Today the house is a home for retarded children.

The WAAF driver delivered me to the Biggin Hill Sick Quarters, where already there were queues awaiting treatment for injuries of every sort caused by the Luftwaffe raids. I felt a bit shifty reporting for a minor head wound, though admittedly my eye was a 'beaut'. The Medical Officer signed me off flying for thirty-six hours.

It was only just after midday. I reported back to the Squadron dispersal, wrote my combat report for Bill Edwards, and decided to get

THE LUFTWAFFE STOKES IT UP

the hell out of it until Monday morning. I hitched a lift to Bromley station and caught the next train to London.

I headed straight for The Boltons where I arrived at about 6 pm. Walking from Earls Court, I could see white vapour trails criss-crossing the blue sky in all directions, and guiltily I knew I should have been up there with them. I had little choice but to make the best of a few hours granted to me.

I arrived back at Bromley Station on Sunday evening, 1 September. There was no transport to Biggin so I started to walk. As usual, condensation trails were filling the sky. I hardly walked half a mile, when suddenly I heard the familiar shrill 'blue note' of an aircraft plunging down in a vertical dive. Looking up I spotted a Hurricane hurtling earthwards, plumes of flames and smoke trailing behind. It plummeted into a copse only fifty yards away from me with a sickening thump, throwing up a thick cloud of ominous black smoke. I was sure no one had baled out, there was no sign of a parachute. I retched and turned away; I could not bring myself to go across to the scene, knowing that whoever was in that holocaust would now be a cinder. For a brief moment, as I resumed my walk, I felt humbled, wondering whether it would be my turn next; I had let the Squadron down and I steeled myself to take whatever was coming to me.

I found the Officers' Mess deserted. Unbeknown to me it had been evacuated during the weekend. Luckily Mortey, the Squadron Adjutant, popped up from nowhere to make last minute arrangements for the pilots to be billeted out. I had been assigned to a country mansion somewhere near Knockholt. An Aircrew Bus had been laid on to run a shuttle service between the various country houses and the Squadron Dispersal. By now it was dusk, and as the light failed air activity grew less. Sure enough, the Aircrew Bus turned up with a dozen or more 72 and 79 Squadron boys who had been stood down. I told them about the Hurricane I had seen 'go in', and Dimsie Stones said it was probably Brian Noble who had baled out, wounded but alive, though badly burnt. I couldn't believe it; it was a miracle that someone could have got out of that Hurricane and survived.

The bus dropped two of us off at a beautiful Georgian mansion, and we were shown to our rooms by a butler called James. The others were driven off to be dispersed at similar establishments dotted round the local area. To this day I am ashamed to admit I do not know where my country mansion was, nor the name of my host and hostess. All I can remember is that my bedroom was a joy, furnished in superb taste with a bathroom and toilet en suite, silk sheets, bedside tables, reading lamps, books, easy

SPIT AND SAWDUST

chairs, in fact 'the lot'. The snag was that as soon as I came off the bus I was capable of one thing only - sleep.

Every morning at about 4 am I was woken by James carrying a silver tray with teapot, sugar, milk and buttered toast. In no time at all came the strident horn of the shuttle and, with fear clutching at my throat, I would dash out into the dark damp air, a typical Autumn morning pointing to a fine, cloudless sky. Another day of combat was unfolding.

My first few sorties found me in a daze. My head was aching and my eye was still half closed. I spent most of the time pulling steep turns in vain efforts to line up deflection shots at passing Me109's, of which there were plenty. All in all I was very lucky indeed not to have been shot down in flames. The next few days saw the same sequence repeated, each night collapsing between the silk sheets, incapable of taking further interest. Not once did I see my country mansion in daylight, the only member of the household I spoke to being the long-suffering James.

After about five days my eye improved and at last I could see properly. My confidence was growing and I was looking for a kill, but instead I had an unnerving experience.

'A' Flight took off in the middle of yet another bombing raid, when to my dismay I suddenly realised that my engine revs were not responding to throttle movement. The Merlin was purring away happily at full bore, and even with the throttle fully closed the revs stayed at maximum. There was nothing I could do about it. By quickly blipping the magneto switches on the off I found the engine would cut in and out without stopping dead, so I decided to return and land by manipulating the switches. I pulled off a reasonable landing, switching the engine off for the last time as I coaxed the wheels on to the grass, coming to rest in the middle of the airfield in between bomb craters. Having no radio I couldn't call ground control, so unstrapping I jumped down and ran towards the perimeter, where I thought I might find a tractor.

Most of the ground personnel where in the Air Raid shelters, but I found a corporal who cheerfully agreed to come out with a 15 cwt truck which had a tow-bar and a length of wire cable. The raid was over by now as he lashed the contraption to my Hurricane, and hauled it out of the way back to the Squadron dispersal. I am ashamed to say I never noted the Corporal's name, events were happening so fast. If anyone earned a medal that day he did.

On 6 September, my eye now completely open, I at last achieved some visible results when I attacked a JU88 which was flying towards Croydon at about four thousand feet. I had the advantage of height and

THE LUFTWAFFE STOKES IT UP

dived down to within about fifty yards, observing strikes along the fuselage and tail plane. Breaking away, still in a steep dive, my gun button stuck, all eight machine guns continuing to fire, raking Croydon High Street with .303 bullets. I saw shoppers running in all directions, and prayed that I hadn't done anyone an injury. There had recently been reports in the press of civilians being fired on in the street by wicked German pilots, so it looked as if I had now joined the Club!. I was credited with '1 JU88 Probable', because a JU88 crashed in the vicinity at the time.

So far 79 Squadron losses had not been catastrophic - one pilot killed and seven wounded - but we had suffered some aircraft casualties from enemy bombing, and very few were left in a serviceable condition. The Battle had reached a critical stage and a high level decision was taken; instead of flying in aircraft replacements, the new strategy was to re-deploy a whole Squadron from a quieter sector in exchange. By the end of the first week in September we were told we were on the move, supposedly to an airfield in Pembury, just east of Tunbridge Wells, which was good news because Teddy Morris said a new airstrip had recently been built there, and that's where we were going. Mortey bribed the driver of the night shuttle to pick us all up at dusk, and drive us over to the White Hart at Brasted to celebrate. When James brought in my silver tray next morning I didn't even know I had been to bed. It therefore came as a bombshell when Harvey Heyworth broke the news that we were going to Pembrey, in South Wales, not Pembury, which had never been a airstrip.

None of us had ever heard of Pembrey. We felt shattered and resentful; we knew we had given a good account of ourselves despite some set-backs. We were aggrieved at the thought of being given the boot when we were just acquiring some hard-won experience and confidence. Inexorably a Squadron Movement Order was issued so there was no going back now.

Those of us detailed to fly out the serviceable Hurricanes, myself included, sadly gathered at dispersal on Sunday morning, 8 September, to take off into the unknown, conjuring up visions of grimy smog-infested villages ringed with slag heaps. My Fitter, SAC Rothwell, a keen and loyal airman, happily volunteered to pilot my Morris 8 on the delivery run to our new Station, taking with him a load of clobber, making the little car look like a 'Steptoe and Son' enterprise.

RAF Pembrey was a hutted camp like Sutton Bridge. The airfield, all grass except for a single tarmac runway, was separated from the sea by

SPIT AND SAWDUST

a wide belt of soft marshy ground, where there was a firing range used by the Army and the RAF. It was encompassed on both sides by the murky sand flats between the estuary at Llanelli, and westwards to the small coastal town of Ferryside, an area famous for its cockle beds and the ladies who picked them. On the north side rose the foothills of the Valleys - a flying hazard, especially at night. We viewed the scene with dismay. It was a depressing prospect after the excitement of Biggin.

Enemy air action was mostly confined to attacking Atlantic convoys on the Western Approaches, and laying mines in the shipping lanes, and in the harbours at Pembroke Dock and Milford Haven. The Squadron was to maintain constant daylight fighter patrols over the convoys, which meant about thirty minutes, with luck, over the convoy and then return to base with just enough fuel for a circuit and landing. Each pilot was doing as many as four convoy patrols a day plus frequent night sorties.

The weather was still holding in late September. HQ 10 Group had established a hook-up with the Royal Observer Corps in the Scilly Isles, to try to intercept the 'Milk Run'. This was the name given to almost daily raids by the Luftwaffe, routed via the Scillies to Southern Ireland, then a turn to the northwest towards targets in the Liverpool and Merseyside area, returning home in the dark. The ROC in the Scillies, as soon as EA were sighted, would phone Group Operations giving the code name 'Lions Den', whereupon Ops would call us up to 'Readiness'. This gave us ample time to work out our take off to coincide with sighting the EA as they approached the Irish Coast. We had no extra fuel tanks in those days, so the timing was critical, added to which we quickly lost radio contact with Ground Control beyond about thirty miles west of Pembroke, so we had to rely on dead reckoning and visual contact to pull of an interception.

In all we had about six calls to the 'Lions Den', and we succeeded twice, the first time on Friday 27 September, the second on the following Sunday, 29 September, which was the last time the Luftwaffe tried this particular caper. The other attempts were aborted due to adverse weather, failure to make visual contact, or low fuel state, but I suppose this tally wasn't too bad considering the factors involved.

It seemed for some reason that my long distance eye sight was particularly good, because I could spot EA seconds before the other pilots. Consequently I was usually in the lead section to show the way on sighting hostile aircraft, substituting for Ground Control so to speak. On 27 September the weather was good, clear skies but rather hazy on the horizon.

THE LUFTWAFFE STOKES IT UP

We had taken off at 1800 hours, when at 1830 I spotted about nine or ten small black dots silhouetted against the haze. We were at twenty five thousand feet, and I could just pick out the coast of Southern Ireland about ten miles to the west. Shouting "Tally Ho!" I pulled the tit and headed full bore towards them, selecting my own target as we drew near. They were HeIII's, and clearly they hadn't spotted us because they carried on, spread out in a gaggle. I throttled back to reduce my overtaking speed as I came within range. Closing to about two hundred yards I let the Heinkel have it with a long burst, seeing strikes all along the cockpit and fuselage. So far as I could tell there was no return fire. A cluster of bombs came tumbling out of its belly, and the undercarriage dropped down as I was breaking away. Turning hard round I kept with the Heinkel as it went into a shallow dive, smoke billowing out from the starboard engine. Then I saw two bodies falling clear as their parachutes opened. The aircraft slowly spiralled downwards until it hit the sea in a great cloud of white spume. Forgetting my low fuel state for a second, I slid my hood back and did steep turns round the two airmen as they dangled beneath their parachutes like plastic dolls. I gave them the 'V' for Victory sign. Poor buggers, they were never picked up. Little did I know then what was in store for me two evenings later.

The fine Autumn weather continued. On the evening of Sunday 29 September I found myself once again in an attack against HeIII bombers just off the southern coast of Ireland. It was a carbon copy of the previous encounter of the 27, with the exception that this time, instead of my two German victims, I finished up dangling on the end of a parachute myself.

Inflatable dinghies for Fighter Pilots were not yet in service; all we had was a 'Mae West' life jacket. I was wearing a brand new uniform from Gieves, plus a pair of shoes I had just bought from the well-known bespoke shoemakers, Poulson and Skone in Duke Street St James, for which I had signed a Bankers' Order for £1 a month. Everything was ruined, including my left shoe, which had a neat furrow cut through the sole by a bullet.

Having spotted the column of smoke rising up through the haze I knew it could only be one thing - a ship. By now I was at about four thousand feet above sea level, so there was no time to waste. I managed somehow to flick-roll the Hurricane and I fell clear. At that very same moment I heard a loud explosion. Bits and pieces of ironmongery were plunging down around me and splashing into the sea. When down to about twenty feet I punched the parachute quick-release box, and the harness fell away as I hit the water hard, going straight under for what seemed like an

SPIT AND SAWDUST

eternity, but I popped up again, lungs full of sea water and choking for breath, kept afloat by my 'Mae West.'

There was a heavy swell on; one moment I was on the crest of a wave, the next I was down in a deep trough. Rising to the top like a cork, I could catch a brief glimpse of the ship only to disappear as once again I was plunged into the hollow. I noted with relief that the ship was altering course and coming closer, in fact so close it was now almost within spitting distance. As it loomed up large above me, a strong current was sweeping me past, and I glimpsed crewmen leaning against the gun-wale looking down at me with clearly no intention of rescuing me, so I screamed as loud as I could

"For fuck's sake get me out of this" and shouting other words in the vernacular, until I was carried way past the ship which within seconds vanished from sight. Under a darkening sky my situation now looked grim, it was too murky to see anything and I began to feel intensely cold.

I didn't know it but already some members of the crew had lowered a lifeboat and started to row towards where they last saw me. By sheer luck they picked up a streak of bright luminous green in the water, and followed it until they found me. This substance was called 'fluoresein', contained in a pack sewn onto the Mae West, which turned fluorescent green on contact with water. This simple little device undoubtedly saved my life, as indeed it must also have saved many aircrew in similar incidents throughout the war.

The next thing I knew I was being hauled aboard the lifeboat by willing hands, I was perishing cold as if struck with paralysis. The skipper pointed to my chest, and as I looked down I saw that my uniform was soaked with a rusty red colour which I mistook for blood. I remember no more until I found myself in a bath steeped in brandy fumes.

After drying out, the First Mate lent me a uniform and we started to talk.

What saved me was the explosion they heard as my Hurricane blew up, otherwise they would never have spotted me. At the time they reckoned I was a German pilot, they had no intention of picking me up until they heard me cursing. The red colour on my uniform was the flourescein which on contact with water goes red, then turns to green. I learned that the ship was a four thousand ton merchantman called the SS Dartford, which was nearing the end of a long lone voyage from the Argentine with a cargo of maize, bound for Liverpool. The Master, Captain S Bulmer, explained that he could not radio a report of my rescue because of the proximity of U-Boats. News of U-Boat activity was

THE LUFTWAFFE STOKES IT UP

constantly being received, and he would make no firm promises when he could get me ashore, so we cruised up and down the Irish Sea for about thirty-six hours, which frankly I enjoyed immensely. I was at last dropped off at Milford Haven early on Wednesday morning 2 October.

I subsequently heard that sadly the SS Dartford was torpedoed and sunk by U-124 on 12th June 1942 whilst bound in Convoy ONS-100 when in 29.19N 41.33W. Twenty-five crewmen were lost. There was a handful of survivors, but two died shortly after being picked up. A tragic ending to what for me was a stroke of incredibly good fortune. I owed my life to those brave men. The First Mate and I swapped our top buttons and I am proud to say I still have his button to this day.

I breakfasted at the Officers' Mess, RAF Pembroke Dock, and telephoned Pembrey to say I was still alive. I hitched a ride on an Anson flying from RAF Carew Cherington to HQ 10 Group, Colerne, the pilot dropping me off at Pembrey en route. I reported to Mortey and found he was busy making an inventory of my personal belongings to be sent to my 'next of kin.' A cheerful homecoming! The final twist was that I was told that the Heinkel I had attacked crashed into the sea, like the one I shot down on the 27th, but I was too late to claim it! I never bothered to do anything about it, life was too short, I had had a miraculous escape from death, so be it.

Soon after rejoining the Squadron I heard the sad news that Paul Davies-Cooke, 72 Squadron, a contemporary of mine in Churchills', Shrewsbury, had been shot down and killed near Sevenoaks on 27th September. I recalled memories of a short camping holiday we had taken together in 1937. Paul borrowed his father's car, a new Riley Kestrel fitted with the then revolutionary Wilson automatic gear box. It was very smart, silver with real red leather upholstery, it was one of the early 'sex wagons'. We drove it down to Salcombe in South Devon in pursuit of a very pretty girl called Jasmine, whom we had met the previous summer. She worked at the box office in the local cinema. We pitched our tent near a beach at Bolt Head, and after the cinema closed we took her back to our camp in a desperate endeavour to persuade her to succumb to our overtures. She allowed us to feel her small firm breasts then, as her nipples hardened, she calmly brushed us aside and walked back to the car, leaving us in no doubt that we were overgrown schoolboys.

After my Irish Sea adventure, I flew my first sortie on 5 October, and soon settled down to the humdrum existence of convoy patrols, night flying and false alarms.

Early one foggy dawn I was sitting in the cockpit of my Hurricane at the take off end of the runway, strapped in, oxygen on, radio switched to 'Ops Control', in a state known as 'Immediate Readiness', when the voice of the Controller shook me out of my reverie.

"Scramble Red Section! Scramble Red Section!"

The 'chore horse' was plugged in and engine warmed up, so all I had to do was press the starter button, wave the 'chore horse' and chocks away, and take straight off, followed by Red 2 and 3. The weather was bad, visibility less than a thousand yards, a gentle drizzle brushing over the airfield. Within seconds we were in cloud.

"Vector 290" came the Controller's voice. "Bogey approaching St David's Head at fifteen thousand feet. Buster! Buster! Then again "Alter course to 235 degrees."

"Wilco, Wilco" I muttered.

I continued the climb through layers of cumulostratus until I struck a clear patch at about twelve thousand feet. There, right in front of us, between the cloud layers, was a Hampden bomber staggering along in a more or less easterly direction. I dived towards it until close enough to wag my wings, signalling to the pilot to follow me. Red 2 and 3 brought up the rear, and together we escorted it back to Pembrey. By now it was daylight, visibility improving despite the 'duty drizzle'. The Hampden followed me in and landed, taxying up to the Control Tower. I parked my aircraft, jumped down, and as I ran across I could see the Hampden pilot wearily stumbling from the exit hatch. I had alerted the Rescue Services on the radio, and already they were helping the crew out, collapsing on the ground as they dropped clear. The navigator and rear gunner had both been wounded.

When the pilot peeled off his helmet I was staggered to recognise the familiar face of Peter Barlow, whom I had last seen in London the previous November in the Blue Lagoon Night Club.

Peter had been on a night bombing raid over Brest. He was hit by flak and becoming disorientated lost his bearings. He thought he was somewhere over the Cherbourg Peninsula. By now dangerously low on fuel, he was contemplating baling out when we intercepted him in the nick of time. It was a fortuitous and alcoholic reunion. I had already started to make arrangements for my marriage in January, and was looking for a Best Man. Peter was an old school friend and had already met Pan, so he was the perfect choice. He readily agreed.

We were married in London on 7 January 1941. The Reception was at Frascatis', an Edwardian Restaurant of some repute near Cambridge Circus, later destroyed in the Blitz. We spent two nights at the

THE LUFTWAFFE STOKES IT UP

Cumberland Hotel, the bill amounting to the prodigious sum of £2 8s. 1d! We motored all the way back to Pembrey in the now somewhat shabby little Morris 8. Within hours I was back on Convoy Patrols.

The official end to the Battle of Britain had been fixed at 31 October. The pressure on day-fighter Squadrons had to some extent been relaxed, the axis of daylight combat now shifting back across the Channel in the form of sweeps, to lure the Luftwaffe into battle, more often than not over hostile territory, although successful, they exacted a relentless toll of fighter pilots, both experienced and raw alike.

Air Operations in the Western Desert were now beginning to intensify, and Fighter Squadrons there were crying out for replacement pilots. A circular went round Fighter Command calling for volunteers. Several members of 79 Squadron submitted their names, including Teddy Morris, DFC, Peggy O'Neill DFC, a veteran Light Bomber Pilot, and a 'press-on' Aussie pilot, Owen Tracey, who within a matter of months was shot down and killed.

We were landed with seven or eight 'sprogs' fresh from Flying School. Harvey Heyworth delegated to me the job of knocking these new chaps into shape by organising a Squadron 'Training Flight'. It bored me to death, and I began to regret that I hadn't volunteered for the Western Desert with the others. I got what I deserved.

As 1941 rolled on, Squadron activities were centred round the same old Convoy patrols, plus night flying operations against the blitzes on Swansea, Cardiff and Bristol. Intercepting EA at night was a hit and miss affair, 99% miss and 1% hit. Airborne radar was a new toy, it was certainly too complex and bulky to be adapted to single-seat fighters. An extra body was required to operate the equipment, so first Blenheims were modified to take it, followed by Beaufighters, and later the Mosquito.

The most the Ground Controllers could do with us was to vector us into the general area from were the EA were dropping their bombs, and from then on it was up to the pilot to get a visual contact.

It was easy enough to see incendiary and HE bombs exploding on the ground below, but it was another matter to flog around the sky above the conflagration, straining one's eyes to get a sight of an EA and simultaneously taking violent evasive action to escape our own searchlights, which had a nasty habit of locking on to us. For a short spell we had a new 'A' Flight Commander, a Canadian called Dickie Dennison. He had a complex about night flying, that it to say, he left us guys to take care of daylight convoy patrols while he spent almost all the hours of darkness airborne in search of the enemy. On the night of 10 March he had his reward.

I was flying on the same patrol line at about ten thousand feet, when we were vectored towards a bandit heading for Pembroke Dock. I heard his cry "Tally Ho!." I suddenly saw a brilliant flash followed by a spectacular spiral of flaming ironmongery pitching downwards, then a conflagration spreading in all directions over the sea below. He claimed a JU88 'Destroyed'. Less than four weeks later, in the same area, he suddenly went off the radar screen somewhere near St Gowans Head, and was never seen again.

Trevor Bryant-Fenn, who had been shot down by Me109's near Biggin Hill on 1 September 1940, ending up wounded in hospital, had just rejoined the Squadron, so he now took over 'A' Flight. David Haysom continued as 'B' Flight Commander. A new airfield was near completion at a site on the Gower Peninsular called Fairwood Common. The Squadron received orders to move there as soon as it was declared serviceable.

In about April 1941, shortly before we moved to Fairwood, a replacement pilot named Alec Chappel joined the Squadron. He was an Old Stoic, like David Niven. Within a few weeks he produced for our delectation his new wife, Fleurettte, an ex-Windmill and Palladium Showgirl. She was a tall graceful blonde with a fabulous figure. Pan had known her briefly during her theatre days, so she and Fleurette had much in common. Perhaps that's just as well, because on about the 30 April, Alec, returning from a daylight convoy patrol, for some unknown reason nose-dived into the ground on the final approach, and disintegrated in a cloud of flame and oil-black smoke. Several of us were standing outside when it happened, it was not a pretty sight. Pan did her best to console Fleurette, and stayed with her to help with sorting things out. She returned to London and we never saw or heard anything more of Fleurette - she was a very beautiful girl.

The impending move to Fairwood came as a bitter blow to the boys, because there was a strong rumour that we were to convert to Spitfires and return to the Metropolitan Sector where all the action was. Suddenly, somehow, as the modern phrase has it, 'we felt deprived'. Harvey Heyworth tried to reverse the decision, but the 10 Group Penpushers had their way. In early June we were uprooted from Winter Quarters at Pembrey in exchange for a quagmire on the Gower.

On 14th June I was detailed to do some trial landings at Fairwood on the only serviceable runway. The approaches were all right, but the airfield was littered with great heaps of building materials and heavy

THE LUFTWAFFE STOKES IT UP

earth-moving equipment of every kind. At the point of touchdown there was no sideways view, because a continuous pile of earth and rubble at least six feet high extended the full length of the runway on either side, making it pretty easy to hit the bank in a cross wind. Clearly something would have to be done about this before the Squadron could operate there, so Harvey gave the Airfield Construction wallahs two and a half days to pull their fingers out. By the 17th the ground had been nearly cleared and we flew our Hurricanes in without incident.

It had been raining solidly for a fortnight so there was mud everywhere, and it was impossible to keep the aircraft clean, inside or out.

Fairwood was built to the new-style airfield design aimed at maximum dispersal of installations, aircraft and personnel. Considerable distances separated the various sites from one another. For example, Officers' sleeping quarters could be as much as twenty minutes walk from the Officers' Mess; once released from duty, one returned to the sleeping site for a wash, with luck, then togged up with raincoat and Wellington boots, one staggered through the mud for about a mile in search of the Officers' Mess, invariably through torrential rain.

Pan was now about four months pregnant. Harvey gave me a day off to go searching for new digs. We found a nice house overlooking the sea at Caswell Bay. We had a bedroom, sitting room and use of the kitchen. Just after we moved in I was detailed for night ops. Ready to go, suitably dressed for the occasion, including my regulation Smith and Wesson revolver, which must be worn by all pilots on operational night flying, I was standing at the sitting room door about to say goodbye when Pan, who was sitting on the large bay-window sea, asked,

"It's not loaded, darling, is it?"

"Of course not" I replied as I drew the revolver from its holster.

"I only cleaned it this morning, the chamber's empty, see?"

With that I pulled the trigger and it clicked once, twice, three times. Pressing the trigger the fourth time there was an ear-splitting bang, followed by a loud crash as a bullet shattered the window behind Pan's head, missing her right ear by a whisker. There followed a scene of panic and confusion. I rushed forward fearful for Pan lest the shock should spark off a miscarriage. Everywhere was strewn with broken glass. At the same moment the landlady dashed in and saw me standing there, in my hand the still smoking gun. She went into hysterics and shrieked,

"Get out of my house! Get out at once."

Clearly she thought I had tried to murder my wife. Pan seemed to be

SPIT AND SAWDUST

OK. We had no choice but to pack up and evacuate, there and then. I contacted Harvey Heyworth and explained the situation. He released me from 'readiness', and we left in the Morris 8 heading towards Swansea looking for a hotel. We got a room in the Mackworth Hotel, an ugly Edwardian edifice which was later destroyed in the blitz.

We were now on the search for digs again. Two or three days later, we spotted a large Victorian style house in the middle of extensive well-kept grounds, trees and shrubs everywhere. It bordered on the southwest corner of the airfield. I drove up the drive and rang the bell. An elderly lady answered the door, and I gave her the usual spiel about did she know somewhere where we could find digs? She beckoned to a dim figure standing behind her, and a disagreeable old gentleman appeared mumbling something about refugees. We hastily explained that we were not refugees, whereupon he turned to the old lady,

"I suppose we'd better take them in."

"As you say, dear."

"Sooner or later we'll be forced to have refugees, so this could be the lesser of two evils."

Turning to us he asked gruffly,

"How much do you want to pay?"

We looked at each other helplessly, we had always been told what to pay, so what could we say?

"As you don't seem to be able to make your minds up, what would you say to £2 each per week, full board?"

Unable to believe our ears we readily agreed.

"That's fixed then, fetch your things and be back for dinner at 7 o'clock."

We had fallen on our feet. We were given a nice old-fashioned double room overlooking a large garden where, apart from copious flower beds, there was also a spacious kitchen garden where apple and pear trees were already fruiting, bedsides raspberries, strawberries, loganberries, and rows of broad beans, runner beans and peas.

The old boy turned out to be Mr Peacock, owner and Director of a chain of stores in Swansea, Cardiff and elsewhere, known as 'Peacocks Stores'. The old lady was his sister, and they lived together in this large house. They had a cook, two maidservants and a gardener. They didn't know what rationing was.

Mr Peacock wasn't that old, perhaps fifty-five/sixty, but he just seemed old to us, being in our early twenties. He obviously enjoyed having us in his house, and his sister fussed round Pan like Mother

THE LUFTWAFFE STOKES IT UP

Goose. He had a storeroom under the stairs where he kept quantities of cigarettes, chocolate, tobacco, and even liberal supplies of knitting wool, which Miss Peacock used for knitting things for the baby. Whenever I left the house to go on duty, be it early morning or late at night, the old boy would always come out from under the stairs with two packets of twenty Players and a bar of Cadbury's chocolate for me.

Since our move to Fairwood, the Squadron had been on continuous night operations, plus of course the usual spate of convoy patrols and 'readiness' states during daylight hours. We operated at night along a patrol line code-named 'Crack', between Pembroke Dock and Swansea, where the Luftwaffe had been carrying out intensive mine-laying operations.

As usual we had to rely on visual contact to pull off an interception, and we seldom got any joy. David Haysom had now taken over from Harvey as Commanding Officer, and he was determined to get a kill. He managed twice to creep up the backside of an EA, one a JU88, the other unidentified, but he couldn't claim more than a 'damaged' for his pains. We were lucky enough to have Roly Beamont as the new 'B' Flight Commander, who joined us at the end of June from 87 Squadron (Hurricane Night Fighters) based at Charmy Down. Later, of course, Roly made history as the Chief Test Pilot for English Electric, testing the Canberra and the Lightning supersonic Fighter.

On the night of 5 July I was detailed to patrol 'Crack', taking off at around 2300 hours. It was a clear night but black as soot. As I turned eastward the Controller's voice came over:

"Several bandits in Swansea/Llanelli area. Vector 100° Angels 15. Buster!" I could see clusters of searchlights beaming up all along my route, when suddenly in front of me I spotted an EA caught in a cone. I was at exactly the same height about two thousand yards behind. It was flying inland from my right heading north, and with the aid of the searchlights I tracked it in a left-hand turn, creeping up behind it to within perhaps four hundred yards, closing up fast. Suddenly the searchlights were doused, and I was plunging into inky blackness like a derailed runaway trolley-car which had missed the buffers. Recovering from this momentary set-back I made a tight orbit, eyeballs straining from their sockets, trying to pierce the darkness for a sight of the EA, but to no avail. As I turned back parallel with the coast, without warning my Hurricane caught fire, flames spreading from beneath the engine cowling, and it seemed all lit up down below where my feet were supposed to be. In seconds flames were licking round the canopy. I had no choice now,

SPIT AND SAWDUST

I had to jump before I was 'barbecued'. Screaming invectives at the Controller on the radio to take a fix on my position, I yanked the hood back, half-rolled and dropped clear, not forgetting first, thank God, to unplug everything. Mercifully the parachute opened. Dangling from the shroud-lines I attempted to survey the scene. All round me there was a vast expanse of dark shadows, which reflected the distant glow of the burning Hurricane as it twisted and spun down towards the coal-black earth. All I could see now were a few stars twinkling above, and the ghostly glimmer of some faraway searchlights.

My eyes grew accustomed to the dark, and I could pick out a jagged line of pearl-white breakers along what must be a beach. I'd no idea of my height, but as I sank slowly down I could see that a gentle offshore wind was coaxing me across the coast line. 'Oh God' I thought. 'For the second time I am heading for a watery grave.'

I feverishly tugged on the shroud-lines to increase my rate of descent, and nearly collapsed the parachute canopy. Suddenly the unmistakeable smell of crops and the harvesting of freshly mown hay assailed my nostrils. I could now hear the backwash of the surf along the shingle. Quicker than I could sink a pint of beer, I hit the ground with a sickening thud and was dragged along on my back, whilst desperately groping for the quick-release box, without the slightest idea where I was except that a rugged cliff-edge could be only yards away. I found the box and gave the knob a vicious twist. The parachute harness gently slid away into the darkness, leaving me lying in a shallow ditch.

I lay there quietly for a few seconds taking stock. Though bruised and scratched, at least it seemed that I was in one piece. It was pitch black. Staggering to my feet, not knowing which direction to take, I started walking. The ground was stubble and pitted, making it hard-going. As I gingerly crept forward I heard muffled movements ahead and thought I saw sinister shadows, even darker than the dark, looming up in front of me.

It's the Welsh Home Guard! I thought to myself in horror. They'll shoot anyone on sight! In a discordant shaky voice I sang out the first few notes of 'God Save the King', then on second thoughts switched to 'Cumre am Bith', in the hope they would take me for a patriotic Welshman, so that perhaps they would spare me the bullet. There followed the instantaneous and sudden rush of pounding feet, as several cows reared up out of the darkness and shied away in the opposite direction, evidently much put out by my song!

I struggled on and eventually spotted a faint light glimmering through

THE LUFTWAFFE STOKES IT UP

the undergrowth. Drawing nearer I saw the outline of some buildings. It was a farmhouse. The farmer took me in, brewed a cup of tea, then ran me in his old jalopy to Llangain Manor, the HQ of a Royal Artillery Ack Ack and Searchlight Detachment about a mile away, some five miles south of Carmarthen. They gave me bacon and eggs, and I shot my mouth off about searchlights and how they fucked everything up. They hastily pushed me into a truck and drove me back to Fairwood Common, in the eager fervid hope that they would never see me again!

It was still dark when I arrived back at Fairwood, so after filling in my Combat Report, I jumped into my Morris 8 and drove straight to 'Chateau Peacock'. I got up to our bedroom just as Pan awoke from a deep sleep. I must have looked a grotesque sight standing there at the end of the bed, covered in dried mud, scorched battle dress and trousers torn. She just couldn't believe it - the second shock for her within the space of a few weeks.

In early July a second Hurricane Squadron arrived, No 504 (County of Nottingham, R Aux AF), commanded by Squadron Leader Tony Rook, an impressive character with a sparkling wit and an enormous black handlebar moustache. Also in the Squadron was his younger brother Mickie. Between the two of them, with the aid of a few 'feeds' and pints, they were as good as any Music Hall Variety Act. It transpired that Tony had been selected to form a new Squadron out of the nucleus of 504, and prepare it for Fighter Operations on the Russian Front. 504 retained its number plate, and was obliged to accept an influx of numerous sprog pilots still wet behind the ears. On 30 July I was posted from 79 to 504 with the acting rank of Flight Lieutenant, as Flight Commander of 'A' Flight. 'B' Flight Commander was Flight Lieutenant Barnes, an old Auxiliary Air Force pilot. The new Commanding Officer was Squadron Leader Trevor Parsons, one of the original 504 members.

After two weeks of intensive training 504 was declared operational on 14 August. Immediately afterwards we were transferred to RAF Chilbolton, a satellite airfield under the control of RAF Middle Wallop. Chilbolton was little more than an emergency landing ground, and had no domestic accommodation. All the pilots were billeted out in private houses. I was assigned to a beautiful old country house near Stockbridge, where the River Test flowed unhurriedly through its extensive grounds. I was surprised and delighted to find that my hosts, or rather hostesses, were none other than the Misses Disraeli, two surviving sisters of the celebrated ex-Prime Minister. In the front hall of the house there were fishing rods, tackle, baskets and all the paraphernalia associated with the sport. I had been taught fly-fishing by my godfather on the River Eden in Cumberland. Suddenly, at the behest of the Disraeli ladies, two miles of fishing on the Test became mine. I wonder what the same stretch would cost today?

Soon after our arrival at Chilbolton, Trevor Parsons decided to get married. The wedding was to be in Cornwall and the reception at the Budock Vean Hotel, Helford Passage. Barney and I each flew a Hurricane down to RAF Porthreath. We bribed the Station Flight to refuel us and, after an excess of champagne made from the black grapes of the appropriately named vineyard Bouzy, we flew back to Chilbolton just before sundown dangerously over-confident which, if the truth be told, was nothing to be proud of.

Once again the Squadron was on the move, this time to RAF Ballyhalbert, a brand new airfield on the Ards Peninsular, in Northern Ireland. There was but one single tarmac runway, allegedly laid down to be in line with the direction of the prevailing wind, but because we were in Ireland, I suppose, quite the opposite was the case! We all became used to landing in 90 degree cross winds of up to fifty knots, but not before we had broken a few undercarriages on the day of our arrival, resulting in damage to at least eight Hurricanes. With so many new inexperienced pilots I almost lost hope, but in October spirits picked up again when we converted to Spitfires.

CHAPTER TEN

SPITFIRE CONVERSION

I was now tour-expired and in November I was posted to No 52 OTU, RAF Aston Down, as Flight Commander 'D' Flight.

Just prior to leaving 504 I took part in a search for the second Eagle Squadron which was supposed to have arrived at RAF Eglington, near Londonderry. Not one of the American pilots made it. The weather was appalling, low cloud, rain and high winds. Having refuelled at Speke on the mainland, they were due to fly across the Irish Sea in the early afternoon of 8 October. Of the twenty Spitfires which had left Speke, all were missing by the expiry of their ETA. The final tally looked something like this:

Ten Spitfires eventually landed at RAF Aldergrove, the pilots not having the slightest idea where they were.

Four crashed into the mountain side of Snaefell in the Isle of Man.

Two pilots baled out into the Irish Sea never to be seen again.

Four belly-landed somewhere near Loch Neagh.

It was a sad introduction to operational flying in the European Theatre. It was the weather that beat them.

No 52 was a Spitfire Conversion Unit equipped with clapped-out Spitfires Mks I and II and several Miles Masters. The Miles Master was a 2-seat Trainer superseding the Harvard. The majority of the staff were 'tour expired' fighter pilots without any 'Flying Instructor' qualifications so it was, at best, a hit and miss affair, but a most enjoyable pastime for all that.

I was reunited with old friends from the 'Battle', Hiram Smith, Birdie Wilson, Lucy Rayner, John Parker, Tony Whitehouse and many others. Later, in March 1942, Tony Rook returned from Russia and took over from Hiram as CFI.

Towards the end of November (1941) I was detailed to conduct a Court of Enquiry on a fatal flying accident at RAF Llandow in South Wales, which was another Spitfire OTU and commanded by a distinguished World War I fighter pilot, none other than Ira (Taffy) Jones. There had been a succession of fatal accidents there recently and Group was getting worried. This time two Spitfires had collided in midair right over the airfield, in good weather conditions, killing both pilots. My brief was to sort it out and allocate blame, if any. It was my first foray at this kind of thing, and a pretty ticklish assignment if I wasn't to tread on someone's toes. There was no evidence of mechanical failure because both Spitfires were totally destroyed. I could have been wrong, but I thought

SPIT AND SAWDUST

I sensed an off-hand attitude among the pupil pilots which, if it were true, could lead to poor flying discipline.

I set up the Court on the morning of 24 November in a small Nissen hut close to Station Headquarters, after first paying my respects to Group Captain Ira Jones DSO, DFC, (and several Bars!). He gave me authority to call for all witnesses I might need to interview, and for all relevant documents relating to the last moments of the two Spitfires and pilots to be handed over. With the use of a Hillman Minx from Station MT, I drove to the location of the crash to see whether any evidence could be found which might reveal clues as to the cause of the accident. I was searching for a needle in a haystack, both Spitfires were totally destroyed. They lay in two main heaps of twisted metal and impedimenta, smaller bits and pieces scattered over a wide area. There was nothing to indicate that either of the pilots had attempted to jump, in any case, by the time they realised what was happening, it was probably too late anyway.

I spent the rest of the day on interrogation. The next morning I recorded my findings on the appropriate AMO Form but, as I have already said, there was no evidence of mechanical failure, but after interviewing a few of the pilots I was sure that flying discipline on the Unit left much to be desired. The spate of seemingly unnecessary accidents, attributable to pilot error, had clearly lowered morale, thus creating a 'knock-on' effect.

I had a long confab with Taffy, and he decided to have a parade of all the pilots the next day outside the mortuary. He made them march in single file past the slab on which the mangled bodies of their two mates were laid out. Taffy had a marked stammer and as they slowly moved round he stuttered:

"If you der der der don't per per per pull our ffffucking ffffingers out you were wer wer will all end up ler ler ler looking like th th th ththat."

I can't say that I approved of this strategy, it was Taffy's idea and he was sure it would work. I know of no evidence to show that it had the desired effect.

During my two and a half days at Llandow I met an ex-17 Squadron fighter pilot called Peter Brett. He agreed to help me lay on a party to celebrate the end of the Court of Enquiry. We had it in the Officers' Mess, which was situated in a fine old country mansion a few miles from the airfield. The party developed into the usual shambles, ending with Taffy Jones letting off fire extinguishers from a gallery, over an attractive wrought iron circular staircase, on to the heads of the drunks below. Infantile, perhaps, but sometimes one had to let one's hair down, there

SPITFIRE CONVERSION

was a war on.

Some years later I was to meet up again with Peter Brett in very strange circumstances.

After Dunkirk, thousands of displaced military personnel from the continent of Europe were being rehabilitated in the UK to form new fighting units. Aston Down was receiving its quota of veteran pilots from the Air Forces of France, Belgium, Holland, Poland and Czechoslovakia. Given the obvious language problem, their enthusiasm and zeal minimised the task of teaching them new techniques and procedures in an alien tongue. It was an exciting and moving experience to take these men, each in turn, in the Master trainer to demonstrate fighter tactics. One immediately sensed their gusto and enthusiasm, their impatience and burning ambition to get to grips with the Luftwaffe to avenge their fallen countrymen.

On one of the rate occasions I was given a day off, Pan suggested we drive over to Cheltenham to visit her Aunt Toby, her mother's sister, the late Rector of Stiffkey's sister-in-law. She lived with her husband, a well-known Church architect, in Imperial Square. On arrival we were introduced to Toby's twenty year old son, Bill Anderson, a 2nd Lieutenant in the Royal Ulster Rifles. Bill was on leave prior to taking a training course with the Parachute Regiment at Warminster. In a fit of generosity I offered to fly him to nearby Netheravon. He readily accepted and on 13 April he turned up at Aston Down rearing to go. I bundled him and his kit into a Master and delivered him safe and sound to his new unit. Fate decreed that I was to see him again when we met up in North Africa less than nine months later.

My time at Aston Down was drawing to a close. The normal tour on non-operational flying duties was about six to nine months and by May I had been there nearly six. Within a week I received a posting notice promoting me to the rank of Acting Squadron Leader. I was to take command of 93(F) Squadron on 7 June 1942. 93 had been a Coastal Command Squadron during the early part of the war, and was now to be transferred to Fighter Command and to reform with Spitfires at an airfield in the Isle of Man called Andreas, which was under the operational control of HQ 9 Group, Preston. I pinched myself to be sure that it was true, that at last I was to have my own Spitfire Squadron.

This called for a celebration. On 5 June I requisitioned part of the anteroom in the Mess for a party, having first set up two kilderkins of Stroud Best Bitter two mornings before to allow time for the beer to settle. I mixed up a concoction for the girls, called 'Knicker-Dropper

Glory', and with unlimited glasses I invited the staff and students of 'D' Squadron, plus anyone who wanted to join in.

The first three hours saw just the beginning of the party which I am ashamed to say disrupted the training programme for the next twenty-four hours, by which time I was happy to say I had escaped and set my course for fields anew.

On 6 June 'Willy' Wheeler, my deputy 'D' Squadron Commander, flew me plus kit in an Old Fairey Battle to Salmesbury, the airfield adjacent to 9 Group HQ at Preston. The Battle had a long slender fuselage. Seating was in tandem, and the length of the cockpit area was covered by a transparent canopy, something akin to an elongated cloche, which trapped together the smells of hot oil, exhaust gases and alcoholic fumes. It was an unforgettable experience.

I was instructed to report to Air Commodore William Dickson, SASO, HQ 9 Group, later to become Air Chief Marshal Sir William Dickson, Chief of the Air Staff. He briefed me on the latest thinking in relation to a tactical, as opposed to a home-based Fighter Squadron. This involved an entirely new strategy, with the emphasis on the Squadron being capable of operating from emergency or captured airstrips in any area at short notice, initially without external support or backup. I was to be assigned an Adjutant, an Engineering Officer, an Intelligence Officer, an Equipment Officer, a Signals Officer, about twenty-five pilots and 'Uncle Tom Cobley and all'.

Inwardly I confess I had reservations about the administrative headaches I would be expected to cope with, in addition to my number one priority which was to clobber the enemy. Nevertheless it was an exciting challenge.

The same evening I met an old friend, Colin Gray, a New Zealander with an already legendary reputation as a fighter pilot. He was at the bar partaking of some liquid refreshment. He also was reporting to Group HQ prior to taking over a Spitfire Squadron. In a somewhat alcoholic haze we talked about this new concept of a tactically mobile Air Force, which we concluded was probably a 'good thing'. Colin was free the next day, so he volunteered to fly me to Andreas in an Oxford from the Group Communications Flight. We arrived just in time for an excellent lunch, after which I watched him heading off in the Oxford, a little unsteadily, in the general direction of the mainland. We were to meet again later on numerous occasions, including an airstrip in North Africa.

RAF Andreas was commanded by Wing Commander Teddy Knowles, DFC, an ex-bomber pilot of some distinction. During the

SPITFIRE CONVERSION

Sitzkrieg', (1939/40) his was the thankless task of dropping leaflets over Germany, flying Whitleys. Don't ask me why, but he had a very special affection for the Whitly, one of the slower and more ungainly bombers of World War II. Teddy was a likeable sort of chap, easy to get on with and fond of his grog which, I am unhappy to say, spelt disaster for him.

After breakfast the next day I started my rounds. I was allotted a new Hillman Staff Car which I drove round the site, until I located 93 Squadron HQ where I found Flight Lieutenant Barrett, my Squadron Adjutant. He owned a shoe factory in Northampton, advertising his wares in the National Press with the slogan: 'Walk the Barrett Way'.

As the week wore on pilots, ground crew, vehicles and equipment started to roll in. By the following Tuesday I had collected about ten pilots, my Engineering, Signals and Equipment Officers, plus some fifty ground crew, plus a few of the ever indispensable Flight Sergeants and Warrant Officers. Spitfire VB's, some brand new, some reconditioned, were arriving, ferried from mainland Maintenance Units by the Air Transport Auxiliary, the work-horse of the RAF. Both Him Mollison and Amy Johnson delivered a Spitfire each, staying the night and taking a swim the next day, before returning to White Waltham in the ATA Anson. The weather was warm and clear, making the island a tempting haven for those with a few hours to spare from the peremptory claims of wartime Britain.

The Squadron was at full strength by the end of June, and I started an intensive programme of shakedown flying. Within a week we were fully operational. Much to our chagrin and disgust, enemy air activity in the sector was minimal; it seemed the Luftwaffe did not regard the Isle of Man as offering worthwhile targets. I'm sure they were right. However, in a way this was to our advantage because we were able to carry on our training with little or no interference.

We arranged practise interceptions with Wellingtons operating from RAF Jurby, almost next door to us, which was a bomber training Station. It was here I first met Jumbo Edwards, the Wing Commander 'Flying' at Jurby. He was an Oxford rowing Blue and Olympic oarsman, and was one of the original members of the Oxford University Air Squadron when it was formed in 1925. His brother, nicknamed 'the Sphinx', also in the RAF, was unfortunately killed in a flying accident before the war. Jumbo led his contingent of Wellingtons from Jurby to help make up the numbers for the first 1000 bomber raid on Germany, 'Target Cologne', on the night of 30 May 1942.

93 Squadron's short spell of three months on the Isle of Man was

SPIT AND SAWDUST

punctuated by two totally unrelated but, to me, significant occurrences. The first happened towards the end of July. One fine midsummer's day a Whitley landed at Andreas to refuel. Nothing unusual about that, perhaps, RAF bombers were often landing unannounced at airfields all over the UK for one reason or another. It happened that this was no ordinary Whitley. The pilot parked his aircraft on the tarmac, and went off to the Mess for a spot of lunch. Teddy Knowles was in the bar with some of his mates, enjoying the usual lunchtime session, when the Air Traffic Controller Officer whispered to him that there was a visiting Whitley on the airfield. Teddy downed his drink, phoned his wife to come to the Mess immediately, at the same time calling for volunteers, including myself, to join him for a joy ride. I had arranged a game of squash with Alan Smith, one of my Flight Commanders, so I declined.

Alan and I had hardly finished a set when we heard the unmistakable sound of a Whitley revving up for take-off. For some reason we froze for a moment then dashed to watch the aircraft rolling down the runway, coming 'unstuck' about halfway along. It continued to rise unsteadily in a nose-up attitude with the undercarriage still down, thereby increasing the drag. Foolishly I yelled at Teddy to trim 'nose down' and give it the gun, but already it was too late. The Whitley lurched drunkenly onwards in an irretrievable stall, until it suddenly dipped and nose dived, like some enormous black predator, into a field beyond. There followed an horrific explosion punctuated by a blinding flash of yellow flame, sending up a fireball followed by an enormous column of thick black smoke.

We jumped into the Hillman and drove full tilt across the airfield, circumnavigating barbed-wire entanglements, rocks, and old dry-stone walls. We were the first on the scene. There was burning wreckage everywhere, about twelve blackened steaming bodies, some still strapped in their seats, the frames stripped of their covers and stuffing, looking like weird wrought iron spidery cages. Teddy's charred body, his wife Valerie next to him, was still bent over the control column assuming a grotesque posture, as if caught in some macabre struggle to escape his bondage, the pathetic remains of Lady, their Labrador bitch, lying incinerated between them.

There were about ten Station Administrative Staff Officers in that Whitley; all were cremated at a stroke. Six airmen had also been persuaded to take a ride; they were in the tail section, which amazingly snapped off on impact throwing them clear with little more than odd broken limbs and bruises. As I said, this was no ordinary Whitley. It was modified as a troop transport and tug for gliders; consequently its

SPITFIRE CONVERSION

handling characteristics and trim settings were entirely different from the standard bomber. Teddy was unaware of this, and when the penny dropped it was too late. This incident illustrates the unnatural strains and pressures exerted on individuals such as Teddy Knowles, a dedicated but spent bomber pilot, banished to the tedium of administering a small station out in the sticks, impatiently waiting for a chance to get back on to ops, a chance which he knew would never come.

This incident was a milestone for me, because in a matter of seconds I was thrust into a situation where I was Acting Station Commander with the grim task of the recovery, disposal and burial of so many fellow Officers, not to mention informing next of kin and initiating a Court of Enquiry. Twenty-four hours later Air Commodore Dickson himself flew into Andreas in his all-black Hurricane, his personal aircraft, sporting a smart non-regulation white flying suit. Surveying the scene he approved the action I had taken, and flew back to Salmesbury to lay on a Group Administrative Officer to relieve me of the chores.

On Monday, 1 August 1942, I was forewarned of an impending move to an unknown destination overseas, and I was directed to fly the Squadron to RAF Valley in Anglesey for a week's Armament Practise Camp. The weather was perfect, the blue sky was reflected in the grey slate crags of the rocky coastline, the motion of snow white surf taking on a velvet hue like an artist mixing his paints.

The first day (Tuesday) we completed a full day's firing on the range. I laid on a similar programme for the Wednesday, when a sea mist rolled in over the sand dunes in the afternoon, followed by a clammy grey fog encompassing the airfield. The air was heavy with moisture, so humid one almost felt one was breathing water. We couldn't see from one Spitfire to the next in the dispersal area. The Metrological Forecast was thick fog until the weekend, so there was nothing for it but to hang around waiting for it to lift.

There was a full-sized billiard table in the Officers' Mess so we started a snooker school. We played all day Thursday and Friday. At about midday the Steward interrupted me in the middle of a break to say there was a call for me from Headquarter Fighter Command, Stanmore. This was nothing unusual, Command was continually calling up to ask when we could fly back to Andreas. As I grabbed the receiver, I immediately recognised a familiar voice from the past.

"Hello Hal, is that you?"

"Hello Dick" I countered "How on earth did you track me down here of all places?"

SPIT AND SAWDUST

"Hal, can you come down to Stanmore? I can't explain on the phone. Perhaps you could pop down here during your embarkation leave. I've something to discuss with you."

"So you've heard we are due for overseas then?"

"Of course, I've been in on the planning. It won't take up much of your time when you're in town saying your goodbyes."

"OK Dick, but why this 'volte face'?" I asked.

"Look Hal, I'll explain it all when I see you. Please accept that I must talk to you before you vanish abroad."

"Very well," I replied "I'll call you as soon as I get my leave sorted out."

"OK Hal, see you soon. So long." He rang off.

My thoughts were working overtime. What in heaven's name did Dick Hillary want to discuss with me? Our relationship had long since gone downhill. Even before we came up to Oxford it was on the decline. Dick had made it perfectly clear that he didn't want to know me, so what for Christ's sake did he want from me now? He had written a brilliant book, had got himself a new set of affluent friends, I wasn't in the same league any more. It had to be something very important indeed to prompt him to ask me for a hearing.

CHAPTER ELEVEN

SPEARHEAD TO NORTH AFRICA

On 9 August the fog lifted and I flew the Squadron back to the Isle of Man. By the end of the month we were packing up. In early September we flew to Kingscliffe, a satellite airfield to RAF Wittering, near Stamford, where we became part of 324 Wing in the new Tactical Air Force, preparing to depart overseas for some unknown destination. We were all allowed ten day's Embarkation Leave from 8 October.

I caught a train to Town and made for The Boltons to spend my last few days with Pan. I was still puzzling over Dick Hillary's strange request, so one morning I took the Underground to Stanmore, arriving at Headquarter Fighter Command around eleven o'clock. I soon found Dick's office, which he was sharing with another Staff Officer, only to be told that he was away on the south coast near Brighton, busy making an Air Sea Rescue Film. It was a wasted journey, there was no possible chance of a second trip to Stanmore. I had no idea when, if ever, I would see Dick again.

My embarkation leave ended almost before it started. We had a family farewell party in Brown's Hotel in Dover Street on the Tuesday. I got very sloshed and remembered little more until I came to on Stamford Station at dawn on Wednesday morning, 19 October, where my faithful Adjutant 'Walk the Barrett Way' met me and ran me back to Kingscliffe. After breakfast I assembled the whole Squadron in the Briefing Room at RAF Wittering, where I bade farewell to all my ground staff until we should meet again in some unknown place at some unknown future date. Group Captain Basil Embrey, the Station Commander, asked all the 93 Squadron pilots back to lunch in the Officers' Mess. We all got paralytic.

On the Thursday (20 October) we boarded a coach for RAF Wilmslow in Cheshire, arriving there in a somewhat disorderly fashion to receive our overseas 'jabs', which included one for Yellow Fever, giving rise to much anxious speculation. Wilmslow was a 'Personnel Despatch Centre', or better known as 'Personnel Despair Centre'. 'Despatch' is defined in the dictionary as 'to send away hastily, to put to death, to dispose of, or to send out of the world.' You can say that again!

After an incredibly uncomfortable night in something little better than an Anderson Air Raid Shelter, the coach transported us to somewhere on Merseyside where, together with 72 Squadron, we embarked on the 12,000 ton 'SS Fort Maclaughlin', one of the new Liberty Ships. We were

SPIT AND SAWDUST

informed that a 'Liberty Ship' took little more than six months to complete from keel to cabin. It was a marvel of marine engineering, so we could only hope that it would continue to hold together if struck by a torpedo.

We each carried a canvas parachute bag with just a few personal items, such as spare underpants, shirts, socks, shaving gear and perhaps a few books, and a pack of cards. The Squadron bulk kit was to be loaded later onto the 'SS Berthier' which, though we did not know it at the time, was scheduled to dock in Algiers by about Christmas time.

The holds of the 'Fort Maclaughlin' were taken up with crated cargo except for the centre hold, which had been modified with fitted bunks in tiers round the sides, below which was a central feature, so to speak, in the shape of a very large wooden table. To reach it we had to climb down clinging to the sides of the bunks like monkeys in a cage. Once down there the table was for eating, drinking and gambling. Spitfires crated up in separate sections were lashed to the decks. Our final destination was a secret, we had no idea where we were going and speculation ran high, from invasion of the South of France to an assault on the Caucasus. Visions of nights on the Cote d'Azur with beautiful women teased our imagination.

After setting sail we joined up with a large convoy from the Clyde, and headed south through St George's Channel, then westwards into the Atlantic, where westerly gales beat up against us as if with protesting, warning arms.

Every day I went up on the bridge to talk with the Master and Officers of the Watch, to try to ascertain our destination by interpreting the constant alterations of course. It seemed we could have been going anywhere, north to Iceland, eastwards to Norway, or south to the Cape. The answer was always the same; 'To foil the U-Boat Wolf Packs'. After about six days at sea, an enormous convoy loomed up on the horizon from the west, with which we duly joined company. Though we didn't know it at the time, it was the American part of the 'Operation Torch' invasion fleet.

This vast group of ships now wheeled round on to a south westerly run and, by Saturday, 5 November, we sighted Spain and the Straits of Gibraltar. Upon arrival at Gibraltar we were told we would be going ashore. Before disembarking we foregathered to drink a toast to the 'Fort', as we called it, and all those who sailed in her. In an alcoholic haze we were transferred to a troopship anchored just off the Harbour. It was crowded with Army, RAF and American Officers, and here we spent the night drinking and meeting up with old friends. The atmosphere was tense with excitement; we all knew now that something big was about to break.

The next day we were transported to a Transit Camp up near the Rock. The food was terrible, by night our beds were infested with a myriad of red bugs which, come daylight, were spirited away as it by some magic spell, but the next night they were back again in full force. Strict security was maintained, we could not leave the confines of the Camp. Our only recreation was an inferior replica of an English Pub called the 'Victory Inn', where we passed the time drinking and conjecturing on our future prospects. We were together in one conglomerate; we were about to witness the birth pangs of a new Tactical Air Force designed to operate in alien, perhaps hostile, territory from strange unfamiliar landing grounds without the comfortable intimate surroundings of our permanent bases at home.

Early on Thursday 10 November, we were all assembled in the Briefing Room. The secret was out, the news we were waiting for broke, the Allies were landing all along the French North African coast from Casablanca to Algiers. 324 Wing's task was to fly its Spitfires off from the Gibraltar strip across the Mediterranean to Maison Blanche, a French Air Force base just north of Algiers. By the time we were due to land it was estimated that all effective resistance would be overcome. This involved a nonstop flight of five hundred nautical miles, which was beyond the Spitfire's normal fuel capacity. The powers that be calculated that an eighty-gallon droppable belly-tank could just about give us the additional range, but with little or no margin for error.

Security restrictions were now lifted so we were allowed into the town and onto the airstrip. With Alan Smith and John Henry, my two Flight Commanders, I went to see the Spitfires being assembled. The scene almost surpassed belief. Apart from the strip itself, which at all costs had to be kept clear, the whole area on every side was littered with Spitfires in various stages of assembly. Indian mechanics were feverishly screwing on belly-tanks, referring now and again to 'blue prints' which were thumb-tacked to the sides of the occasional empty crate, under the supervision of a few RAF Technicians. We were not allowed the chance of an air test to check the fuel flow. The procedure was for each pilot to take off on main tanks, then offer up a prayer as he transferred to the belly-tank until it was empty, which only became apparent when the main fuel gauges in the cockpit started to drop. Then the tank had to be jettisoned immediately in order to reduce the drag.

SPIT AND SAWDUST

The whole spectacle presented the Luftwaffe with a heaven-sent target. Remarkable though it may seem, no such attack materialised.

At first light on Saturday, 12 November, I led 93 Squadron off from the strip with eighteen Spitfires, and headed west biting my nails. Apart from the extra drag induced by the belly-tank, our Spitfires had also been fitted with a clumsy modification under the nose called a Vokes filter, presumably to prevent the engine from stopping in sand storms. It was quite superfluous, it merely knocked off six knots or so from our air speed, which we found out to our cost later. 152 Squadron, led by Jackie Sing, an old friend, took off immediately after us. Within half an hour one of his pilots called up to say he had lost his belly-tank, followed shortly by another shouting that his engine had cut. This was a tragic start to 152 Squadron's debut; two pilots lost before landfall, and there were no special facilities for Air Sea Rescue.

After about an hour, we ran into scattered but heavy cumulus cloud, and I was forced down to two thousand feet when, as we broke cloud, I saw to my surprise we were flying immediately above a large fleet of warships. We were greeted by a hail of tracer and ack-ack. We flew straight on through and by a miracle not one of my Spitfires was hit. It must have been part of the Italian Fleet! It might have been a different story if it had been the RN. From then on the weather cleared, and I saw Algiers Harbour crammed with shipping, smoke rising from numerous bombed-out ships. All eighteen of us landed safely with almost empty tanks.

It would be a flagrant understatement to say that the situation at Maison Blanche was chaotic. The airfield was packed with aircraft of all sorts, from those damaged or burnt out from air attack, to those now preoccupied with the follow-up to the invasion, Spitfires and Hurricanes landing and taking off, Dakotas flying in supplies, others waiting to take off for new dropping zones.

We were directed to a corner of the airfield, where a Servicing Commando Unit refuelled us and carried out inspections. I found the Station Commander, Group Captain Edwardes Jones, universally known as EJ (the late Air Marshal Sir Humphrey Edwardes Jones, KCB, CBE, DFC, AFC, BA), together with Group Captain Ronnie Lees, OC 324 Wing, and our Wing Leader, Wing Commander D A P McMullen, who flew with 222 and 54 Squadrons during the Battle of Britain. They beckoned me over to a small cafe near the perimeter. We were all starving, so after a brief discussion I brought the boys to join us, to eat slices of French bread, cheese, and delicious tomatoes washed down with

SPEARHEAD TO NORTH AFRICA

Algerian wine.

EJ stood us down for the rest of the day to give us time to get our bearings and find somewhere to sleep. We stayed by our Spitfires and made rough shelters out of empty petrol tins and pieces of canvas from an old French Army tent. Throughout the following day we were on convoy patrols to protect shipping entering the Harbour. From then on, until 21 November, we were continuously on patrols, providing cover over the airfield and shipping, and also escorting some Dakotas dropping paratroops near Djidjelli. We saw no EA.

On 21 November, the Squadron was ordered to Bone, a port about four hundred and fifty kilometres along the coast, near the Tunisian border. We landed on the airstrip nearby, which had already been taking a pasting from the Luftwaffe. I reported to Ronnie Lees, who briefed me to carry out an armed reconnaissance from Nefza to Medjez-el-Bab, and then to land back at an airstrip, if it could be called that, on the outskirts of a village called Souk-el-Arba, which was about a hundred and twenty kilometres west of Tunis. The strip had been captured the previous night by British Paratroops. It was very easy to spot, because almost the entire field was littered with abandoned Army parachutes, which from above looked like a patchwork quilt of brown and yellow tortoise shells. On landing we weaved our way through them, trying to prevent undercarriages and tail wheels being snagged with parachute silk and shroud lines. One complete parachute wrapped itself round my tail plane. We all made scarves out of the silk panels. I never flew again without my parachute scarf, which I have to this day. It transpired that Souk-el-Arba was a French army outpost, and the strip was an emergency landing ground for L'Armee de L'Air. The parachutists met with some resistance, but fighting had ceased by the time we arrived, and French soldiers were laying down their arms.

Ronnie had briefed me to look out for an Army Liaison Officer, who was supposed to hang out in the village school/infirmary, who would let me know the latest score. I also found Alan Bromley, my Intelligence Officer, who had taken three days to get there from Algiers. He had rustled up some RAF Servicing Commandos who were to look after our Spitfires. Whilst chatting with the ALO, he told me that a Captain Bill Anderson had led the parachute drop. He was none other than Pan's cousin, whom I last saw when I flew him from Aston Down to Netheravon in a Master the previous April.

There was nowhere to kip down, so Alan had liberated about four old French Army bell tents, plus a couple of dozen palliasses. We pitched the

SPIT AND SAWDUST

tents round the perimeter alongside our Spitfires, near to a large dump of one hundred octane petrol tins. After a feed of 'Compo' rations provided by the army, we settled down for the night. I could boast without fear of contradiction that 93 was the first Spitfire Squadron to operate from Tunisian soil.

My first task was to maintain a standing airfield patrol of four Spitfires from first light. The Germans had reacted swiftly to the Allied Landings, and already by 9 November troops were landing at El Aouana Airport, Tunis, followed by the deployment of at least three Luftwaffe Jagdverbaende, comprising nine Staffel (Squadrons) of Me109 G's and Focke Wolfe 190's.

Hardly had the first patrol taken off, when two Me109's streaked across the field strafing, and dropping bombs, taking us completely by surprise. Fortunately we suffered no damage, but we quickly moved our tents, putting hundreds of yards between us and the petrol dump. We now started to dig in and pitched two of our tents over some bomb craters in the simple belief that lightning never strikes in the same place twice. We suffered two more attacks before dusk that day, one by six FW 190's, the other by three JU87 dive-bombers escorted by Me109's. I had increased our standing patrol to six Spitfires and, as luck would have it, we damaged one Me109, two FW 190's and claimed two JU87's 'probably destroyed', one of which I got myself. As far as I can remember, that was the last time the Luftwaffe used JU87's on airfield strikes in Tunisia, but they continued to be used for dive-bombing British and American Army targets.

It's easy enough to make excuses, but the fact is that the Luftwaffe was operating from established airstrips, with concrete runways, located in the vicinity of Tunis, and they had radar and homing facilities, whilst we had neither early warning or navigational aids. Interception of enemy aircraft depended entirely on visual contact.

The next day, 23 November, Jackie Sing arrived with 152 Squadron in the middle of a raid. Two of my Spitfires were damaged on the ground, and one of my pilots was killed. Two Spitfires of 152 were shot down in the circuit, killing both pilots. For 152 it was an inauspicious start to an already sad beginning, after having lost two pilots in the wastes of the Mediterranean.

Throughout the next two or three days we continued to receive the attention of the Luftwaffe, then the raids eased off when the rains started on 6 December. All told we had lost six Spitfires destroyed on the ground, the petrol dump had been hit, and several houses in the village including the school, were damaged. One of my pilots, Sergeant Mincher, was missing. About four of my airmen had been injured in ground attacks.

Ronnie Lees now arrived, and set up an 'ad hoc' Control Centre near the infirmary, where we used to have nightly Wing briefings. Mac McMullen, our Wing Leader, had succumbed, and returned sick to Algiers. We were still without any form of radar, so we continued to rely for airfield defence on standing patrols. Calls for close Army support reached us via the ALO, who maintained a tenuous telephone link with the front line. This meant that more often than not we reached the scene after the bird had flown. Bitter complaints about lack of air support for the troops were frequently hurled at us, but regretfully there was very little we could do about it.

72 Squadron, commanded by Squadron Leader Bobby Oxspring, DFC, arrived on 24 November which helped to step up our efforts to give air support to the Army, enabling us to mount some armed reconnaissances over the battle zone, where a bitter struggle with the Germans was developing some twenty to thirty miles to the east in the Beja/Mateur/Majez-el-Bab area. During the thirty-eight days between 23 November and 31 December I led 93 Squadron on forty-one operational sorties in support of the Army, involving the ground strafing of German road convoys and troop concentrations, escorting Hurribombers, and frequent air combats over the battle front.

By the end of the year 93 Squadron's score was sixteen EA destroyed, twenty-nine damaged, for a loss of three pilots missing and three wounded. We also shared a JU88 'destroyed' with 72 Squadron on 29 November, who on the same sortie claimed a further two JU88's 'destroyed' which they caught dive-bombing British Army positions near Mateur. On 5 December, 111 Squadron, commanded by Squadron Leader Tony Bartley, DFC, arrived from Bone, so now 324 Wing was in effect complete, including 225 Squadron (Hurribombers) commanded by Wing Commander John Barker, an old BNC man.

Both Bobby Oxspring, in his book 'Spitfire Command', and Tony Bartley in his book 'Smoke Trails in the Sky', failed for some reason to acknowledge that 93 was the first Spitfire Squadron to fly on fighter operations in Tunisia following 'Operation Torch', being the first Squadron to be based at Suk-el-Arba, and the only Squadron to give close support to the Army from an impromptu airstrip near the front line at Medjez-el-Bab. I make this point merely to put the record straight for the sake of 93 Squadron's history. Bobby and Tony were good friends of

SPIT AND SAWDUST

mine, as well as being first-class Fighter Pilots, with a record of achievements which left me standing.

After McMullen's debacle we were without a Wing Leader, so it was up to the four Squadron Commanders, Bobby Oxspring, Tony Bartley, Jackie Sing and myself, to liaise together to keep the momentum going, not forgetting Ronnie Lees, himself a brilliant fighter pilot, who had to carry the added burden of Wing Administration as well as overall Operational Control.

On 4 December I had just returned from shooting down a JU88 (confirmed by the Army) when Ronnie Lees told me he had chosen 93 to operate a Detached Flight from an improvised strip at Medjez-el-Bab. It was four thousand metres or so from German Army positions, well within their artillery range, and only about fifty kilometres from the outskirts of Tunis. I need hardly say I protested strongly, bearing in mind that, apart from the close proximity of the enemy ground forces, the Luftwaffe had established undoubted air superiority. Our Spitfires Vc's with the tropical filter were scarcely a match for the Me109's and FW190's at altitude, although it is fair to say that we could hold our own below twenty thousand feet, and the Spitfire was an excellent ground-strafing platform. We were due to re-equip with the Spitfire IX, which had a much improved performance, but would not be with us until the Spring of 1943

Anyway, it seems the Army insisted we should at least give it a try although Ronnie agreed with me, that it would be little more than a token, if not suicidal, gesture. That night I briefed Alan Smith and five of his A Flight boys to brace themselves for a pre-dawn take off, destination Medjez, myself in the lead. A small detachment of Servicing Commando had already left by road with ammunition, tool kits and several extra vehicles to pick-up adequate supplies of 100 octane, lubricants, etc. Medjez was only twenty minutes flying time away. The seven of us just managed to scrape in 'over the hedge' as the sun came up, braking like crazy to avoid running into a heap of rocks at the end.

We taxied over to a fairly dense olive grove, where the ground crew had cleared a rough dispersal area which afforded us some cover. We were greeted by a cheerful Coldstream Guards Officer who explained that he was the link between us and a Forward Observation Officer, who was to select our ground targets! Our arrival didn't go unnoticed, because within the hour we came under shell fire. Luckily for us the Pioneer Corps had dug slit trenches. We stayed there all day pinned down by constant shelling. To add insult to injury, FW190's made frequent passes at the field, strafing and dropping bombs, mostly wide of the mark, thank

No.93 (Spitfire) Squadron
Prior to departure for North Africa on Operation 'Torch', 1942

A handful of Belgian and Free French pilots converted onto Spitfires, period March-May, 1941. 'D' Squadron.
L-R: Plt Of Prince de Merode (Belgium), Plt Off Creteur (Fr), Self, Plt Off Collingnon (Fr), Plt Off Dopéré (Fr), Plt Off Lawton (Br), Plt Off Wilkin (Belgium)

F86 'Sabre' Conversion Course at RAF Wildenrath, 1956.
L-R: U.K., Flt Lt Rideout, Flt Lt Shelton, U.K., Sqdn Ldr Roy Chatfield 234 Sqdn, U.K., Sqdn Ldr Ian MacDonald 20 Sqdn, Flt Lt 'Danny' Daniels, U.K., GHNE, Flt Lt Alan Woodcock, Flt Lt Galletley
(Photo: Crown Copyright NIL RAF 634/G)

French General (Giraud), GHNE, Sir Humphrey Edmondes-Jones, Sqdn Ldr Ken Smith, CO 26 Sqdn on Tactical Air Exercises under canvas at RAF Butzweiterhof, BAOR, 1953

SPEARHEAD TO NORTH AFRICA

God.

This was hardly the lot of a Fighter Pilot, I mused, far better to leave this sort of thing to the Army who were geared up to it. Towards dusk I managed to contact Ronnie via a land line connected to Souk-el-Arba by the Signals Corps. Without hesitation he agreed that we should take off just before first light, strafe any German troop concentrations we could find, and head back for Souk. In the event we didn't get away until well after sun-up, because two Spitfires had been damaged by shrapnel and the runway, if you could call it that, was pockmarked by the shelling, so the Pioneer Corps were busy filing in the holes.

Having finally got off the ground, undercarriages barely retracted, we were suddenly bounced by Me109's. Pulling hard round I nearly stalled as I caught a glimpse of my No 2, Brose Haley, plunging earthwards below me. Then I saw another Spitfire belching smoke. That left five of us. Being able to out-turn the Me109 at low level, we fought them off, Alan Smith getting one and I claimed a 'damaged'. Within seconds the Me109's vanished. That strange phenomenon when one moment the sky is black with twisting gyrating aircraft, and the next moment totally void, manifested itself. We reformed and made straight for base.

Ronnie bluntly refused to authorise any more close Air Support operations from Medjez, much to the relief of the whole Wing. We later heard that Brose Haley had belly-landed behind the German lines and was taken Prisoner of War. The other casualty was Flying Officer Hector Keil, a Rhodesian, reported missing. He was never seen again.

Between shelling I had one surprise visitor in the olive grove, Pan's cousin Bill Anderson, the 'captor' of Souk-el-Arba airstrip. Crouching together in a slit trench we compared notes. After Souk his next assignment had been a drop at Jebel-el-Ahmera, a mountainous ridge running north from Medjez, nicknamed 'Longstop Hill'. From here the Allies could dominate the main German supply route along the flat plain from Tunis to Massicault. His story was one of 'move and counter-move'. After the Paratroopers took it, the Guards relieved them, and held on until they were ordered to hand it over to the Americans. The latter in turn were overrun by the Germans, so the Guards were called in again to retake it, but being already fully committed at Medjez they hastily handed it back to the Paratroopers. Bill with his detachment of Paratroopers spent all the next night holding on. He related the story of how, in the early hours before dawn, in pitch blackness, they heard the unmistakable sounds of movement close to their position.

It looked as if they in turn were to be overrun by the Germans, so

SPIT AND SAWDUST

the Colonel ordered 'Open Fire', and they let fly with everything they had. Come the dawn they looked down the slope to see the landscape littered with dead goats!

On 6 December the rains descended upon us. Until now the surface of the airfield had been so hard you could scarcely drive a wooden peg in between the cracks. By dawn on the 7 it was a quagmire - a sea of mud - Spitfires bogged down, tents awash.

George Tye, my Engineer Officer, arrived back from the Tibar Monastery, in the Atlas Mountains, with a load of wine and brandy he had collected in empty petrol tins which the monks filled up in lieu of bottles, which were unobtainable. These tins were the pre-Jerrycan type, each one retaining about a quarter of a pint of 100 octane in the bottom which was impossible to draw off. After swapping quantities of second-hand dried tea leaves for fresh eggs with the Arabs, a massive omelette party ensued, accounting for at least six dozen eggs. It continued till dawn, rain pouring down in torrents.

We drank the Monastery wine mixed with 100 octane so we all got paralytic. Duggie Hine, a staunch and trusty Squadron member, vanished outside to take a pee, but by now we were becoming anaesthetised, so his absence went unnoticed until I also staggered out of the tent for the same purpose. Pausing unsteadily for a moment or so, deep in mud, I heard a ghastly gurgling, choking noise. Looking down I saw a body lying sprawled in the wet soft earth, its head immersed face downwards in a deep puddle. It was Duggie about to drown in the North African gunge. I yelled for assistance and several chaps stumbled out of the tent. Together we dragged Duggie inside. One of the boys knew something about life saving and applied artificial respiration. After quantities of bilge and vomit were evacuated from his lungs, he slowly came to. Much to his disgust I kept him off flying for a week.

After a day or so the rains eased off and we recommenced operations. The heavy sticky mud make it very difficult to handle the Spitfires on the ground without nosing over, so we made it a rule that between taxying out and lining up for take off, an airman should bestride the tail plane to weigh it down. This was working well until one morning a 111 Squadron Pilot, Tommy Tinsey, forgot to signal the wretched airman to jump clear as he took off. The Spitfire lurched drunkenly round the circuit almost on the stall, the airman hanging on for grim death. It was an astonishing sight to see a Spitfire flying round with a body and legs dangling from the tail. Tommy managed to land safely back into the mud, the airman falling off with little more than a few bruises and severe shock. He earned his ticket back to Blighty.

The Pioneer Corps had been lying down a wire mesh runway which, with the rain, rapidly vanished beneath the mud. When at last things started to dry out, the wire mesh sections became warped and twisted, thus creating yet another hazard when taking off and landing. One of my boys, Hoppy Hopkinson, was coming in to land when a main wheel was caught up in the mesh, and the Spit literally spun round 360 degrees, ending up on its nose, dragging up half the runway in the process. Hoppy was OK and damage to the aircraft was slight. It was flying again as soon as George Tye came back from Setif with a replacement prop.

Similar wire mesh runways were now being laid down at two new airstrips at Suk-el-Khemis, where we were to move shortly. We called them Waterloo and Paddington.

Ronnie Lees now decided that he, Bobby Oxspring and myself needed a break. He got a lift in a Dakota on Wednesday, 14 December, and on Thursday Bobby and I took off in two Spitfires, which were to be delivered to the MU (Maintenance Unit) at Setif for major inspections. Feeling almost released from bondage, we formated together in an exuberant mood, smoking cigarettes all the way, tossing flying discipline and butt ends out of the open cockpits. We met Ronnie at the Aletti Bar, Algiers, for lunchtime drinks, and proceeded to get plastered. We stayed that way right through till Saturday, when we sobered up enough to board a plane back to Souk.

We arrived to be greeted with the news that the 'SS Berthier', with all the Wing's personal kit aboard, had been sunk by a mine off the North African coast, so bang went a change of clothing. By now we were shaking hands with our socks and underpants.

Also at Souk to greet us were two War Correspondents, Randolph Churchill and Jack Profumo, who were paying a visit to 324 Wing. I knew Jack briefly when, as a post-graduate in BNC, he occasionally dined in College. I need hardly mention that, as everyone knows, he was obliged to bow out of the political scene, so abandoning a highly promising Parliamentary career. Today many could say "There but for the Grace of God go I."!

They both spent some time with the Squadron, making a point of talking to the ground crew who didn't often receive the praise and recognition they deserved. We entertained them both with Tibar Monastery wine and brandy. About a month later Jack revisited the Squadron to inform me of Dick Hillary's death.

On 7 January 1943, it seems he flew into the ground at night in a

SPIT AND SAWDUST

Blenheim Mk 1. He was taking a conversion course onto Night Fighters at RAF Charter Hall.

So after all, following my abortive visit to his Office at Stanmore the previous October, the chances of discovering what Dick wanted to talk to me about were lost for ever. I have never ceased wondering what it was that Dick was so concerned about, sometimes I even tried the Ouija Board which sounds a bit stupid, I suppose, but Stuffy Dowding used to consult it now and again, so perhaps it wasn't that stupid. So far the answer I look for has eluded me, and no doubt it always will. There was just one occasion towards the end of the war when I thought I might have found the answer.

After our short break in Algiers my first commitment was to lead the boys on a strafing mission to destroy a German Army Headquarters at Massicault, a few miles west of Tunis. We took them by surprise before the flak started. When it did, three of my boys were hit, but all returned safely. A Hurricane pilot was briefed to reconnoitre the area to assess the damage, and reported that the place was a shambles, later confirmed by the Army. The Germans had evacuated, and the British Corps Commander conveyed his personal thanks to the pilots.

The RAF was still taking some hard knocks for the lack of Army close support, so this small word of appreciation came as a welcome change.

Following the demise of Mac Mc Mullen with 'Tunisian asthma', we now at last had a Wing Leader, none other than Wing Commander 'Sheep' Gilroy, a Scottish mountain farmer and a prewar weekend flyer with No 603 (City of Edinburgh) Squadron, R Aux. AF, with whom he flew during the Battle of Britain. He took some of the load off Ronnie Lees' shoulders and introduced a spot of badly needed cohesion into the Wing.

On 21 December, 93 Squadron moved up the road to Suk-el-Khemis where the two new strips 'Paddington' and 'Waterloo' were almost completed. We set ourselves up at Paddington, and looked round for a suitable domestic site, as far away as possible from bombing and strafing.

I was introduced to a French family farming the area, headed by a Monsieur Dureaux, who had an attractive daughter aged about nineteen called Martine. He invited me and my two Flight Commanders to dinner one evening and granted us the use of a wooded site well away from the airstrip. Here we established the Squadron's quarters, enabling us for the first time to enjoy some semblance of comfort. Inevitably, of course, he came to be known as Monsieur Durex.

SPEARHEAD TO NORTH AFRICA

'Sheep' led us on our first sweep from Paddington on 23 December, the target being Medjez-el-Bab. The weather started to close in, heavy rain and thunderstorms were approaching and 'Sheep', who was still unfamiliar with the area, lost himself. I took over the lead and eventually we all landed back unscathed.

There now followed about a week's rain, and once again we were grounded in a sea of mud, except for maintaining the essential airfield patrols against air attack. The Luftwaffe took advantage of the situation. A JU88 suddenly dived out of a cloud, bombing and strafing the Squadron dispersal areas. The next day about nine or ten FW190's suddenly appeared overhead, dropping bombs and shooting up the strip. They shot down two Spitfires from 152 Squadron on airfield patrol. Ronnie ordered us back to Souk, where the mud wasn't quite so bad, but operations continued to be very restricted until the ground started to dry up.

Once more we 'upped sticks' and moved back to Khemis, this time to 'Waterloo' where we were joined by John Barker and 225 (Hurribomber) Squadron. On 31 December, just after we left, Souk-el-Arba was bombed by six FW190's. A Beaufighter from 600 Squadron was destroyed and two airmen killed. We got away just in time!

In January, two new pilots arrived delivering replacement Spitfires. They were both attached to 93, namely Flight Lieutenant Wilf Sizer DFC, who I had known back in the Aston Down days, and Flight Lieutenant Mortimer-Rose DFC. Ronnie broke the news to me that before long I was to be sent back to the UK 'tour expired', and Wilf was earmarked as my successor. Mortey was also due to take over one of the other Squadrons, but I never knew which because on 28 January, 'Sheep' Gilroy, whilst leading the Wing back from a ground strafing mission in the Tebourba area, collided in mid air with Mortey Rose.

It happened when 'Sheep' was joining the circuit to land at Paddington. I was just behind leading 93 in to Waterloo, when I saw two Spitfires slicing into each other, then a body fell clear, and a parachute opened split seconds before the aircraft hit the ground. Mortey didn't jump, his Spitfire plummeted straight down like an arrow, he never had a chance. 'Sheep' was picked up and the Wing Doctor drove him to Monsieur Durex's house (where he was billeted) and put him to bed.

I managed to purloin a bottle of brandy and drove straight over to the house, to find 'Sheep' lying back in luxury between cool cotton sheets. He was shaken and bruised but otherwise unscathed. Whilst regretting the absence of good old Highland Malt, he was delighted to see the brandy. We polished off the bottle drinking a toast to poor Mortey. The Wing had

SPIT AND SAWDUST

lost a brave, able and experienced pilot, all the more tragic because it was so unnecessary.

Late in the afternoon of 1 February we escorted twelve Hurribombers of 225 Squadron on a strike against a German tank concentration near Pont du Fahs. The Hurricane boys did a fantastic job, coming down out of the sun, taking the Germans completely by surprise, dropping bombs, strafing and generally creating chaos. We followed down with our 20mm and .303, destroying a number of trucks and Volkswagen Jeeps. Bodies sprawled everywhere, and flames from the fuel dump leapt into the air, spewing up black smoke and clouds of debris. The flak was swamped as we continued to press on with the attack until we ran out of ammunition. I called up the boys to reform and return to base, as I made one final low level pass to inspect the damage.

I suddenly realised that my No 2, a new boy called Lloyd Hunt, was no longer with me. He must have 'bought it', or perhaps his radio had packed up, I thought, as I did a wide sweep which took me practically over the centre of Tunis. There was no sight or sound of him and I didn't like it. Turning westwards at about three thousand feet I suddenly spotted four sinister silhouettes orbiting at speed in line astern immediately above me. They were 109G's. I could tell they had seen me because they were lining up for the kill. The sun was now sinking over the mountain tops, blazing red, its rays casting deep shadows across the valleys below. What was I to do now? They had the advantage of me in both height and speed, and my ammunition was spent. To turn and fight without my guns would be senseless bravado, if not suicidal and, besides, I was now dangerously low on fuel. At full throttle, the 'tit' pulled, I nosed-dived towards the ground as two of them turned steeply round ahead of me all set to swoop down in a head-on attack. In a split second they shot past me a few feet above my canopy. Clearly they had misjudged my height - so far so good. By now I was right down on the deck heading West hugging grimly to the contours of the valleys, the blinding red sun just above the rugged horizon. In my mirror I spotted two Me109's side by side rapidly closing up behind and, as they came within firing range, I pulled the nose up to fly directly into the sun. The 109's shot past me firing their guns into space, tracer bullets flashing by my wing tips. They had completely missed me. The other two 109's had now wheeled round, and were coming up behind me and, as before, I watched them in my mirror waiting for the moment to pull up into the lowering sun and, Glory be to God, they also lost me. By now I was nearing friendly territory, the shadows were lengthening, and I must have been well nigh invisible in the darkening obscurity of the hillsides. That's the last I saw of them. I landed back at Waterloo in the twilight, fuel gauges on the zero mark, shaken but elated, the only damage a bullet through the spinner, and two bits of shrapnel in the radiator, probably flak.

I flew several more sorties between the 2nd and 10th February on escort and ground strafing missions, finally handing 93 Squadron over to Wilf Sizer on 13 February, to my regret, yet also in many ways to my intense relief.

On 2 February the Luftwaffe gave Waterloo its first real pasting, when a mixed pack of twelve Me109's and FW190's caught us on the hop, bombing, strafing and getting away before the airfield patrol could intercept them. Several Hurribombers of 225 Squadron were destroyed. The very next day they returned, this time eight FW190's zooming in at deck level with about six Me109's as top cover, clobbering 111 Squadron's dispersal, killing thee airmen and writing off two Spits.

Squadron Leader Desmond Hughes, an ex-University Air Squadron chum of mine from the 'other place', flew me back to Setif on 15 February in one of the 600 Squadron's Beaufighters. He was to have come on to Algiers with me for a couple of days' break, but unfortunately on arrival he was recalled to fly a serviceable Beaufighter back to Souk.

I boarded the 'SS Nea Hellas' in Algiers Harbour on 17 February bound for Southampton. The voyage was uneventful affording me a much needed rest. On board there was a bunch of Luftwaffe pilots destined for a Prisoner of War Camp somewhere in the UK. Among them was a Lieutenant Richter, a FW190 pilot shot down over Bone. His father was a Brigadier General on the Russian Front. I was occasionally able to exchange a few words with him in the Dining Saloon where all the Officers ate, RAF, Allied Air Forces and the Luftwaffe together, the latter segregated from the others, of course, and closely guarded by MP's. He was a confident self-assured young man convinced of ultimate victory for the Fatherland. He expressed a healthy respect for the Spitfire, but rightly maintained that the tropicalised Mark V was no match for the FW190 in the dive and zoom climb. All one had to do to say alive, he said, was to avoid close encounter involving dog-fights, and always to attack from above out of the sun; then shooting at Spits was like shelling peas. As for his own dismissal, he maintained it was flak that got him. He claimed at least ten victories over the Tunisian battle zone. Somehow he managed to lay his hands on an inexhaustible supply of Schnapps, and we would surreptitiously drink many toasts to all the Fighter Pilots throughout the world.

CHAPTER TWELVE

BACK TO BLIGHTY

Upon disembarking I made straight for London. I had very few belongings, owing to the sinking of the 'SS Berthier', apart from flying gear and a bottle of genuine French perfume, so I arrived in The Boltons adequately equipped, as I thought, for my first encounter with the family.

I was greeted with the news that my parents had sold up Rugeley and had bought a pub in Cornwall. They had asked Pan to go down with them to help with the 'handover', so she had already left with our one year old son Patrick. My brother-in-law, Ronnie Collier, who was married to Pan's sister Paddy, was staying at The Boltons prior to leaving for the States. He had been appointed the Daily Mail correspondent in Washington, and was ready to embark any minute on the 'Queen Mary' which was sailing back to New York, having previously disgorged thousands of American troops at Southampton on Saturday (25 February). Ronnie and I had a night out together, starting at the Mucky Duck in Magpie Alley, behind the Daily Mail Offices in Fleet Street.

Here I met for the first time one Leslie Illingworth, the celebrated cartoonist. The three of us ended up at about four o'clock in the morning in the Bag of Nails. Leslie was a Welshman and a true friend. We retained a close relationship for the rest of the War.

It took me all next day to sort myself out. I managed to discover the name and telephone number of the Cornish pub and, having phoned Pan, I caught the night sleeper to Penzance on the evening of Monday 27 February. The pub had the inauspicious name of 'The Whitesands Bay Hotel', situated on the seafront in a small fishing village called Sennen Cove. I was turfed out of my sleeper at Par and finally arrived at Penzance Station at about nine o'clock on Tuesday morning. I was met by Pan and my mother.

The pub, later to be called by its old name 'The Old Success Inn' dating back to 1651, was to be our first 'Spit and Sawdust'. I didn't know it then, of course, because there was still a war to be won, but on my father's death in 1945 not long after VE Day, I was granted a six months' Compassionate release from the RAF to help my mother to derequisition the pub, which, throughout the war, had been an RAF Officers' Mess for the large Radar Unit established near Land's End, but that's another story.

At the end of February we returned to London and I reported to 'P' staff to find out what they wanted me to do next. Much to my chagrin they had a job lined up for me as an 'Air Planner' at the new Combined Operations HQ at No 1A Richmond Terrace, headed by Lord Louis

BACK TO BLIGHTY

Mountbatten. I had hoped for another Spitfire Squadron but it wasn't to be, so I resigned myself to sweating it out for a while. As it happened it didn't turn out too badly.

After a short 'Combined Ops' course in Scotland in an outlandish place near Greenock, I returned to be told to sit at my desk and write a paper on 'The Fighter Squadron in the Close Support Role'. My boss was a pleasant enough chap called Group Captain Peter Broad, who had little or no experience of Fighter Operations except for a few Fighter Sweeps across the Channel, so he left me to it. He arranged for me to have the use of an elderly Spitfire 2 which was kept at Northolt. From there throughout April and May I flew to various Stations in Fighter Command's 10 and 11 Groups, preaching the gospel on the 'Air Aspect of Combined Operations.' I never thought a lecture tour could be so entertaining. I met scores of Fighter Pilots of all sorts and nationalities, I covered a lot of new ground and made many new friends, but most importantly I was able to keep my hand in on the beloved Spitfire.

Owing to the house in The Boltons being so conveniently situated, it was becoming increasingly crowded with numerous male members of the family who were now in the Armed Forces. They used it for temporary accommodation in transit from one posting to another, or whilst on leave. Pan and I decided to look for somewhere on our own. I was talking to my sister on the phone one day when she said some old friends had grown weary of London and the bombings, and had evacuated their three-storied terraced house at 48 Addison Avenue, Holland Park, to go and live in the country. Would we like to 'caretake' it for them at a nominal rent of £1 per week? We jumped at it. We had already been to see two or three other places, notably a large house owned by a well-known lady called Mrs Van de Elst, famous for her 'one-man' crusade against hanging. She was once a friend of the late Rector of Stiffkey. The house was situated near Abbotsbury Close, not far from the Russian Embassy. It smelt of must and decay, most of the furnishings covered in dust sheets and cobwebs, reminiscent of Mrs Havershams's house in 'Great Expectations'. The rent was too high and besides, it needed a hundred maids with a hundred mops to clean it up! So 48 Addison Avenue it was.

Although somewhat old fashioned, the house was clean and airy, fully furnished including linen, crockery, etc., and even a Bechstein grand piano. There were five bedrooms, a bathroom and toilet, a large drawing room, study and dining room, and a kitchen and scullery in the basement with a gas cooker, not forgetting two terrapins in the garden pool at the back. Once again we had fallen on our feet.

SPIT AND SAWDUST

One beautiful spring day I took an extra hour off during the lunch break to go and visit Rosa Lewis at the Cavendish Hotel in Jermyn Street. I hadn't seen her since my Oxford days. The puzzle of Dick Hillary's phone call to me at RAF Valley, Anglesey, shortly before I departed on Operation 'Torch', was still niggling me. It occurred to me there might be an outside chance of Rosa throwing some light on the mystery. On enquiring at Reception I was told she was in and would be pleased to see me.

Rosa had a small private office at the far end of the Hall where she sat amidst piles of letters, documents and invoices, accumulating in untidy heaps on the top of a very large ornate Victorian style bureau. The walls were obscured by hundreds of photographs and pictures dating from pre-World War One days to the present time. She remembered me all right, which flattered me, because she had never known me quite so well as the others, I couldn't afford to stay there every weekend.

Entering the 'Holy of Holies' I spotted almost at once a large photograph of Dick standing out amidst a glut of pictures.

"I've come to pick your brains, Rosa."

"What is it, dearie? What d'you want to know?"

I told her the story of how Dick had tracked me down in North Wales saying he had something very important to discuss with me, how I had missed seeing him when I went down to Fighter Command, Stanmore, and how, within a few days, I was on the high seas heading for an unknown destination.

"Ah, Dick!" She sighed "I was very fond of that boy. Though I loved all the boys, of course, he was without doubt one of my favourites. What a tragedy!"

"Yes, indeed it was," I replied. "Can you remember when you last saw him?"

"Oh dear me now, when was it? I think sometime during last summer before he went back onto flying. Foolish boy, he should never have done it."

"Did he say anything about wanting to contact some of of his old school and Oxford friends?"

"I can't say for sure, duckie, it was quite a long time ago you see, although I do seem to remember he said he had some scheme afoot. I couldn't say for the life of me what it was though. Have a Champagne Cocktail with me, luvvie, just for 'old times' sake."

After a few minutes an elderly waiter, whom I thought I recognised from the old days, entered with a silver tray on which were two tall

BACK TO BLIGHTY

familiar goblets containing Rosa's favourite beverage.

"To Dick, the dear boy, wherever he may be now."

Our glasses clinked. Rosa was far away, my quest for information long forgotten. After a few minutes I thanked her for the drink and sadly stepped out into the sunlight on Jermyn Street. The next time I saw the Hotel, the old Cavendish had been demolished and replaced by a large modern structure which somehow dispelled all the happy memories of the past. I never saw Rosa again.

Towards the end of May 'P' staff phoned to ask whether I would like to go on the Army Staff College Course at Camberley. I unhesitatingly replied "No", whereupon a posting notice was promptly despatched to Peter Broad stating that go I must, which frankly got on my wick. Why ask me first if it was already a 'fait accompli'? A Staff College course, Army, RAF or what you like, was the last thing I wanted to do. I was still a Volunteer, I reminded myself, not one of those haughty career-conscious Regulars. I considered that within reason I was entitled to some choice in the matter, and said as much to Peter. It was no use, 'there's a war on, don't you know?' Volunteers were always the first bodies to be pushed around. I had been to Oxford, Cambridge and Cranwell, and now I was expected to graduate as a qualified Army Staff Officer in blue, a ludicrous and contradictory situation.

I duly reported to Camberley on 2 June, to find that I was to be accommodated at Minley Moor, a pleasant country house about three miles from Camberley, close to an RAF aerodrome called Hartford Bridge Flats, now better known as Blackbushe Airport. Minley Moor was an annexe to the main Staff College down in the town. I was joined at Minley by another RAF Officer, none other than Bill Edrich, the Middlesex and England cricketer. He and I were the only 'blue types' amidst about fifty or more 'brown jobs'. We were both subjected to many jibes and quips, mostly harmless and light-hearted. As time passed we came to realise that the RAF was distinctly unpopular with a small minority of the regular, class conscious Army Officers, who belonged to the more prestigious, or one might say, glamourous Regiments.

It happened that I had to share a room with a Marine, Major Nigel Beale, an exceptionally smart officer with a magnificent array of uniforms for all occasions, which were closeted in a large built-in wardrobe at one side of our bedroom, my modest RAF gear being in a similar cupboard on the other side. Nigel was of small, wiry stature, slightly thinning shiny black hair, and pointed features with the hint of a port-wine complexion. As we got to know each other I found him an agreeable, easy going

SPIT AND SAWDUST

companion, with a more than average understanding of the air aspect of military operations.

We were divided into Syndicates each with about eight students, headed by a member of the Directing Staff, known as DS. Although Bill Edrich and I, for obvious reasons, were never in the same syndicate, we spent much time together off duty. There was a large mock-Tudor style pub on the edge of the airfield within walking distance of Minley. Bill and I would repair there most evenings to enjoy a pint or two together.

Bill would yarn about his cricketing days, the tours to India, Australia, New Zealand and the West Indies. He just couldn't wait for the war to finish, he longed to get back to his beloved bat and ball. Nevertheless, he had done well in the RAF, and was awarded the DFC for his part in bombing raids, mostly on Blenheims. I considered that anyone flying bombers deserved the VC, let alone the DFC. I was grateful that the unseen hand of Providence had guided me into the world of the Fighter Pilot, where at least one was one's own master and, up to a point, with some control over one's own destiny.

The aircrew casualties in Bomber Command during the war make awesome reading - fifty-five thousand killed, twenty thousand wounded and twelve thousand made Prisoners of War. Nearly seventy-five thousand chopped down in their prime, for what? None of them, perhaps not even the legendary Guy Gibson himself, could claim to have survived solely through his own skill and cunning, because there were so many factors to be accounted for: the responsibility of the Captain for a crew in whose eyes one must be seen to be without fear; the hazards of wide variations in the weather pattern, on flights involving many weary hours over long distances; the deadly German flak; the Luftwaffe night fighter assailing the bomber stream almost undetected; the risk of aerial collision over the target area; even the possibility, slender perhaps yet very real, of damage or destruction by bombs falling from above, during those mass saturation raids. By comparison the Fighter Pilot's lot was a happy one. He could kill or be killed on a one-for-one basis, he was well placed to evade trouble, and to get the hell out of it quick and, dare I say it? - fit and ready to fight another day.

It was not long before my Syndicate colleagues were pestering me to take them up flying. They argued, quite reasonably, that with an airmen in the side they had the edge over the other Syndicates, because I could provide them with the means of aerial reconnaissance when we played our war games. Okay, I said, I'll see what I can do.

I paid a courtesy call on the Station Commander at RAF Hartford

BACK TO BLIGHTY

Bridge and, as was the custom even this far into the war, left my card. I duly received an invitation to lunch, and introduced myself to Group Captain Lusada, the Station Commander, and Wing Commander Peter Wykeham Barnes, another legend in his time, who commanded a Mosquito Squadron operating out of 'the Flats'.

From this moment I established an agreeable easy-going relationship with them both, and I was given a free hand to fly the Station Proctor whenever I liked. With a spot of dual from Peter I also flew the Mosquito solo for the first time. I triumphantly reported back to my Syndicate that an aircraft was at our disposal.

The Proctor carried three passengers, one beside the pilot and two behind seated side by side. An amiable but persistent member of the Syndicate, Captain Ian Ramsay of the Seaforth Highlanders, continually badgered me for a flight. He was a frail diminutive figure in a kilt which looked more like a mini-skirt. He had chubby cheeks and hair the colour of winter fodder. His sole ambition was to learn to fly. Every time I took someone up he insisted on coming too.

On 30 July I arranged to take my Syndicate leader, Major Peter Robertson MC, plus Major Tony Haslerigg and Captain John Will, Guardsmen both, on a recce of the Winchfield-Hook area. Ian Ramsay insisted on coming too, so we squeezed him in at the back. At the time I didn't think his extra weight, perhaps eight stone, would be a problem. I took off, climbing to about a thousand feet over Phoenix Green. Peter was intent on examining the ground close-to with his binoculars, and nudged me to reduce height, as if we weren't already low enough. At that moment the engine coughed, the propeller ceased to rotate with a spasmodic hiccup and there we were, hovering in space, with only about eight hundred feet to spare.

This was a novel situation for me; I had never flown passengers before I came on the course, and now I was saddled with four 'brown jobs', all dependent on me for survival. They clutched desperately to their seats, whilst I feverishly tried to figure out my next move. On the west side of the Fleet to Aldershot road I spotted a large meadow; it was my only hope, it was just within gliding distance. As I made my approach, due to the extra weight, the aircraft started to sink, the air speed rapidly dropping off, until I stalled into the ground with a dreadful thump. I sat there waiting for the undercarriage to crumple but, incredible though it may seem, the Proctor trundled on for a few more yards and came to a juddering halt. As I opened the side door Ian Ramsay reached out and was violently sick.

SPIT AND SAWDUST

The other three were in a state of semi-shock, unable to grasp that they were still in one piece. I bundled them out in double quick time in case of fire, and simultaneously spotted one of my favourite pubs just across the road at Hartley Wintney. We hastily assembled there, downing a swift 'double', then phoned Hartford Bridge to send a car for us.

The 'Plumbers' came to survey the scene and found that the engine had seized up. Apart from that there was no damage done. A Queen Mary was despatched to load up the Proctor and take it back by road. Group Captain Lusada was most apologetic for being indirectly responsible for nearly writing off four distinguished Army Officers, and congratulated me for pulling of an extremely difficult forced landing. I thoughtfully forgot to remind him that we were overweight. He asked us all round for drinks and canapés the following evening.

In about June 1943, we acquired a nanny for Patrick so Pan started to look around for some sort of war work. A friend of her sister's, an Australian called Frank Kemp, had a splendid job as Manager of Portland Place GI's Club, near Marble Arch, so she went along to see whether he wanted any staff. He didn't, but he suggested that she should try her luck with the Employment Department in Grosvenor Square. When she got there she was asked to fill in a form on which she entered, under 'Any previous experience', Theatre and Stage work. Within minutes she was ushered to a door marked 'Leighton K Brill, Entertainments Director, American Red Cross'. She knocked and entered. Leighton K Brill was seated at a large desk littered with numerous telephones. On either side of him were two glamorous looking secretaries, one with an armful of files, the other trying to take a shorthand letter to his wife.

"Goddam it woman" snapped Leighton "Tell'er I'm Okay, tell'er I'm too busy, Aw hell, tell'er any old crap."

He was holding one of the phones and started to hurl obscenities at it whilst at the same time a wretched little man was standing on a chair nervously plucking at a guitar. The scene was pandemonium, phones ringing, Leighton shouting, the secretaries in hysterics, and a man trying his best to impress with his guitar.

Leighton looked up.

"Whaddyer want gal, cain't yer see I'm busy?"

"Excuse me Mr Brill, but you see I was sent up to ask you for a job."

"For a what?" Leighton exploded "Holy mackerel, what next?"

"But I was told you were auditioning for a show," persisted Pan as she handed him the application form. Leighton stared at it for a few

BACK TO BLIGHTY

seconds. Suddenly he shouted "Can you produce?"

"W-well, it depends what you mean Mr Brill."

"Why, showbiz production you dumb cow."

Pan felt like crying. "I-I-I've never done any stage production" she stammered "But I'm willing to give it a try."

"Atta girl" Leighton beamed, his mood changing, "Talk to my secretary here, she'll sign you up and get you measured up for a uniform."

Pan was stunned by this sudden transformation. She felt a small thrill as she realised she had got through. Leighton turned his attention again to shouting abuse down the telephones, this time reserving a special obscenity for the miserable guitarist.

Leighton K Brill until recently had been a Hollywood Film Director. He had a sallow complexion, sharp features, pointed nose, lantern jaw and abundant iron grey hair. When he stood up he seemed quite tall, six foot two or three maybe, but on the lean side. He always wore a shiny dark green plastic eye-shade secured round his forehead with an adjustable tape, an open neck long-sleeved shirt, the sleeves pulled back and held round his forearms by elastic bands. Several pencils were sticking out prominently from over his ears, and he chewed a fat cigar between his teeth. He was the text-book Hollywood Film Magnate.

Pan introduced herself to one of the secretaries, a very attractive blonde called Miss Jordan, who got her to sign more forms, then took her to be measured up for a uniform. She then introduced her to Miss Jean Tate who was in charge of Administration and Finance. Without any delay or formality Miss Tate placed Pan on the payroll. She was to receive the very handsome sum of £12 per week, a lot of money in those days, for doing something about which, in all honesty, she knew very little. For the next few days, until the uniform was ready, Miss Jordan took Pan round to the various locations where the American Red Cross organisation performed its functions. These functions were a kind of cross between those of the NAAFI, the YMCA and the Malcolm Clubs, covering such items as family welfare, comforts, canteens and so on. And now the Entertainments Division of the ARC was about to be formed to provide stage shows for the Troops, something like ENSA, so this is where Pan came into the picture.

Her uniform was an exceptionally smart one, skilfully tailored, made out of best quality Air Force blue baratbea, a neat little forage-cap with the letters 'ARC' in red on one side. A shoulder flash with 'Great Britain' in red letters was sewn on each sleeve. To finish off the ensemble, she

SPIT AND SAWDUST

wore a white silk shirt, sheer nylon stockings with seams up the back, and smart black shoes. Altogether she looked a sight for sore eyes, if I may be forgiven the cliché, and I say without bias that it was by far the most attractive of all the girls' uniforms in the Allied Services. Basically Pan's job was 'talent spotting' by means of weekly auditions held in the Hans Crescent Club every Wednesday. This Club, which was specifically for American GI's, was between Knightsbridge and Sloane Street. It was beautifully appointed, a smart reception centre for booking rooms, massage, theatre tickets, etc., attractive lounges, cafeterias, bars, hairdressing salon, tailor's shop, in fact the lot. It also had this splendid ballroom with a stage, where Leighton would come to see the acts which Pan sorted out for him.

At the end of July the Army Staff College took a 'half term' seventy-two hour break. I caught a train to Waterloo, having arranged to meet Pan at Leighton K Brill's office in Grosvenor Square. It was the first time I had met him.

At first I was astounded by his liberal use of four-letter words in front of the fair sex. After being introduced he told us to fuck off to Hans Crescent, where Pan was due to take some auditions. No one raised so much as an eyebrow. We stepped out into Grosvenor Square to look for a taxi. In those days London taxis where almost impossible to get, especially if one was in British uniform; taxis were the Yankees' prerogative because Yankees had all the money. However, I realised it was different with Pan. In her pale blue American style uniform and nylon stockings, taxi drivers would almost queue to pick her up.

The job was becoming too much for Pan to cope with on her own, and it was not long before a lady called Cissy Sewell joined the outfit. She was very experienced, having done many stage productions for Noel Coward. Luckily she and Pan hit if off really well, and they made a great team. They were now starting to work up for their first Revue, which was called 'Corn on the Cob'. It was not very good, but as they went along they improved, and Cissy and Pan produced some really successful shows including 'Hit Parade' and the 'Black and White Minstrels' Show. One of the problems was that ENSA had got in first with what talent there was available - and that wasn't much! - so they had to rely on trying to spot natural ability from dozen of old-time Music Hall artistes well past their prime, or from embryo 'Cochran Young Ladies', aiming for instant stardom, or from mobs of young factory girls thinking they could sing like Vera Lynn, or act like Carole Lombard. Cissy and Pan had to audition the lot, Chinese Jugglers, contortionists, magicians,

BACK TO BLIGHTY

ventriloquists, fire eaters and even clairvoyants.

When our course finished in September, Bill Edrich and I decided to celebrate. After a few pints at the Hartford Bridge Pub, we took a taxi down to Camberley. I don't remember very much more of this escapade. How, I don't know, but we made it back to Minley, and managed to crawl into bed. In the middle of the night I woke up bursting for a pee. In total blackness I struggled out of bed, making for where I thought the bathroom door should be, which was in fact just to he left of Nigel Beale's wardrobe. Hopelessly disorientated, and groping blindly round the walls with my hands, I touched a door handle and gave it a twist. Need I say more? Nigel's clothes, including his best ceremonial uniform, were drenched. In the morning he shook me out of my stupor, though for a few moments what I had done just didn't register. I lay back and groaned.

"You dirty sod."

"Why? What have I done?"

"You've only pissed all over my uniforms, that's all!"

I had committed the unforgivable sin of urinating in a Marine Officer's wardrobe! I was abashed and cast down. How was I to do penance? Should I offer to pay the cleaners, perhaps? Nigel remained calm and self-controlled, saying he would be sending me his tailor's bill for a new dress uniform in due course. Seeing my horrified expression, he flopped back onto his bed in paroxysms of laughter. It was all over, he was human enough to see the funny side of it, and, being the gentleman he was, he forgave me.

CHAPTER THIRTEEN

NEXT STOP NORMANDY

The build-up for 'Overlord' was now under way. A new Tactical Air Command, already in embryo upon the invasion of North Africa, was being planned and prepared to carry the war into Western Europe. It was to be independent of the home-based RAF structure of Fighter, Bomber and Coastal Commands, although in close co-operation.

After Camberley, I was posted supernumerary to HQ 83 Group, Gatton Park, waiting for a Squadron. Unluckily for me the Staff College course had been three weeks too long, because I missed the chance of commanding a Spitfire Squadron, beaten by a short head by another Squadron Leader who shall be nameless. All that was now on offer was No 231, a low level Photographic Reconnaissance Squadron, based at RAF Redhill equipped with Mustang I's, powered by the American Allison engine.

I hadn't flown Mustangs before, which wasn't a problem, but I had never done any aerial photography, which was. My AOC, A V M William Dickson, decided I should first do a short conversion plus photo-recce course at No 41 OTU, RAF Hawarden, near Chester.

I reported to Hawarden on 26 October. Hawarden was a 'peacetime' RAF Station, with permanent brick buildings and tarmac runways, and comfortable domestic accommodation. It was adjacent to the industrial areas round Stockport, Birkenhead and Merseyside, which didn't help the weather factor. I was obliged to drop my 'Acting Squadron Leader' rank.

I was sent off on a Mustang straightaway. It was very easy to fly, it had a typical American cockpit layout, with plenty of room on either side to manipulate and scan the various knobs, levers, switches and instruments, it was like sitting in an armchair compared with the confines of the Spitfire, but without the Spitfire's supreme individuality. The unfamiliar bit were the camera installation and control panel. Photographs could be taken from both sides of the fuselage, and from the underbelly, depending on one's position relative to the target. The terminology was; 'port or starboard low level obliques, or line overlaps'. From then on it seemed to be a hit or miss affair, depending on the pilot's ability to navigate at both low level and high speed. The Allison-engined Mustang was almost untouchable at five hundred feet, but on the climb it rapidly lost power, and was a sitting duck at altitude.

Unfortunately, the November weather was exceptionally bad, and it was December before I could leave Hawarden to take over 231. I first reported to Air Commodore Dermot Boyle, the SASO at 83 Group. He

NEXT STOP NORMANDY

broke the news to me that Redhill, now officially designated No 128 Airfield, 2nd TAF, was to be handed over to the Royal Canadian Air Force, to become exclusively a Canadian Wing, and that about the end of January, 231 Squadron would be disbanded. From then on, the role of low level reconnaissance would be taken over by a Canadian Mosquito Squadron. Thus I was dealt a double blow, I had lost the chance of a Spitfire Squadron, and now I was to lose a Mustang Squadron.

Dermot Boyle, for whom I had the greatest respect, (he was one day to be come Chief of the Air Staff after Sir William Dickson) explained that a new Wing Commander post had been created, namely, 'Fighter Operations Liaison Officer', to be attached to the 9th United States Army Air Force, and that I was a candidate for the job after winding down 231. How did I like the idea? It was a hard decision to take. I wanted time to think. I still had a month's operational flying to go with 231 before disbandment and, knowing how swiftly situations changed, I thought, or rather hoped, that something more to my liking might crop up.

I formally took over 231 Squadron on 10 December. One of my Flight Commanders, Dickie Turley-Geroge, had just been badly wounded by flak on a low level sortie in the Pas de Calais area. My other Flight Commander was Kit North-Lewis, who later made a name for himself after D-Day, creating havoc and destruction, flying Typhoons on ground attack in Normandy.

I have to admit that I found flying the Mustang I on low level reconnaissance was nothing if not exciting. We used to head out for the English Channel at nought feet, following the contours of the countryside inland, and then skimming over the waves at 'deck level', as we approached the French coast. At full throttle we could maintain a ground speed of well over four hundred knots. No German fighter could bounce us. We winged it across the Channel just like I did in the old days with Sergeant Jenna in the Avro Tutor, at ninety-five knots round the Folkestone Pier! The Mustang would buffet just above the waves, almost like playing ducks and drakes; it was indescribably exhilarating and against all the rules of flying discipline, but nobody seemed to care, there was still a war on. Provided we had a ceiling of five hundred feet we could operate in most weathers.

Photographic reconnaissance had by now revealed a new threat, the unmanned missile, the Flying bomb, or the 'Doodlebug', as it was called. Maximum effort was to be directed to pinpointing their launching sites. During the last few weeks of 231 Squadron's existence, our major task was to take low level oblique photographs of their locations, called

SPIT AND SAWDUST

'ski-sites', because of the shape of the take off ramp. These ski-sites were set in wooded coastal areas in the Pas de Calais region, incredibly difficult to locate, well camouflaged, and heavily defended. We were also allotted the task of photographing certain river and railway bridges in Normandy which were equally heavily defended, in this case by 'flak trains', which were never in the same place twice. Regrettably these operations were short-lived.

On 10 January, 1944, 83 Group sent a signal confirming the disbandment of 231 Squadron with effect from the 15th. We sadly handed over to the Canadian Air Force, and packed our bags. We arranged for those of the boys who could make it, to meet up in the West End for a farewell party, on the evening of the 16th.

About twenty-five of us, including a few wives and girlfriends, met in the Tartan Dive of the 'Sussex', a pub in St Martin's Lane, at about 6 pm. It was already blackout time and, before long, the pub ran out of beer. We decided to walk towards Holborn via long Acre in the hope of finding a pub somewhere, when we spotted a chink of light through a blackout curtain, revealing a bar counter, so we all piled in. Apart from an elderly couple up at the other end of the bar, we were the only ones there. There was no shortage of beer, and we carried on drinking until a message was passed down the bar: 'Follow the little man in the green hat', whereupon we spotted that the couple had split up. Only the man remained, and sure enough, after a few minutes he reached for a green hat which was on the peg, put in on his head, and vanished through the blackout curtain. We quickly drank up and followed him. It seemed a long walk, we had no idea where we were going, except I felt sure we were somewhere near Chancery Lane. Then the man in the green hat stopped, took out a key, and opened a door leading into the lounge bar of a pub. The lady preceded him, and was now behind the counter, having lined up drinks for us all along the bar; she had even taken a note of what the girls were drinking.

It was a most unusual room, the bar was semicircular, the wooden doors, panels and fittings all in dark mahogany, but the unique feature was a circular minstrel's gallery above, enclosed by a heavily carved black hardwood balustrade. I had never seen a pub quite like this. We must have been drinking there for at least two hours, when Pan reminded us that the Underground trains stopped running at midnight. The Landlord resolutely refused to accept any money, and led us all the way to Holborn Station, where we arrived with about three minutes to spare. We flung ourselves down the escalator, when without warning, someone switched

NEXT STOP NORMANDY

it off, the momentum throwing us downwards to the bottom, landing in a heap of knotted bodies. We just made the last train.

About a fortnight later, I was up in Fleet Street having lunch with Leslie Illingworth at the Mucky Duck, prior to taking up my new appointment with the IXth USAAF, which I had accepted, albeit with some misgivings. I told Leslie about the pub with the minstrel's gallery.

"I must try to find it to thank the Landlord."

"Nonsense, Hal," Leslie retorted "Publicans try to help the Services as much as they can. Call it their 'war effort' if you like, he wouldn't expect your thanks."

"Maybe, but he was no ordinary Publican. Somehow, I had an intuition that he took special pains to lead us through the blackout, first to his pub, then to the Underground, as if we were the Lord's 'lost sheep.'"

"Balls, Hal, you're getting over sentimental."

"I don't care," I replied "I'm going to find him."

After lunch, I strolled down towards Ludgate Circus, and passed a policeman standing on the corner of Farringdon Street. I paused and turned. Shall I ask him? I thought, feeling a complete idiot.

"Excuse me, Constable, I'm looking for a pub with a semicircular bar and a Minstrel's Gallery."

"A Minstrel's Gallery? A circular bar? You young fellows get more kinky every day, you don't want much, do you Guv?"

"No, Officer," bestowing him with instant promotion, "You misunderstand me. I mean I'm trying to find a particular pub near here answering to that description."

"Now let me see, Sir. Would you be referring to the Black Lion in Gough Square? It's the only pub in the City which has a Minstrel's Gallery."

"Yes, I think that must be it. Which way?"

"Up St Bride's Street and turn left, but you won't find it there any more Guv, it's flattened."

"But I was drinking there the other evening. Do you mean....?"

"I do mean Sir, it was blitzed last December, just before Christmas, the 'Guvner' and his wife both killed. You must be mistaken."

I stood momentarily dumbfounded. As I walked up St Bride's Street I looked to the left, there wasn't a building standing. My stomach turned inside out, I felt dizzy and light headed. There was something about this I just couldn't fathom, what did it all mean?

I reported to the Headquarters of the Ninth USAAF on 2 February

SPIT AND SAWDUST

1944. It was located in a large country estate called Sunninghill Park, near Virginia Water. I was to share an office with Wing Commander George Lerwill DFC, the RAF Bomber Operations Officer. In the next door office were our opposite numbers, two USAAF half-Colonels, responsible for American Fighter and Light Bomber Operations. They briefed us on the Command layout, including all the airfields in the UK manned by American Flying Units. Last but not least was the HQ Communications Squadron, based at a small grass airfield in Windsor Park called 'Smith's Lawn', which was owned by the King.

It took a while to absorb and to acquaint ourselves with our new surroundings, amidst a bevy of unfamiliar khaki-clad Airmen constantly chewing gum, and eating so-called 'biscuits' and maple syrup for breakfast.

Before long I was introduced to Lieutenant General Brereton, the Commander in Chief, a breezy genial character who was pleased to see me, and wanted to know all about my background. He asked me whether I had a car of my own, because Staff Cars for the use of Lieutenant Colonels, or equivalent rank, were in short supply. There was a fair amount of travelling to do, he said, to get around all the Bases, so 'wheels' were essential. I replied "No." I didn't think I could raise the money to buy a car anyway.

"Waal" he said "Mebbe you could borrow one or sumpen, huh?"

"I'll see what I can do, Sir" I said, as I headed for the door.

"Hey!" he called after me "Tell yer what, how about having one of our light aircraft at Smith's Lawn for your own use?" I turned in surprise.

"You really mean that Sir?"

"You bet I do buddy, I'll lay it on rightaway."

So I found myself allotted a Fairchild. I was given a short checkout by a Captain Steinhoff, and I was away. I spent the next four months flying pretty nearly all over the UK, though mostly in the south east and west country. The setting at Smith's Lawn was delightful, and with Spring on the way I began to enjoy myself. The GI's in the US Service Flight where a good bunch, and always put themselves out to find me another aircraft whenever the Fairchild was unserviceable, which was not infrequent. I flew a variety of American light planes, including the Cub L3 and L5, even the Cessna Crane, a twin engined monoplane something like the Anson, but smaller and much smarter.

With this newly acquired freedom of movement, it wasn't long before Pan's boss, Leighton K Brill, who had just allotted her the job of going on tour in charge of ARC Productions, hinted that I might take advantage

NEXT STOP NORMANDY

of the situation, and airlift her to the various Show locations.

Her first assignment was to take the 'Black and White Minstrels' Show to several units in the west country. She was due in Exeter on 16 February, so I agreed to fly her down there in the Fairchild, provided I could obtain the blessing of higher authority. I consulted HQ 83 Group, my Parent Unit, but they were unwilling to carry the can, so I tackled the Colonel 'Exec' at Sunninghill.

"Sure thing, bud, you're welcome to fly your wife wherever you wish, but mebbe you'd better ask the RAF!"

It was a kind of Catch 22 situation, but the Colonel's unofficial blessing was good enough for me, so on 15 February we took off for Exeter. Pan was scheduled to put the 'Black and White Minstrels' Show on at an American Base at Tisbury that same evening. While she was out with the Show, I booked us in for the night at the Rougemont Hotel in Exeter.

Afterwards Pan came back to the Hotel with an extraordinary story.

Apparently no one knew, least of all the American Red Cross Tour Manager, that the Unit at Tisbury was one hundred percent coloured. As soon as the curtain went up, there were boos, shouting and hissing, followed by a near riot. In desperation Pan hustled the cast back behind the stageset to scrub off their black grease paint. The show never really got started, it went over like a lead balloon.

Next day, I phoned through to the US Navy HQ at Fowey, to ask first whether there were any coloured men on the Unit, and secondly for a staff car to meet us at their airfield at Dunkerswell. No problem, the Base Commander, Captain Aldrich himself, would be on the tarmac to welcome us! Exeter to Dunkerswell was a mere ten minutes flight time. Joining the circuit I made my approach far too high, but for some inexplicable reason, I didn't go round again to make another stab at it. Instead, I allowed the Fairchild to dip towards the concrete in a series of horrific bounces, as if I was playing some silly game with a beachball. As I taxied up to the Control Tower, I was shocked to see a group of dark blue uniformed Naval Officers waiting to greet us. We stepped out from the cabin to be welcomed with cheers, clapping and laughter. Despite it all, we were entertained to a first class lunch in the Officers' Club. It transpired that Captain Aldrich was Gertrude Lawrence's husband. Leaving Pan to get on with her tour of South Devon, I returned that evening to Smith's Lawn in a chastened but happy mood.

For the first few weeks at Sunninghill, I was having to put up with a daily grind on the train from Town, because there was no overnight

SPIT AND SAWDUST

accommodation at the Headquarters. George Lerwill had already acquired a comfortable billet for himself in a farmhouse nearby, so I now started to look around for suitable digs for myself. The idea of appropriating a car still appealed to me. I was racking my brains about how to lay my hands on one, when I decided to consult Leslie Illingworth, who was a great man for solving people's problems. I phoned him at his office in Fleet Street, and he suggested coming up to Town for a spot of lunch. We met as usual at the Mucky Duck.

"Hal, I've got an old car you could have" he said, as I joined him at the bar. "I just remembered about it. It hasn't been out of the garage since before the war, so I can't guarantee it will go. You're welcome to give it a try."

I was tickled pink, knowing Leslie, the car couldn't be all that bad.

"Where is it?" I enquired.

Then Leslie revealed that he had a mistress called Miss Clayton, who lived in his house near Horsham, in Sussex, where he had a four acre smallholding. Miss Clayton looked after the animals and chickens. The car was jacked up on bricks in one of the outbuildings. Miss Clayton had a key. If I decided to go down there and a take a look, I would have to bring petrol and oil with me, Leslie said. This could be a snag, I thought, but not insuperable.

The next morning, back at HQ IXth USAAF, Sunninghill Park, I made straight for the Transportation Officer, Captain Jury, an important person to keep in with. I asked him where I could get some petrol. To my surprise he asked me how much I wanted. I knew I couldn't handle more than a gallon or two travelling by train.

"Would a full jerrycan be asking too much?" I enquired.

"It's a deal" he replied. "You can pick it up here whenever you like."

Thanking him profusely, I began to figure out how I could get it up to Victoria. I consulted George Lerwill, who had a car. He volunteered to drive me up to Town early the next day, plus the jerrycan, and drop me at the station. All went well, I grabbed an empty compartment on a train to Horsham, and within the hour I found a taxi to drive me to Leslie's house, where I was greeted by Miss Clayton, a pack of barking dogs, a few goats and some turkeys. Leslie had already briefed her, of course, so without further ado she showed me where the car was housed.

Upon opening the double doors of a large shed, a flock of squawking chickens flew out amidst a fog of feathers and flotsam. I could see the vague outline of a car underneath the straw so together we brushed it

NEXT STOP NORMANDY

clear, until revealed before me was a magnificent Daimler Sports Drophead Coupe.

I was bowled over. Leslie said an 'old car', yet here was the latest 1939 model, probably one of the last to be produced before the war. We managed to get the car off the bricks using a jack. Lowering it down onto all four wheels I was amazed to note that the tyres, which had seen little use, remained inflated. We cleared out the rubbish, straw and chicken muck, we even found some eggs. The bucket seats were in genuine cream leather upholstery, the body being a light fawn colour. Miss Clayton produced a large funnel through which I poured the contents of the jerrycan into the tank. I filled the radiator with water, checked the oil and battery, then turned on the ignition. The engine fired immediately. After a few more goes it was ticking over nicely.

Miss Clayton made me some delicious sandwiches, which I washed down with a bottle of Alton Ale, and set course for Ascot. Leslie had even registered and insured the car for me, so I could now apply for petrol coupons. When I popped in to tell General Brereton the good news, he signed a chitty authorising me to fill up with gas at any USAAF Base in the UK!

I quickly discovered that wherever I took the Daimler, people assumed I was wealthy. One early summer evening, Pan and I drove to Sonning to have dinner at one of our favourite pubs, The White Hart, on the banks of the Thames. We had a splendidly expensive meal, the ingredients doubtless procured on the Black Market. On paying the bill I found I had exactly half a crown left, which in normal circumstances would have been a fair tip. As we left, the waiter dashed out white with rage, exhibiting the solitary coin in the palm of his hand, and shouting:

"What the hell d'you think this is indeed?"

"A half crown I presume!" I retorted. With that I took it from him and drove off.

In May we were on 'full alert' for Operation 'Overlord'. Just prior to D-Day, I was invited to a dinner party by one of the US Ops Officers called Major Napier Pallato, a strange combination of Maltese by birth, American by adoption, and Etonian by education and accent. His wife Blossom, a large but very ravishing brunette, was our hostess. General Brereton being the chief guest, sat next to Blossom at the table. It seems he was playing footsie with her, because she suddenly jumped up, and poured a bowl of soup over his head. Luckily the soup wasn't hot but the dinner party broke up in confusion.

The new threat of the V1, plus frequent air raids on London, and my

SPIT AND SAWDUST

imminent departure to somewhere in Normandy, persuaded me to leave Addison Avenue, and move the family to Datchet, where I rented a bungalow on the banks of the Thames almost opposite Egham. I spent my last few days there.

Late one evening I heard the harsh discordant note of a VI. Curiosity getting the better of me, I walked across the law towards the river bank to get a clearer view. I stood rooted to the spot as the V1 motor cut out. Suddenly there was an almighty explosion, and I was blown to the ground by a searing hot blast of air coming from across the river. The next morning, with the sound of the bang still ringing in my ears,I fond out that the V1 had scored a direct hit on the 'Bells of Ouseley', completely demolishing it. One of my favourite pubs had bitten the 'sawdust'!

On 17 June, with my fellow American Ops Officers, I boarded a C47 'Dakota' for the beach-head. Approaching the airstrip the scene below could best be likened to an ants' nest. Conglomerations of vehicles, tanks, half-tracks and Jeeps jammed together in the parking lots, boxes and crates scattered round the perimeter, and everywhere trucks driving off in all directions except towards the sea.

A truck took us inland to a pre-arranged RV in a field, where we set up the Operations Control Centre in a large tent. An American Signals Unit had laid on radio-telephone communications, and within twenty-four hours we were monitoring ground attack strikes against German troop concentrations in the Bayeux/St Lo sector. The stench of dead bodies and cattle persisted everywhere, a smell I can never forget. We were within range of German artillery, the sound of gun fire constantly with us day and night.

A sudden spell of dry weather caused thick layers of dust to settle on houses, hedgerows, vehicles and uniforms, with the result that the Americans began shooting up the RAF contingent, mistaking us for German soldiers in their Field Grey. General Pete Quesada, commanding the IXth Tactical Air Command, issued an order authorising all RAF personnel to wear US Army battle dress. In my new outfit I looked a veritable mongrel - RAF peaked hat, American Officers' battle jacket, with Wing Commander's stripes on the epaulettes, RAF Wings, my Smith and Wesson revolver, in its blue webbing holster, strapped round my waist, pink trousers and light brown suede US Officers' Army boots! God knows what the Germans would have made of me had I been taken prisoner. In all probability I would have been shot as a spy and no questions asked.

The beach-head expanded daily, and soon we moved to a more

NEXT STOP NORMANDY

comfortable site near a farmhouse, where we found ample supplies of Calvados. Our facilities were improving, we acquired a Mess Tent, and set up a well stocked bar. Vast quantities of French Brandy and Liqueurs had been liberated from a Château, near Beaux, which had been a German Officers' Mess. The most popular drink was Brandy and Benedictine mixed - three quarters Brandy to one quarter Benedictine, served in half pint glasses, no charge. 'B & B' became a recognised Liqueur after the war.

About mid-July, just prior to General Patton's breakthrough, my opposite number, Lieutenant Fred Dollenberg and I were detailed to drive to the outskirts of St Lo to witness a massive bombing of the town. We found a handy spot on top of a hill occupied by a US Army forward observation post.

The day was fine and sunny with good visibility. Wave after wave of bombers flew over, first the Flying Fortresses, then the Marauders, clusters of bombs pitching and tossing earthwards over our heads, as they tumbled from the bomb bays like confetti. The noise was deafening, the destruction horrific, flames soaring skywards accompanied by thick clouds of dust and black smoke. One group of bombers jettisoned its bombs several miles back from the target, pulverising concentration of American troops and transport. On our way back we hit a mighty traffic build-up, the scene was one of chaos and confusion, bomb craters everywhere, vehicles upturned and scattered round like pieces of twisted Meccano.

At morning briefing one of the Ops Staff, Captain Jesse Calhoun of the US Cavalry, gave out that a cheese factory near Carentan had been liberated. No one seemed interested, but having a passion for Camembert, I decided to investigate, and took off for Carentan in my Jeep. Carentan was still being shelled by retreating Germans, but it was no deterrent. I soon found the factory, and introduced myself to the manager, who welcomed me in the traditional fashion. He then spotted my strange uniform, momentarily throwing him off his balance. Fortunately I spoke tolerably good French so he accepted my explanation. I drank quantities of Calvados, whilst listening to his tales about the horrors of German occupation. Before I departed he presented me with a carton of twelve fresh Camemberts in their little round boxes.

It happened that I was sharing a tent with two Lieutenant Colonels, both sociable and easy-going characters, and when I left to go on watch, I deposited the Camembert cheeses on my camp bed without a thought. Entering the tent the following morning, I was surprised to see the other two camp beds plus personal effects had vanished. A note was pinned to my bed: 'Sorry, bud, we couldn't stand the smell. We've found another tent and warned everyone not to come near you. Best of luck. Signed: Bob and Clarke'.

The cheeses were nowhere to be seen, until I discovered them wrapped up in a blanket under my bed. Making my way to the Mess Tent for breakfast, I couldn't help chuckling to myself at the American attitude towards food and hygiene, which was so different from the British. Even before D-Day, at Sunninghill Park all fresh foods were imported from the States, including meat, poultry, dairy products and so on. Americans were very squeamish about eating British food, preferring their tasteless, antiseptic tinned products to local fare. Their butter and cheese, which came in cans, were bland and flavourless. I didn't much care for their coffee either, although the boast was that only Americans could brew good coffee. I tried hard to persuade them to taste the Camembert, but the only one to react favourably was my boss, Dyke Myers, the Senior Ops Officer, a full Colonel and a very experienced Fighter Pilot, having fought against the Japs in the Pacific, chalking up a score of some twelve aircraft destroyed.

Fate then stepped in, in the shape of Spike Jones and his 'City Slickers', an internationally known jazz group with a comical twist. They arrived straight from the States into the Normandy mêlée. They were a great bunch of boys, and spent two weeks with us under canvas, giving shows to American combat units. Spike couldn't leave the Camembert alone. Between us we demolished the contents of the remaining little round boxes. The 'City Slickers' were screwballs, getting stuck into 'B and B', which they drank daily in vast quantities between shows. Spike presented me with their recordings of 'Cocktails for Two', 'I went to your Wedding' and 'Laura'. I wish I had them today.

General George Patton, commanding the US Third Army, who regularly turned up at the IXth TAC nightly briefings, was now poised for his break-out from the beach-head, codenamed 'Operation Cobra'. St Lo fell on 18 July, and by the 26th Patton had overrun Brittany, bypassing Vire and Avranches. He held a German counter-offensive on 7 August at Mortain, trapping the 5th Panzer and 7th Army in the 'Falaise Gap'. The Allies took fifty thousand prisoners, and the Germans left ten thousand dead. I drove down to see the destruction wrought by RAF Typhoons, which had rocketed a vast concentration of German tanks, half-tracks and trucks, caught between Mortain and Domfront, creating a massive jam of burning vehicles and equipment, stretching for about twenty miles. I cannot find words to describe the scene of death and destruction; it was

NEXT STOP NORMANDY

a miracle that any Germans escaped at all.

On 24 August George Patton was at the gates of Paris. Pete Quesada ordered Fred Dollenberg, Bill Mallison and myself, to take the Jeep and drive straight to the French Capital, with instructions to recce a suitable site for the Ops Centre, in the Versailles area.

We arrived on the outskirts of the City on the 26th, after it was liberated. We waited by Les Étoiles until General de Gaulle had passed down L'Avenue des champs Elysée, on his triumphal procession, proclaimed by all the people of Paris. We slowly followed in its wake, crowds packing L'Avenue, the road bestrewn with flowers thrown to the columns of troops, and crushed underfoot as they marched by. Several girls clambered onto our Jeep, one sat in the back with Bill, and two sat on the bonnet. The occasion was unforgettable. Slowly we approached the Place de la Concorde, turned left into the Rue de Rivoli, then left again into the Place Vendôme, where we parked the Jeep outside the Ritz Hotel. We had developed a thirst, so we went in and ordered champagne, which came up by the bucketful. The welcome was rapturous, the mood one of triumph and ecstasy. It seemed the whole of Paris had gone mad. Without so much as a word the manager insisted we stay in the Hotel for free. I was shown into a suite which, the manager explained, had always been reserved personally for King Farouk, prior to the German occupation. Reception, Writing and Dressing Rooms, all with priceless Louis Quartorze furnishings, led into a large bedroom with an eight foot four-poster bed, and beyond a bathroom in marble and gold, the bath the size of a Jacuzzi. I hadn't had a bath since landing on the beach-head. I stripped off ready for the plunge, only to find the water was stone cold. I phoned down to Reception to be told that the heating system was kaput, but I could have hot water and warm towels sent up. Within minutes, two attractive girls appeared and, after scrubbing my back, wrapped me up in an enormous bath towel to dry off. Now fully restored, I dressed and went downstairs to meet up with the others. As we drank more champagne, we concluded that a night club sortie was now on the cards.

The last Paris night club I had been to was 'Bobbys', in Montmartre, before the war. The manager thought it was closed, but he recommended the 'Chat-Noir'. Paris was without mains electricity. We drove the Jeep through the lampless streets, amidst the milling rejoicing crowds, lighting their way with car headlights, torches and paraffin lamps. Naked flares illuminated the 'Chat-Noir'; we descended the stairs into the smoky chasm, packed with heaving bodies, pulsing to the beat of a group of a coloured jazzman. The crowded tables round the tiny dance floor,

SPIT AND SAWDUST

reflected the flickering flames of a myriad candles. The atmosphere was wild and abandoned, we were mobbed by the girls, many of them intrigued by my strange regalia. We drank champagne until it came out of our ears, eventually weaving our way back to the Ritz in time for a late breakfast.

27th August was a lost day. Early morning on the 28th, we drove out to Versailles to look for a suitable site for the Ops Centre. We found a superb spot amongst the trees, from where we could look along the line of the Grand Canal, to the Water Terrace in front of the Palace. A US Signals Unit was soon laying land lines, and in no time at all the tents were going up. Within twelve hours we were in business. Out of the blue an RAF Officer with a DFC poked his head in, and asked whether we were the Headquarters, IXth TAC. He was a short stocky young man with a round face and an infectious grin.

"Sure" I replied "Come on in."

"I'm Flight Lieutenant Grey, Sir, one of your US Squadron Liaison Officers!"

"Good God man, how did you find your way here?"

I was conscience stricken. I had several RAF Officers farmed out to various US units, but in the frenzy of the moment I hadn't spared them a thought.

"I was hoping, Sir" he said "you would show me something of Paris, now that it's liberated."

He was Jimmy Grey, whom I later came to know well when, together with his brother Douglas, he was the landlord of the County Hotel, Haverfordwest, Pembrokeshire.

Fred, Bill and myself continued to live in the Ritz for the next ten days, but before long Fred found himself a ravishing French blonde, and moved in with her. She lived in a stylish apartment just off the Boulevard Haussmann. Fred could hardly speak a word of French, so he was having problems. One day, when we were off watch together, he asked me to go along to the apartment to do a spot of interpreting.

Upon arrival we found the girl, whose name was Claudette, in her bathroom - a combination of boudoir and dressing room - with a large central bath, a beautifully upholstered chaise longue on one side, a loveseat on the other. There were fitted cupboards faced with mirrored glass, and perfumes and make-up enough to stock Galaries Lafayette. She slipped off her gown and stepped into the bath while Fred and I made ourselves comfortable; she had a breathtaking body. She asked me to give her some English lessons. Finally, like Aphrodite, Claudette rose from the bath, and slipping on a Kimono, vanished into the bedroom. I decided I had had enough, so taking my leave of them both, I headed for the Ritz and a bath of my own, before going on watch at Versailles.

The next evening Fred turned up looking distraught.

"What's eating you, Fred?" I asked.

"Claudette's been arrested. They've taken her away." He replied.

"Who's taken her away, and where?"

"Don't ask me, I was nearly taken myself. Luckily there was just time to get dressed, and when they saw my uniform they backed off."

"Who are they?"

"They certainly weren't Gendarmes. One of them spoke English, and said Claudette had been the kept woman of a notorious German Officer."

We had hard stories about how young French women, who had collaborated with German Occupation forces, were stripped and shaved, then driven through the streets like cattle, whilst being pelted with rotten eggs and tomatoes. The lovely Claudette's fate can only be left to the imagination.

The Allies continued to thrust eastwards. August saw the successful landings in the South of France, near Cannes, codenamed 'Anvil.' IXth TAC was soon on the move again, and after the liberation of Brussels on 3 September, we set up the Ops Centre in Charleroi, where for the first time we were under a roof instead of under canvas. Within days we moved to Namur, then on again to Liège, where we requisitioned the Central Hotel, remaining there until 14 October.

During this period I was able to get in a fair amount of flying. I was allotted a Cessna Crane which I flew on visits to the various Fighter Strips in IXth TAC and 2nd TAF areas, and I flew several missions on Mustangs with 366 Fighter Group, based near Laon, mostly escorting Marauders attacking targets east of the Moselle. The Luftwaffe was seldom in evidence. The whole outfit, which now consisted of the IXth USAAF HQ as well as the IXth TAC, moved south to Luxembourg on 14 October. At this juncture we came under the overall command of General Hoyt S Vandenberg, who was to be American Chief of the Air Staff after the war. A new airstrip known as 'A 97 C' with a pierced steel planking runway, was located about two miles east of the City, and operated by the HQ Communications Flight. General Vadenberg kept his personal Mustang there, a beautiful highly polished Mark 3 which he allowed me to fly.

On the morning of 16 December, before first light, I was on watch in the Ops Room, when the telephone came alive with calls from all along

SPIT AND SAWDUST

the First US Army front line positions, reporting a massive enemy artillery bombardment. It looked like it could be a breakthrough, but no one would believe it possible. The Bosche had been well and truly beaten, how could he possibly launch a full-scale offensive when he was already in headlong flight, having suffered enormous losses? We were in the middle of the pre-dawn briefing, attended by General George Patton, and General Courtney Hodges of the First US Army. Both expressed the view that it must be one huge bluff. The Metrological Officer gave his forecast, which was for heavy snow within twenty-four hours. I asked General Vandenberg if I could take his Mustang and reconnoitre the bomb line. He agreed, and after phoning the Flight to have the General's Mustang on the line, I drove my Jeep post haste to the airstrip, and took off just as the sun was coming up.

It was a fine clear morning, light wind and some scattered cumulus. I headed north towards Echternach and St Vith flying at about ten thousand feet. I spotted fires burning amongst the densely wooded areas, and here and there I could make out columns of vehicles advancing westwards along the roads from Bitburg, Prum and Blankenheim. Swooping down low I could identify Panthers, one or two Tiger tanks, and convoys of German trucks and half-tracks, strung out for several miles. I spotted gun flashes, shell bursts and fires flaring up, as trees and buildings were set alight. There was very little flak as I pressed on to Malmedy, transmitting everything I saw back to Ops Control. I had been airborne for well over an hour, but my attention was so riveted to the scene below, that I failed to notice that the weather was closing in. Heavy black clouds were gathering, and already the ceiling was down to about two thousand feet, with winds freshening from the east, bringing scattered snow showers, sporadically blanking off the horizon. I reported the weather deterioration, and turned for home.

Over Verviers, I was down to a thousand feet, the ground below me to the south rugged and hilly. I had to hedge-hop to Bastogne, where I managed to pick up the main road back to Luxembourg. It was snowing heavily as I banked left over the City, following the road to the village of Sandweiler, on the airstrip perimeter; I was down to about a hundred feet, with very little forward visibility. I couldn't see the strip, but the warm orange glow of the flarepath infiltrated through the murk. Then swinging to port, undercarriage down, I made a final nose-up approach from fifty feet, with almost full power and half flap. There was a strong twenty-five/thirty knot crosswind, forcing me to crab in at an angle some forty-five degrees to my line of approach, in order to keep the Mustang

NEXT STOP NORMANDY

tracking down the runway centre-line, the flares dimmed by a fresh flurry of snow. The wheels hit the deck as I slammed back the throttle. I fought to keep the aircraft straight with the rudder, but it was no use, the strip was like a skating rink. Caught by the crosswind, the aircraft sliced diagonally along the ice like a frenzied crab, heading straight for a line of GI tents, pitched some two hundred yards to my right, which I bisected like a knife through butter, leaving a trail of torn canvas, guide ropes, broken cots and tent pegs. The Mustang stopped rolling as it gently buried its nose into a deep drift. There was a loud hissing noise from snow melting against the red-hot exhaust stubs. A miserable end to what should otherwise have been a successful sortie. I unstrapped and climbed out wondering what sort of bollocking I would get from the General.

A small tracked vehicle appeared, driven by the Tech Sergeant, who hitched up and towed the aircraft clear. Believe it or not, as we looked for signs of damage, there was none to be seen, apart from some guide ropes wrapped round the prop. Luckily there were no casualties, the tents were unoccupied at the time. The Sergeant towed the Mustang in for a detailed inspection, while I drove directly back to Ops Control to file my report, after which I sneaked away to the Mess Bar to fortify myself with a pint of B & B. Later that evening the General joined me in the Bar for a drink, and to my amazement offered me his congratulations. Apparently, Generals Bradley and Hodges were more than delighted with the information I had passed over the radio, and he said the occasion called for champagne. He said to forget about his Mustang, no damage had been done apart from some camping kit. I could fly it again any time I wished, with his blessing! I had got away with this incident very lightly indeed. I owed it to the General, he was a great guy! Believe it or not, he put me up for a Mention in Despatches, which was published in the London Gazette on 1 January 1945!

After about ten days the situation in the Ardennes stabilised. Group Captain Noel Clifton, the Senior RAF Liaison Officer to the IXth USAAF HQ, had to return to the Air Ministry on business, so he asked me to fly him to the UK in the Cessna. We took off for London on 24 December. The Cessna was due for a Major Inspection back at Smith's Lawn, so I dropped the Group Captain and his Orderly Room Sergeant at Northolt, and then made the short hop to Smith's Lawn. I had previously managed a quick shopping spree in Brussels to buy presents for the family. I bought a radio set, and a pair of very smart red shoes, for Pan, a train set for Patrick, and a selection of delicatessen, including a large goose liver pate. I ordered a turkey from a Luxembourg poulterer, and purchased a mixed

SPIT AND SAWDUST

crate of French Liqueurs, Brandy, Pernod and Champagne, from the PX, for next to nothing. Pan was in Cornwall at the Old Success, so I was anxious to get down there before the turkey went off.

It was just getting dark when I landed at Smith's Lawn. I switched on the landing light as I taxied across the field towards the Maintenance Flight. There was no sign of life, everywhere was in total darkness. Cursing under my breath, I went to open the door. It was jammed tight. Try as I could it just wouldn't budge. There I was, locked in the Cessna on Christmas Eve!

At least I wouldn't starve, I thought to myself, nor go without a drink or two. I kept banging and shouting for what seemed like an age when, through the side window, I saw a torch flashing, then a voice called out:

"What's the trouble in there?"

"I can't open the door," I shouted desperately "For God's sake find something to wrench it open."

After some thumping noises the handle gave way, and an American's 'Snowdrop' helmet appeared in the doorway.

"How come you're her at this time of night? Where yer from?"

I explained the situation. The 'Snowdrop' was on night patrol with a fiercesome Alsatian on a leash checking round the buildings.

"Can you find me a phone?" I asked.

"Sure man, I have a key to the Tower, follow me."

I got through to Rear HQ, Sunninghill, to report my arrival, then I booked a taxi to take me to Reading, where I was pretty sure I could pick up the night Mail Express to Penzance. By this time it was about 10 pm. It was a tough job humping all my clobber round the place, but I finally arrived at Reading station. There was enough time for a couple of drinks, before the train pulled in at the platform, belching smoke and steam. It was packed with troops on Christmas leave.

I had a First Class ticket but I didn't find a seat until some Army Officers got out at Exeter. I bribed the Guard to keep an eye on my merchandise, which I had deposited in the luggage van. I slept the rest of the way, and woke up in Cornwall on Christmas morning. No one knew I was coming, so I phoned Zachie Nicholas, who ran the Garage at Lands End, from where he used to drive clients in an old prewar Wolesely Taxi. Within the hour I was in the Old Success.

We had a great Christmas together, the red shoes fitted Pan like they where made for her, and all the luxury foods went down a treat.

I was due back in Luxembourg on New Year's Eve. I managed to

NEXT STOP NORMANDY

reach Smith's Lawn very early in the morning, where I found Sergeant Couteur, the Orderly Room Sergeant, waiting for me with the news that Group Captain Clifton had decided to stay on in London, so we were to fly back without him. On New Year's Day, I checked in at my office in the HQ, just in time to testify to the Luftwaffe's last full scale effort of the war. It took everyone by surprise, by mounting widespread air attacks at dawn on most of the Allied Airstrips west of the battle front, with more than seven hundred aircraft, destroying nearly two hundred Allied planes on the ground. It was a far more telling cure for post-New Year's Eve hangovers than prairie oysters!

By February the Battle of the Bulge was over. Life in Luxembourg assumed an aura of jubilant carefree deliverance. There were parties on every night, sleep became a rarity. On the 12th, I was detailed to fly the Cessna to the UK, to deliver important documents to the Air Ministry. I was more than happy to oblige. On arrival at Smith's Lawn, I was met by a Staff Car and driven to Whitehall. I deposited the Despatch Case with an Air Commodore who exclaimed,

"What on earth's the matter with you, old boy? You look ghastly."

"Do I, Sir?" I faltered "I must admit I've been feeling a bit groggy lately."

"You look like a cross between an Aborigine and an Albino. You'd better pop across to Hallam Street and see the Quack."

Straightaway I took a taxi to Hallam Street Hospital, where I reported to Reception. The MO took one look at me.

"To bed with you at once! You've got jaundice."

By now I was running a high temperature, and felt like death. For the first week I was semi--delirious, I couldn't eat or drink anything without bringing it up. Then I slowly started to come to, but I was kept on a lousy fatless diet for nearly three weeks. Yuk!

Gaining normality, I noticed one day a lady wheeling a trolley through the ward with books and magazines. Suddenly the penny dropped. She was Mrs Edwyna Hillary, Dick's mother. The last time I had seen her was when I was staying at Shirley Cottage, Gerrards Cross, in 1937. She recognised me at once. We started to talk about Dick and the old days, how we used to spend our school holidays together. I told her how we drifted apart when we went to Oxford, how Dick didn't seem to want to know me any more. Then I told her about the unexpected telephone call he made to me in North Wales, when 93 Squadron was fog-bound at RAF Valley. He asked me, as a matter of urgency, to see him prior to our departure overseas on Operation 'Torch'. I told her how I turned up one

SPIT AND SAWDUST

morning at HQ Fighter Command, only to find that he was away making an Air-Sea Rescue Film down at Brighton. Mrs Hillary was intrigued by my story, but just as puzzled as I was. What was it that Dick was so anxious to see me about? During the last few months of his short life, she told me, he was working on a new book, she thought perhaps this might have had something to do with it. Well, maybe so, but it was pure speculation, and a mystery it will remain forever. I promised to visit the Hillary's at the first opportunity, after leaving hospital. Regrettably, it turned out that I never did, because something happened which was to have a vital bearing on my future in the RAF.

CHAPTER FOURTEEN

CORNISH INTERMISSION

The MO at Hallam Street informed 'P' Staff, Air Ministry, that there was no question of my being fit enough to return to Luxembourg for several months. Prior to release from Hospital, I had a final medical check, and was told that under no circumstances should I indulge in alcohol for at least a year, and after that, only one pint on a Saturday night for the next year! Undeterred I walked out, crossed over the road, and went straight into the Golden Cockerel. I ordered myself a pint of draught Worthington in a pewter tankard, making myself comfortable on a bar stool, slowly savouring the glorious tang of hops and malted barley. After a few more pints I weaved my way to Oxford Circus, finally fetching up at The Boltons.

Pan was still down in Cornwall. When I phoned her at the 'Old Success', she told me my father was seriously ill, and had gone up to Birmingham with my mother to see the family doctor, Sir Guy Dain, who at that time was Chairman of the BMA. I caught the next train to Penzance. I arrived to find that the RAF had just confirmed the de-requisitioning of the 'Old Success'. My father was dying, he had cancer of the colon (there was no colostomy in those days) so Pan and I found ourselves having to cope with the hand-over. I had about a fortnight of sick leave left.

The 'Old Success', although I call it a pub, was a small Hotel with about fifteen bedrooms, Dining Room, Lounge Bar and Kitchen. A small Public Bar with a separate entrance was maintained for use by locals and visitors, lorded over by an ex-Merchant Navy seaman called Jack Chope. My sick leave at an end, I returned to London to report to 'P' Staff, to give them my story. With the war nearly over, scores of Officers had pressing business or family problems to contend with, so there was a new Air Ministry Order out which permitted temporary and/or compassionate release from the Service, for those with a good case. I filled in the form and awaited results. My application was approved, and by the end of March I was back in Cornwall, having been granted a Compassionate Release for six months without pay, with an option to extend if proved necessary.

I must admit I was quite pleased about this, although it went contrary to my original plan, which was to apply for a Permanent Commission, as soon as the wartime standstill on granting PC's was ended.

We now turned our attention to restoring the pub to its original state. Under the terms of the de-requisition order, the RAF was to

SPIT AND SAWDUST

redecorate the premises throughout, settle the bill for furniture storage in Penzance, and the cost of removal of same, back to Sennen Cove, which took six removal van loads. We now had a problem. After a lapse of five years, how could we find out where all the furniture went? Which curtains fitted which rooms? And there were many other knotty questions. The all-important thing was that we must get a cash flow going as soon as possible. The only money coming in was from the takings in the Public Bar, just enough perhaps to pay Jack Chope's wages.

Therefore the first priority was 'Summer Bookings'. We advertised extensively, and began accepting reservations before we even knew where anything fitted, and even before we had engaged the necessary staff, including a chef, to produce meals for our prospective clientèle.

The RAF Contractors didn't finish redecorating until the end of May. All we could do now was to cross our fingers, in the hope that we weren't heading for a monumental snarl-up. After the painters left, we had about a fortnight to get everything into place, bedroom and dining-room furnishings, kitchen equipment, linen, crockery, cutlery, etc.

Staffing was a problem. We kicked off with a chef, engaged on spec from an ad in a London paper, a waiter called Pennaluna from St Just, a chamber maid, and Mrs Hollow the cleaner, more commonly known as 'Mrs Oller'. At the last minute, we inherited a porter-handyman called Martin from, the Land's End Hotel, which had been bombed out during the war. That left Jack Chope, still exercising his authority over the Public Bar, and ourselves as general dog's bodies.

We opened on 1 June 1945. The Hotel was situated at the base of a steep bill leading down into the Cove, only a narrow road separating it from the rocky foreshore. The situation was idyllic, a long sandy beach, stretching north-eastwards towards Escalls Cliff, well suited both for swimming and surfing. Little wonder, then, that we had an abundance of bookings. The summer weather was perfect, attracting throngs of ex-servicemen down to the west country, pockets full of money after demob, looking for relaxation, diversity and excitement. Although we 'cocked up' a few reservations, including that of a Brigadier, who wrote from Whites Club, to demand a double bed for his honeymoon which he didn't get, things passed off peaceably.

The popularity of Jack Chope's Bar increased daily, it exuded the right kind of atmosphere. It was frequented by native fishermen on the cadge for drinks. George George, better known as Double George, was the favourite. Greeting strangers with a knuckling of the forelock he would say:

CORNISH INTERMISSION

"Marnin, sorr, wud yer harve a drink wiz an orld Corrnish Fisherrrman, sorr?"
to which the standard reply was,
"No, no, my man, you must have this one on me."

Such technique seldom failed, it was rare indeed for Double George to pay for his pint. His capacity for beer was vast, he consumed perhaps as many as twenty-five pints daily, sleeping it off lying in the bottom of his boat, or in the bushes alongside the cliff path near his cottage.

Spittoons were still commonly used in pubs, and Jack Chope's bar was no exception. Double George's brother, Steve George, continuously smoked an old foul smelling pipe from which he would produce, at intervals, a shaft of thick brown spittle, spearing it unerringly into the sawdust. Standing next to him one day, when he was about to bazooka a warhead of black pitch onto the floor, he paused in mid-course, and nudged me to kick the spittoon away from between his feet, in case he mis-aimed and spat in it! These dreadful pots had to be cleaned out occasionally, perhaps he thought he was doing me a favour!

We toiled on through the summer, getting very little sleep, and once in a while having a spot more to drink than was good for us, though sometimes it helped.

By this time I was looking forward to returning to the RAF. I had decided that running a pub was not for me. I realised it wasn't the sinecure it was cracked up to be.

In September my mother returned from Birmingham with my father, who was still hanging on, but with weeks rather than months to live. My Compassionate Leave now ending, I was under orders to report to 'P' Staff, Air Ministry, to find out what they wanted to do with me. They posted me to RAF Sudbury, Suffolk, on the Staff of a Recruit Wing, where monthly intakes of raw recruits were put through the mill.

The unit was commanded by Wing Commander Frank Aiken, a motor racing enthusiast, who drove his own Cooper 500cc speed model at Silverstone, Oulton Park, and similar race tracks.

One evening Pan phoned me to say my father had died, and Frank Aiken granted me a few days' leave to attend the funeral. Dressed in civvies, I took a morning train down to Kings Cross. With several hours to spare before catching the midnight sleeper from Paddington to Penzance, I deposited my suitcase in the Left Luggage Department, then took a taxi up to Mayfair, to spend an hour or two at a small pub called the 'King and the Prince of Wales', which was in a Mews behind the Berkeley Hotel - long since demolished, to make way for a new block of flats.

I knew Ken Jackson, the landlord, quite well; he had been down to Sennen Cove once or twice, and I frequently popped in for a drink whenever I was in Town. Whilst having a beer in the Snug Bar, I heard a rumpus next door. Above the fracas I discerned the querulous voice of an American female, raised in anger against several male voices. It was already gone three o'clock, afternoon closing time. I poked my head round the cut-glass partition, and before I could say a word, Ken grabbed me shouting:

"For Christ's sake be a pal, go and fetch a taxi. Help me get this bloody female off the premises."

I found a taxi, and waved it round to the side door, while Ken bundled her out onto the pavement.

It was my first chance to get a close look at her. She was well made up, and wore very smart clothes, including a typically American style coat with a heavy fur collar, nylon stockings, and expensive high-heeled shoes. She carried a large leather handbag with a long shoulder sling. She was blonde, very attractive, and though I didn't think she was a prostitute, to stretch a point she could perhaps have been a lady of comparatively easy virtue. She certainly wasn't more than thirty, if that. As I opened the taxi door for her, with a violent tug she caught me off balance, propelling me backwards on to the seat of the cab, slamming the door, and in her convincing American accent told the driver to take us to Park West, Edgware Road. Evidently she had an important appointment, and needed someone as an escort.

By this time we were nearly at Marble Arch, there seemed little point in lodging a protest until we arrived at our destination. Park West is a large apartment block, only a few hundred yards down the Edgware Road. As the driver pulled up at the main entrance, the woman plonked her handbag onto my lap, muttering something about my hanging on to it while she took a lift to the fifth floor, then she vanished inside. Several minutes went by, the taxi meter was ticking away relentlessly, I was getting worried. Where on earth had she disappeared to, and why was she so long? I now had visions of forking out a lot of money to pay the taxi fare, which I could ill afford. After about a quarter of an hour, I had a sudden brainwave, perhaps I might find some money in her handbag. The idea of prying into her personal belongings caused me a twinge of conscience, but I braced myself and opened up the bag.

To my amazement, it was packed tight with five and ten pound notes, it was stuffed so full, several notes spilled out onto the floor of the cab.

CORNISH INTERMISSION

Hastily I picked them up and grabbing a fiver I thrust it into the cabby's hand. With a surprised but delighted look, he accepted the pay-off and left. I found myself standing there looking like a proper Charlie, clutching a lady's handbag to my chest as if it was a hot water bottle.

Where to now? I asked myself, perhaps the lift to the fifth floor? I entered the lift, and punched the fifth floor button. I stepped out onto a landing stretching away into the distance on either side of me. For a moment or two I stood listening, then sure enough, I heard the same unmistakable American female voice coming from down the passage to my right, so I 'homed in' on the sound, which brought me face to face with the door of an apartment, behind which I made out several voices raised in altercation. Clutching the handbag I pressed my ear to the door when, without warning, it was suddenly yanked open, so propelling me across the threshold out of control.

"Ullo! Ullo! Wot's all this?"

In the same second someone grabbed the merchandise from my hands.

"So you're the boyfriend, eh? You're in real trouble, matey. You'll have to come along with us."

"Darling, darling, thank God you've come." The woman screeched, as she rushed forward to embrace me.

"Tell them the truth! Tell them we're engaged, darling. Tell them we're to be married tomorrow!"

With this outburst, she surprisingly reverted to an unmistakable Cockney accent. I was speechless, the sinister reality dawning on me. I was caught red-handed in a trap as an accessory. How could I talk my way out of it, with this bloody woman fawning all over me? Anyway, it was now obvious to me that her admittedly convincing American drawl had been 'put on'.

Meanwhile the plainclothes men, for that was what they were, were having trouble dragging her off me. We were both unceremoniously conducted down to the ground floor, bundled into a Police car, and driven to Bow Street, the woman by now in hysterics, her behaviour making it impossible to talk sense to anyone. Once inside we were separated, thank God, and I was taken before a Detective Sergeant, who proceeded to question me. I tried to give him my side of the story, but I just couldn't get through, he was absolutely convinced I was an accomplice. When I told him I was an RAF Squadron Leader, waiting to catch the midnight train to Cornwall, he laughed his head off.

It took a great deal of time and patience to persuade him to check my

SPIT AND SAWDUST

story, until grudgingly he agreed to telephone Ken at the King and the Prince of Wales, who readily testified that I had been doing him a favour by removing the woman from his pub, but the Officer was still unconvinced. Despite what Ken said, how did I explain being in possession of a great deal of money? They had counted the notes which added up to over a thousand pounds.

"Talk your way out of that one, old boy." He said. "You're properly in the shit now."

Finally, he agreed to put a call through to RAF Sudbury. It was now about seven pm. Frank Aiken was nowhere to be found, but he allowed me to talk to the Station Duty Officer, Flight Lieutenant 'Hank' Oldfield, whom luckily I knew well. Hank promised to track the CO down, and get him to ring back as soon as possible. I sat for the next hour biting my nails, and jumping out of my skin whenever the Sergeant's phone rang, which was pretty often. Finally the call I desperately needed came through. It was Frank Aiken on the line. He did his stuff, backing me up to the hilt, telling the Sergeant it was just one big mistake, I was the innocent victim of a con trick etc., etc., and would he please let me go on my way. At last the Sergeant seemed convinced that I had spoken the truth after all. He asked me to sign a statement to the effect that I absolved the Police from any blame for wrongful arrest. After that, one of the plainclothes men drove me to Paddington Station.

I still had over an hour to spare, so my first thought was to grab a stiff drink to steady my nerves. I invited the copper to join me. He became talkative, and gave me the low down on the woman. She was pure Cockney, he said, and she already had a police record. For over a year she had been living with an American Air Force Colonel, who showered her with expensive gifts and money. This Colonel had lately been absent on duty for long periods, so she had improved the hour by flogging many of his possessions, including such items as jewellery, radio, radiogram, typewriter and so on. Also she had access to the PX where, with the help of a collaborator, she stole thousands of cigarettes and other valuable goodies. The Colonel smelt a rat and asked the police to put her under surveillance, which is where I came into the picture. Phew! It was a close shave! It was all over now, but none the less an experience I shall never forget.

The moral of my story is never get involved with strange attractive ladies, who carry large leather handbags stuffed with stolen money!

After the funeral, my mother put pressure on me to finish with the RAF altogether, on the pretext that she would give the pub to us. Now

CORNISH INTERMISSION

that my father had gone, she argued, she had no further incentive to carry on. The 'Old Success' was there on a plate waiting for us. Like the impressionable fool I was I fell for it, and on my return to RAF Sudbury I told Frank Aiken I had decided to pack it up.

I was demobbed on 2 January 1946, and the next day I returned to my chores at our 'Spit and Sawdust' Mark I, with foreboding and many misgivings, knowing that in my heart of hearts it stood very little chance of working out, my mother being the sort of character she was. To make the best of it, Pan and I decided to rent a cottage in the Cove in order to have a bolt-hole whenever things got on top of us, which they did, frequently! We knew now that my mother had no intention of taking a back seat, she had tricked me.

At this juncture Fate stepped in and took a hand in the shape of one Ernest Phipps, a very wealthy solicitor from Kidderminster, a widower and former flame of my mother during World War One. Ernest had a finger in every pie, from Cinemas to Carpets. He even owned the Star Hotel in Worcester. Before long he and my mother became engaged. This coincided with the delivery of an official looking letter from the Air Ministry, enclosing details of a new scheme, whereby RAF Officers who had been demobbed could apply for a 'Five Year Extended Service Commission'. It didn't take me more than a couple of seconds to make my mind up. With Pan's wholehearted approval I filled in the application form and sent it off.

We had seen the summer season through, my mother now had her boyfriend, so I had no compunction about leaving the business to return to the Service I loved.

CHAPTER FIFTEEN

ANOTHER FLYING START

I was granted an Extended Service Commission with effect from 4 November 1946, when I was to report to RAF Uxbridge, where I put in an application to go back on to flying. On 19 November I was posted to No 1 Flying Refresher School, RAF Enstone, in Oxfordshire.

It was one of the severest winters on record. Enstone was closed down and we moved to Moreton-in-Marsh, but it was just as severe there, so when it was announced over the BBC one night that the lowest temperature recorded in the UK was at Moreton-in-Marsh, the Station Commander decided, with the blessing of higher Authority, to cease operations, and to grant everyone indefinite leave until the thaw, which came at the end of March 1947.

I completed my Refresher stint, and was posted to Central Flying School (CFS), RAF Little Rissington, on 9 April, to join No. 100 (All purpose) Flying Instructors' Course. Even then, with Spring all but over, it was still bloody cold in the Cotswolds, and snowdrifts lingered on in the hedgerows until May, but I had the satisfaction of knowing that I was back in the RAF.

I had never contemplated becoming a flying instructor, I had assumed I would go back on to fighters, but after more than a year out of the Service, I could hardly expect to dictate my own terms. I thoroughly enjoyed the Course. I put my all into it, in fact perhaps too much so because, having ended up with a 'Special Distinction', to my intense disappointment I was selected to remain at CFS to replace Squadron Leader Eddie Langhorne as Chief Ground Instructor (CGI). Eddie was a brilliant lecturer, especially on the 'Theory of Flight', having previously succeeded Squadron Leader Kermode, an equally talented instructor, who later became a 'boffin' - no disrespect. Eddie opted out, and went to Cheltenham as Headmaster of the Junior School, Dean Close.

However, I suppose it was an honour to be selected to join the Staff of CFS, so I stuck it for two years, during which time I was fortunate enough to be granted a Permanent Commission.

The Chief Instructor was Wing Commander Ben Boult AFC. He had a pleasant and amenable disposition, combined with a highly orthodox sense of duty and behaviour, an admirable trait, but one which tempted the students on the yearly post-war courses, almost all of them seasoned and much decorated operational wartime pilots, to pull his leg. Through no fault of his own, Ben had never flown operationally, because he was far too valuable as an Instructor. I knew this weighed heavily on him, and

No.8 Flying College Course.
Sqdn Ldr Dunn, Sqdn Ldr Barber, Sqdn Ldr Furner, Sqdn Ldr Slade, Wg Cdr Mackie
Wg Cdr Lewis, Lt Cdr Black, Sqdn Ldr Royston, Wg Cdr Horsley, Maj Fairbrother, Wg Cdr Gard'ner
Wg Cdr Nelson-Edwards, Wg Cdr Burton, Wg Cdr Everitt, Gp Capt Strong, Wg Cdr Witt, Wg Cdr Davis, Wg Cdr Dennis

RAF West Raynham — Day Fighter Leaders Course, March 1953
Seated at the centre is Wg Cdr John Merrifield, the course chief, who broke the Atlantic crossing record in a Mosquito after WW2. George Nelson-Edwards is seated third from the left, to his right Sqdn Ldr Hemmingway and Flt Lt Hibbert, to his left Flt Lt Hazelwood and Flt Lt Nineass

No. 25 N.A.T.O. Transport Support Course — 7th-17th December, 1959
Rear Row: Sqn Ldr Evans, Capt. Anderson, Capt Weir, Lt Lavender, Capt Chapman, Flt Lt Kirkbride, Capt Edwards, Capt Langham, Capt Palmer, Maj Prahl, Maj Newton.
Centre Row: Maj Savage (DS), Lt Holmes-Higgin, Capt Rega, Lt Jones, Capt Paesschierssens, Capt Bennetts, Capt Francis, Lt Innes, Sqdn Ldr Teager, Maj Waymouth, Lt Morris, Sqdn Ldr Clifton, Maj Bridge, Capt Potts, Sqdn Ldr Turner (DS).
Front Row: Maj Bardell, Maj Turner, Lt Col Breese (DS), Wg Cdr Nelson-Edwards, Lt Col Colby, Gp Capt Tacon (DS), Col Howarth, Wg Cdr Owen, Maj Buchanan, Wg Cdr Meharg (DS), Maj Edmonson

ANOTHER FLYING START

frequently drove him to over-react. Nevertheless, we got on pretty well, and he allowed me the use of the Station Tiger Moth most Saturday afternoons and Sunday mornings, to scour the countryside for empty houses and cottages.

In those days there were only four Officers' Married Quarters, one for the Station Commander, the others for the three Wing Commanders. One weekend, I spotted a row of four derelict cottages in Oddington, a small village about two miles southwest of Stow-on-the-Wold. They where entirely of Cotswold stone, the roofing in the traditional handmade stone slates, in use for centuries, until Canadian pine shingles and synthetic tiles came in. At the first opportunity, Pan and I drove over to Oddington to inspect my find. We fell for it, and decided on the spot, provided we could discover the owner and persuade him or her to part with it, to knock the cottages into one, and make it our house.

The question of money hadn't entered our heads, we had none anyway. The cottages hadn't been lived in for over ten years, brambles and nettles growing shoulder high on the ground floor. We discovered that the fourth cottage, luckily the inside of the row, was occupied by squatters. We had befriended a certain Mr Pritchard, of Messrs Taylor and Fletcher, Auctioneers and Estate Agents, through meeting him over a pint in the Bar of the Unicorn, Stow-on-the-Wold. That's our man, we thought, so up to the Unicorn we went.

Sure enough, Mr Pritchard, was in the Bar, so without delay we told him all about it, and asked if he could find out who owned the property. He thought we were mad, of course. The craze for renovating old cottages hadn't caught on yet, and he tried to flog us a rather nasty little bungalow instead. We said nothing doing, so he promised he would look through the records in his office, and if he came up with anything, he would let us know. We were beside ourselves with excitement for the next few days, waiting for Mr Pritchard to turn up trumps.

We met him in the Unicorn the following Saturday, when he informed us that he had found the owner, a widow called Mrs Pullen, an octogenarian, living in Kingham. Without delay we dashed over to Kingham and found the old lady. She was taken aback by this sudden intrusion, but, despite her age, she was in full possession of her faculties, although she admitted she had almost forgotten about the cottages, it was such a long time ago. In any case she couldn't understand why anyone in his right mind would want to buy them. However, when she realised there was a chance of a few quid coming her way, she soon perked up. She finally agreed to the handsome sum of three hundred pounds for the lot.

SPIT AND SAWDUST

As we left, we looked at each other scratching our heads. Where on earth was the money coming from? Three hundred pounds was a great deal of money in those days, at least it was to us. I suddenly started to get cold feet, but Pan's heart was set on it. Reluctantly I phoned my mother at Sennen Cove, expecting a flea in my ear, but to my surprise she agreed to forward a cheque for three hundred pounds to my Bank in Oxford. She also surprised me by saying she wanted to buy a pub in the Cotswolds, and asked me to keep my eyes open for something suitable.

I mentioned this to Mr Pritchard, who told me Taylor and Fletcher were auctioning the Noel Arms Hotel, Chipping Campden, in a couple of months time. We popped over to see it one Sunday morning, and were very taken with it. It was a typical old Coaching Inn, with a Courtyard and stables at the back, all in Cotswold Stone. My mother came up from Cornwall for the auction, and bought it, but tragically Ernest Phipps died of a heart attack, so she was landed with two pubs and no husband. However, being a very resourceful lady she weathered the storm.

We finalised the deal over the cottages with Mrs Pullen's solicitors, and secured the Title Deeds, but this was just the start of our problems. The bombshell came when we called on the RDC Planning Officer, Moreton-in-Marsh, who informed us that the cottages were the subject of a Demolition Order, which meant there was no possibility of planning permission. What could we do now? The situation looked hopeless.

We did everything possible to persuade the Authorities to rescind the Demolition Order, all to no avail. Then, as a last resort, I phoned the MP for Gloucestershire, The Rt. Hon. Ivor Morrison, Speaker of the House of Commons, who lived at Winchcombe. The upshot was that he overruled the Local Authorities, and we got our planning permission. However, these negotiations took time, I had already been at Rissington nearly a year, so we had very little time to make the cottages habitable before the summer ended. Nevertheless, with the help of a local jobbing builder and two Sergeant 'Chippies' from Station Workshops, who came in the evenings to make a new wooden staircase and built-in cupboards, we were able to move in by June, 1948. Building materials such as timber, cement, plaster, bricks, etc., were all on dockets or restricted allocation. We needed ten new doors but our timber dockets all went on the roof and staircase.

Talking with a local in the Unicorn bar one day, he told me the Admin Buildings at RAF Enstone, where I had been briefly during the bitter winter of 1946/47, where being dismantled. He said if I went over there, I might stumble on some pickings. I did just that, coming away

ANOTHER FLYING START

with a set of ten oak-veneered flush, doors which suited the rooms admirably! To give us more privacy, we decided to build a dry-stone wall down one side of the garden. I found a retired stonemason called Jack Scarrott, who agreed to take it on for his beer money. We filched loads of Cotswold stone from a derelict site near The Slaughters, and Jack made a magnificent job of it.

Whilst at Rissington, I renewed my connection with the Oxford University Air Squadron, meeting for the first time Wing Commander J R A Embling, the Commanding Officer. John Embling was bent on getting an RAF Rowing Club going, and he asked me whether I would help him. For the second time in my life I became involved with the river. John's aim was to form an RAF Eight to enter for the Head of the River Race on the Tideway in London, and he sent a questionnaire round all the RAF Commands, asking for details of anyone who had had rowing experience.

The response was good. We held a meeting at the HQ in Manor Road, and sorted out a squad of about eighteen potential oarsmen for preliminary trials on the Isis. We hired boats and oars from Slaters, the Boat Builders at Foly Bridge, and after many weeks of training throughout the winter, we had an eight fit and ready for the 1948 Reading Head of the River Race, which was the run-up to the Tideway Head in April. We didn't make much of an impression, but at least it was a start. Shortly afterwards John was posted and was succeeded by my old friend and contemporary, Christopher Foxley-Norris, destined in later years to become an Air Chief Marshal.

That summer, Christopher was engaged to be married, and I received an invitation to his Wedding Reception at the Oxford University Air Squadron Headquarters in Manor Road. It was a beautiful day as I drove my open-tourer Standard Flying Nine to Oxford, arriving in time for a fabulous party, where I met Flight Lieutenant Peter Horsley, the Squadron Adjutant, for the first time. After an excess of food and wine I took off for Oddington feeling buoyant and detached.

The night was clear, it was full moon, the Cotswold air rich with lush smells of harvest. Upon turning left at the pub called the Quiet Woman, I ran out of road, and rolled over into a deep ditch just short of Adlestrop. There was no way I could drive out of that gully. I walked the three miles back to Top Cottage with plenty of time to reflect on the day's events. Despite the fact that my car was undamaged, my high spirits and optimism became somewhat dissipated.

Within a few weeks of John Embling's departure, I also received a

SPIT AND SAWDUST

posting notice, which unhappily meant that we would almost certainly be compelled to sell our cottage. My new appointment was to the 'Organisation' Directorate in Air Ministry, Bush House. The Branch I found myself in was known as 'OA 1', which was responsible for RAF aircraft establishments worldwide. I took over from Mike Le Bas, whom I was to meet again later when he was the Wing Commander 'Flying' at RAF Wildenrath. An old 79 Squadron colleague, Trevor Bryant-Fenn, was also in OA1, so I was in good company. We had to live in London, of course, and we eventually found a nice flat in St Margarets, near Twickenham, from where, for the next two years, I commuted daily to and from Waterloo on the 'Metro' line.

It wasn't long before John Embling contacted me again. He wanted to enter an RAF Eight for the Thames Cup at Henley Regatta and asked me to join the squad. John went to great lengths to persuade higher authority to grant time off for training. He gained the wholehearted approval of the Air Staff, who deemed it would boost recruiting. Several senior RAF Officers supported the project, including Marshal of the Royal Air Force the Lord Elworthy, who rowed for Trinity College, Cambridge, and was elected a Member of Leander Club in 1931; the Principal Medical Officer, Air Marshal P C Livingstone, who was a Cambridge rowing Blue; Air Marshal K V Garside, who was an Oxford rowing Blue; Air Vice Marshal H E C Boxer, an Old Salopian, who rowed in the exceptional Shrewsbury School Crew which won the Ladies Plate at Henley in 1932; last but not least, Group Captain 'Jumbo' Edwards, whom I first met during the war when he was 'OC Flying' at RAF Jurby. He was well known for his part in coaching several successful Oxford Boat Race Crews. The Rowing lobby at Air Council level was therefore pretty formidable.

Permission for the project having been endorsed, the Squad, comprising eight oarsmen and a cox plus two spare men, commenced a period of intensive training, from mid-May until the end of June, when the 1950 Henley Royal Regatta was due to start. Accommodation for the Crew was provided by HQ 90 Group, Medmenham Abbey, in the Officers Mess. The location was ideal, being close to the banks of the Thames near Marlow. This brief spell of rowing for the RAF did me the world of good, both physically and mentally. I had never thought I could be capable again, after nearly ten years of drinking and smoking, of getting down to strict training, and achieving the high degree of fitness demanded by this exacting sport. I gave up smoking, went 'TT' and soon I was a different person, which more than made up for my having to fly a desk

ANOTHER FLYING START

in Bush House for two years.

By the start of the Regatta, we had hardened into a tip-top Eight, thanks to the splendid coaching of Wing Commander 'Two Legs' Hellyer, who used to coach the Cambridge Crew, and 'Jumbo' Edwards who took us over for the last ten days. We were all experienced oarsmen, including Ian Lang, a Cambridge Blue, and E N Clarke, a Cambridge Trial Cap. We also had a first-class Cox - John Brignell, Sidney Sussex College, Cambridge, a regular RAF Officer. I was Crew Captain and stroke. It very much looked as if we were in with a chance. As luck would have it we were beaten by half a length in the semi-final by Harvard University, who went on to a comfortable win in the Final.

My stint in Air Ministry, Bush House, ended in August 1951. For the next eight and a half years I was lucky enough to remain on full flying duties, except for the first few months from September, when I was posted to HQ 2nd Tactical Air Force, Bad Eilsen, Germany, as Wing Commander 'Organisation', another Staff job. However, fate stepped in, in the shape of ACM Sir Harry Broadhurst, who took over from ACM Sir Robert (Pussy) Foster as C-in-C. I knew Sir Harry of old, so I lost no time in seeing him to ask if I could have a flying job. He immediately offered me the Wing Commander 'Flying' post at a new Jet Fighter Airfield, due to become operational in April, 1952, at Oldenburg, a pre-war Luftwaffe base. He said I was first to take a Vampire Refresher Course at RAF Chivenor, in North Devon.

It was fixed up for me to go in February, so I was a couple of months at Bad Eilsen enjoying myself, mostly gliding at Scharfoldendorff in the Harz Mountains, an old German Gliding School, which had been taken over by 2nd TAF as an Officers' Recreation Centre.

Another most agreeable diversion was a week's free holiday with Pan in Field Marshal Herman Göring's Villa in West Berlin, which had been appropriated 'lock stock and barrel,' by the British Military authorities. This was the highlight of my brief sojourn at HQ 2nd TAF. The senior WAAF Officer, or 'Queen Bee', Group Captain Mirabelle Pitter, came with us and we had a memorable week. All the original furnishings and trappings were there, plus most of Frue Goering's personal servants. We had the daily use of a Staff Car and a German driver, who took us all round Berlin, including the Russian Sector.

After completing the Chivenor Course I officially took over the Oldenburg Wing in April, although the Squadrons could not assemble until the new runway was completed. The Station Commander designate was Group Captain Desmond Wheeler, DFC, a bachelor and mad keen

SPIT AND SAWDUST

sailor. We soon managed to scrounge a Vampire Mk 5 apiece and we started flying unofficially, evaluating the runway and familiarising ourselves with the area. Oldenburg is situated on the North German Plain, a very large area of flat countryside something like East Anglia, a good thing for flying, but otherwise uninteresting. The new 'outfit' was designated No 124 Fighter/Ground Attack Wing, comprising three Vampire Squadrons, Nos 20, 26 and 234, commanded by Squadron Leaders Ian Macdonald AFC, Ken Smith DFC, and Roy Chatfield DFC, respectively. By the end of May the Wing was at full strength.

The Station had been splendidly renovated by a Unit of the RAF Airfield Construction Branch, under the command of Squadron Leader Bill Herbert (a civil engineer in uniform), who was a genial but forceful character, especially when dealing with the German Service Organisation which provided the labour. The original Luftwaffe Officers' Mess was a fine, solidly built edifice, with all the usual offices, plus a magnificent Beer-Keller. The whole set-up was eminently suitable for social gatherings of every sort. The Wing Commander 'Admin' was Philip Halford DFC, an ex-bomber pilot. His wife Phyllis took over in lieu of the Station Commander's wife, and went top of the pecking order. One day, without consulting anyone, least of all me, she unilaterally gave permission to a nearby British Tank Battalion to carry out manoeuvres on the airfield. I had the whole Wing up at the time on ground attack exercises, and returning to the circuit I was shattered to see a squadron of tanks slowly proceeding down the runway. The shit hit the fan.

Throughout my tour as Wing Leader, apart from the 'Tanks and the Mrs Station Master' affair, everything went like clockwork. I took the Day Fighter Leaders' Course at RAF West Raynham in early 1953, which greatly added to my professionalism I led the Wing on the Coronation Fly-past in June, together with the other Fighter Wings in 2 Group, from Celle, Wunsdorf, Jever, Gutersloh, Wahn and Fassburg. This was followed by a trip to Toulose-Blagnac in southern France, where we won an International Formation Aerobatic Competition against Teams from the Dutch, Belgian, French, Italian and American Air Forces. Afterwards, the Mayor of Toulouse gave a fantastic Champagne party and dance in the Town Hall, music provided by the Hot Club de France, from Paris.

There was one notable exception to this happy background. Many of my pilots, not all in the same squadron, were finding that the improved Vampire Mk.FB9's, which had replaced the FB5's in the Oldenburg Wing, were revealing some disturbing handling characteristics. There was no obvious cause, the FB9 was in all respects the same as the FB5, except

ANOTHER FLYING START

for a few minor modifications.

For instance, it was fitted with the new TR 1932 ten-channel radio set, a G4 compass, and a new refrigeration system, hardley enough to shift the centre of gravity.

Anyway, between April and mid-July,1953, we lost three pilots. The first was a segeant pilot who spun into a block of flats over the centre of Cologne, very nasty! The second was when a 234 Squadron pilot, whose name I forget, spun into the ground from a great height, and the third was a very experienced pilot from 20 Squadron called Terry Long. He spun into the ground, also from a considerable altitude. These last two incidences showed a remarkable similarity. Both pilots had been authorised to carry out high altitude aerobatics above 20, 000 feet. On each occasion the weather was perfect. We assumed that there was no technical fault, otherwise we might have expected some sort of distress call, but there was not a peak from either of them.

On July 15th, a beautiful cloudless day, I decided to investigate this phenomenon for myself. I flew my Vampire, WR186, a nearly new aircraft, up to 30,000 feet, and gave it a full work-out. I had often carried out similar exercises before. As far as I was concerned it was nothing new. I did a few stall turns, rolls, and loops. Nothing unusual occurred. I then rolled off the top from about 20,000 feet, the Vampire behaving quite normally. Levelling off, I decided to climb to 35,000 feet. At this height the controls becomes very floppy and the aircraft flounders about like a kite. I entered a steep dive, followed by a pull-up into a half-loop and roll-out at the top. I estimated that I was then at about 25,000feet. As expected, the controls were very sluggish, but I felt no concern as I started the roll-out, and fell into an inverted spin. Nothing new about this, I was well versed in recovery proceedures. After a couple of turns, I realised I was not getting a positive response.

I continued upside down, spiralling earthwards whilst I tried everything in the book - rudder, throttle, dive brakes, flaps etcetera. I even tried selecting under-carriage 'down', but no response. By now I was becoming disorientated, I couldn't focus on the instrument panal. One thing was for sure, I was approaching terra firma at a rate of knots. Even then, I couldn't persuade myself that I must abandon ship; this was impossible, I thought, yet I knew it was inevitable.

I managed somehow to shove back the canopy and unfasten the safety belt and other encumbrances. I started to push myself out of the cockpit. I seemed to be stuck to the side of the fuselage like a fly on the ceiling. Suddenly, I became unstuck, and as I fell clear, one of the tail booms

SPIT AND SAWDUST

struck me a severe blow on the shin. I was now desperately groping for the 'D' ring of the ripcord. I found it, pulled hard, and the parachute opened. I felt the sudden jolt in the crutch as I hit the silk. There I was, for the third time in my life, dangling helplessly like a corpse on the end of a rope. Simultaneously, I heard a loud explosion as my Vampire hit the ground. It was a close shave and no mistake! I had a soft landing on marshy ground near a village called Barghorn. After reassuring myself that no bones were broken, I set out across boggy fields, until I came to a farmhouse where luckily there was a phone. I got through to Oldenburg, and they sent a Landrover to fetch me back.

Upon returning home, the first thing I did was to drive to my quarter and announce to my wife that I was still in one piece, and wanted a hot bath! I later submitted a full report to Group HQ, resulting in a relevant amendment to the flight Order Books which did little to get to the root of the problem. I was certain in my own mind that what I had experienced was precisely what happened to those two pilots who had left it too late.

The Accident Record Card for Vampire FB9, serial number WR186, merely states:-

"Failed to recover from spin at top of loop at 23,000 feet; abandoned Barghorn, BZG."

The Wing was scheduled to re-equip with F86 Sabres in July. To this end a Sabre F86 Conversion Unit was set up at RAF Wildenrath to familiarise all pilots. The unit was run by Squadron Leader 'Danny' Daniel DFC, whom I knew when he was in 72 Squadron in Tunisia. He had just returned from a tour on Sabres in Korea, so he was the very man for the job. The Station Commander was Group Captain 'Johnnie' Johnson CBE, DSO, DFC, distinguished RAF Fighter Pilot and one of the World War Two Top Scorers. The transition from Vampires to Sabres was a big step, the latter being an early example of the new generation of swept-wing fighters capable of flying through the sound barrier.

Unhappily my time at Oldenburg was drawing to a close. Early in October 1953 a postagram arrived appointing me to command the Oxford University Air Squadron in December, a job I had often dreamt about but never really thought I would get.

Suddenly it was a reality. The be CO of the University Air Squadron at any one of the three senior Universities, Oxford, Cambridge or London, had always been regarded as a 'plum job'. I considered myself very lucky.

We had a few weeks left in which to pack up and hand over our very splendid Married Quarter, and to throw a Wing Party to which even

ANOTHER FLYING START

'Mutti'; the Prima Donna of the local hostelry, was invited. She was so overcome she showed up the next morning at the Station, with an enormous bunch of flowers, as we were boarding the train for the Hook of Holland.

My non-smoking, non-drinking campaign whilst rowing at Henley was long gone overboard. Returning to the UK meant we would have to face up to a significant rise in the cost of living, since the time we left in 1950. For instance, the cost of a packet of twenty Players had risen from around 2/- to 4/11. Cigarettes in Germany were so cheap, it was said that one couldn't afford not to smoke! I made up my mind to stop smoking for good, and selected the twelfth stroke of Big Ben at midnight on New Year's Eve, 1953, as the precise moment when I would take my last drag, and throw the butt-end into the fire's dying embers. Prior to our departure, I packed a suitcase with about two dozen cartons of Senior Service, enough for us both to smoke our heads off until the last toll. Knowing we would be doing a fair amount of entertaining, once settled in Oxford, calling for liberal supplies of spirits and liqueurs, we purchased a dozen or so stainless steel bottling cans. Each can had a capacity of about thirty fluid ounces, and a 'snap-on' lid with a rubber seal. We labelled the cans 'Plums 1952', 'Strawberries 1953' etc., and filled them with liqueurs, such as Cointreau and Benedictine, so that when shaken they would give off a thick rich slurping sound.

In due course we arrived at Harwich where we had to pass through the Customs.

"Anything to declare?" asked the Customs Officer.

"No, except for 4,800 cigarettes in that suitcase."

"What!" He almost exploded, his eyes popping out like organ stops. "Do you mean to tell me that you have nearly five thousand cigarettes in there?"

"Of course, Officer. Anything wrong?"

"Wrong? I should say so, you must be mad, do you know how much it will cost you?" Then softening "Tell me, Sir, why are you doing this?"

I could sense he was beginning to show signs of concern for my predicament.

"Well, Officer" I said, "It's like this. In Germany we pay 1/- for a packet of twenty, here it is now 4/11. I can't afford 4/11, so I am bringing in enough cigarettes to last my wife and myself through to New Year's Eve."

Then I told him how our last drag would be on the twelfth stroke of Big Ben on the BBC at midnight, 31 December 1953, the signal for us to give up smoking for evermore - whatever we had left over we would give away.

"Well I'll be damned! I've never heard anything like that before. What a good idea!"

With that he took his piece of white chalk, drew a large cross on the case, and wishing us the best of luck, waved us on! Honesty pays off sometimes. In my excitement I had forgotten all about our pickling cans of liqueurs!

I took over the Squadron from Wing Commander Andrew Willan DFC, an old Etonian, on 7 December 1953. Andrew flew Lancasters during World War Two until eventually he was shot down over Germany, to spend the rest of the war in Prisoner of War Camps. We decided to take over his Hiring, an old fashioned Edwardian style house at No 19, Northmoor Road, and moved in just before Christmas. By the beginning of the Hilary Term, which was on 10 January, we were comfortably settled in.

It now meant that I would be flying Chipmunks and Harvards, of course, a bit of a come-down from swept-wing jets, but very rewarding all the same. It was magic, even awe-inspiring, to find myself once again midst the 'dreaming spires' and my old familiar haunts.

The Squadron HQ hadn't changed, it was still in the old World War One Hangar converted to provide space for ground training lectures, the same old Avro Tutor, coated in yellow dope, parked on the wooden floor of the main lecture room, and a line of doors down one side, leading to the Offices of the CO, the Secretary, the Adjutant and the Orderly Room. At the opposite end of the Hanger, at the far corner, another door gave on to a passageway into a spacious Anteroom, Bar, Dining Room and kitchen quarters, all housed in an old wooden lap-jointed hutted extension, doubtless of pre-World War One vintage. At the back ran the Holywell Mill stream, a narrow reedy tributary of the Cherwell, into which we used to throw our silver tankards after a wild party, to be retrieved from the muddy bottom the next day by Jack Acres, our long suffering Chief Ground Instructor, Flt Lt J B Acres, MBE, RAFVR. He was awarded an Honory MA on 28th February, 1953, by which time he had been appointed Secretary of the Frilford Heath Golf Club.

Miss Olive Round MBE, who had been the Secretary from the very day the Squadron was founded in 1925, still reigned supreme over administrative affairs. Having luckily kept up contact with her through the years, I found no difficulty in establishing a close and personal relationship in which she was my mentor and confidant. She had an intimate, almost encyclopaedic knowledge of the protocol, conventions and proprieties revolving round the world of 'Town and Gown'. To give a simple example, one of my first courtesy callers was Air Vice Marshal W MacNeese Foster CBE, DSO, DFC, who, prior to retirement, had been AOC No 6 Group. He was now on the City Council and the Senior Resident RAF Officer in the County. He arrived unannounced at Miss Round's office who, excusing herself, discreetly came through to my office to brief me not to receive the AVM whilst seated at my desk, but to rise, go outside, and greet him at the door! Being a venerable member of the City Corporation his local knowledge and opinions commanded respect, when it came to acting as an intermediary between University, Local Authorities and the Services.

One of my first priorities was, of course, to reintroduce myself to BNC. Entering the old Lodge Gate, opposite the Radcliffe Camera, the first person I encountered was Harris, the Head Porter, with a ruddy complexion like a Cox's Orange Pippin.

"Haven't seen you for a long time, Sir, the last time must have been when I spotted you climbing into College from the Rector of Lincoln's garden!"

As I talked with him, Bert King, my old Scout was passing by, hobbling as usual, he was born with a club foot. Bert had a thick crop of fair wavy hair, but I noticed that it had turned grey. He had aged considerably, but I knew he was still his same cheerful self when he invited me to come and have a pint and a game of shove-halfpenny with him at the Turf Tavern, as we used to do before the war.

Passing through the Cloisters, I glimpsed the windows of my old room which overlooked the Chapel, thence to the Principal's Lodgings. 'Sonners' was long since deceased, having inexplicably fallen from the Paddington to Oxford midnight express, after attending a Law Dinner. I paid my respects to his successor, Hugh Last, a Professor of History and Economics, and then called on my old 'Moral Tutor' Maurice Platnauer, who was still the Vice-Principal, and occupied the same rooms on Staircase 1 in the Old Quad, as he did when I was an Undergraduate. The ageing Henry, the Senior Scout, continued to administer to Maurice's needs, and we had a yarn about Dopey Leonard, the Australian Cox who once ran the Boat Club into debt, through his inability to steer straight!

Before long, I received a note from Maurice informing me that the Principal and Fellows of BNC had elected me to Honorary Membership of the Senior Common Room, a privilege I accepted with due modesty and pride. This enabled me to entertain guests at High Table. I took full advantage of this prerogative during term time, dining in College perhaps three or four times a month. The custom of passing the snuff box round with coffee and port lived on. In no time at all I acquired the habit, doubtless sparked off by withdrawal symptoms created from nicotine deficiency. I was soon taking as much as an ounce of snuff a week. My two favourites were 'Otterburn' by Smiths' of Charing Cross Road, and 'Princes' by Freiburg and Treyer, in the Haymarket.

Another early caller was the current BNC Captain of Boats. He asked me to coach the College Eight, first in the Torpids, then in the 'Summer Eights' towards the end of the Trinity term, which were the equivalent of the 'Mays' at Cambridge. As CO of the Squadron I was encouraged, indeed expected, to participate in College activities as a sort of RAF flag waving exercise. I agreed to take on the coaching. It wasn't long before I found myself coaching crews of other Colleges, including Christ Church, Pembroke and Worcester. I must admit it was a painless way of coming to know a fair cross-section of Undergraduates and Dons, as well as being frequently invited to dine in other colleges.

We were asked to dinner one evening by AVM McNeese Foster at his house in Lynton Road. He wanted us to do him a favour. It seems he had an annual commitment to present a Silver Trophy to the winning team in the Oxford City Speedway Championships. He couldn't manage it this year, because he was going on holiday abroad, so would we do the honours for him? The event was an important one to the locals. Naturally we agreed, and asked him to brief us.

"Nothing to it, old boy. You just turn up at about six o'clock in the evening of the appointed day, have a drink and a sandwich, then present the Cup to the winner."

"What about dress?" I asked "Uniform or civvies?"

"Uniform with medals, of course," he replied, with an unmistakable glint in his eyes. "In fact, 'the lot' my boy. Oh yes, and Pan will have to tart herself up as well, with fancy hat, long gloves and all that."

"Very well Sir, I've got the idea. I only hope we don't make a faux pas."

"No problem George, you'll have a most entertaining evening, believe me."

When the great day came we got ourselves up like a couple of costermongers, and duly arrived at the Speedway Stadium on the dot of six pm, to be greeted by a cacophony of noise, the strident scream of revving engines mixing with the sound of voices spewing from the 'Tannoy'. We felt embarrassed, no one was there to receive us as we

ANOTHER FLYING START

stood waiting in the vestibule, looking like proper 'Charlies'. We turned to go.

"Hey, are you the RAF bloke old McNeese said he was sending? Hang on a mo."

Glancing back I saw a character looking like a cross between a skin-head and a scuba diver, with open-neck shirt, oily jacket, breeches, and calf-length leather lace up boots which had seen better days.

"Sorry," I faltered weakly "I though I had come to the wrong entrance. Yes, we're supposed to be deputising for the AVM."

"Of course, of course," he said reassuringly "but you aren't half poshed up though, aren't you Guv? Old McNeese always turns up in a pair of old slacks, and a polo-neck sweater, it gets pretty draughty here you know."

I didn't know, but I was beginning to agree with him. It was a cold February evening, and blowing an Easterly. The penny dropped, as I remembered that wicked glint in the AVM's eye when he was briefing us. We were fall guys and no mistake!

With that the one-man reception committee invited us into a room something like a NAAFI canteen. There was a bar at one end, where numerous similarly dressed characters were eating sandwiches, and scoffing back pints.

"Come on in, make yourselves at home! Why don't you shed some of that gear for Chrrissake?"

I took off my for jacket, medals and all, and was presented with a sweater somewhat the worse for wear, soiled with grease, and what seemed and smelt like residue from the dirt track. One of the ladies produced a sort of cardigan for Pan, as she removed her fancy hat and long gloves. Within seconds a gin and tonic was thrust into her hand, and I found myself clutching a large tankard of beer.

We were ushered to the VIP seats, from where we watched the last few heats of the Championship, machines roaring round the track kicking up showers of cinders, and making a noise like squabbling tomcats. It was all very pally and informal. After presenting an enormous cup to the Captain of the winning team, we repaired to the canteen for sandwiches and more drink.

On the AVM's return from holiday a few weeks later, he popped round to see me, and when I told him all about it he laughed his head off, as I knew he would.

Before long we were finding that the upkeep at Northmoor Road was draining our resources. The long 1954 winter cost us a bomb in heating, so we closed up most of the rooms (there were six bedrooms plus an attic). After learning that a Professor's wife had committed suicide in the kitchen, by putting her head in the very same gas oven we were now using, it put us off the place even more.

Within the year we had bought a new bungalow in the small village of Hampton Poyle, about a mile to the west of the main road to Bicester, very convenient, both for flying at Kidlington and my office in Manor Road. We called it 'Picket Piece'. There was an extensive frontage and plenty of ground at the back, so we set about creating a new garden.

I was dining in BNC one evening, and was seated next to the Principal of St Hilda's, Miss K Major, B Litt., MA. She was telling me how they were building an extension to the College which necessitated the removal of the lawn in the Quad. I pricked up my ears. This is where our garden comes in, I thought, it could save the hassle and bother of starting grass from seed. I asked her what was to be done with the turf, and she replied that I was welcome to it for nothing if I could arrange transport to take it way. I hired a lorry, picked up the turf at St Hilda's, now neatly cut up by the College gardeners, and looking like massive muddy Swiss Rolls, deposited the load at Picket Piece. Almost overnight we had a lush matured lawn mindful of a billiard table, no weeds, no wild herbs, a tiny piece of history one might say, something to be proud of.

I had completed almost two and a half years as CO of the Oxford University Air Squadron, when I was informed that I had been selected to attend No 8 Course at the Flying College, RAF Manby, in Lincolnshire, starting in April 1956. I first had to do a short stint of Meteor refresher flying at the satellite airfield at RAF Strubby, chiefly to renew my 'Master Green' Jet Instrument Rating.

Manby could be likened to a Senior Officers' Staff College, with the accent on flying several of the latest types of Service aircraft, such as the Hunter, Javelin and Canberra, on simulated wartime air operations. It was considered a 'Career Posting', so it now looked as if I was all set for a promising future. Yet it was a sad moment when I bade farewell to Oxford. I felt deeply grateful for the privilege of having tasted an unforgettable second round of University life. I handed over command of the OUAS, on the 29 April, to Wing Commander Michael Constable-Maxwell DSO, DFC, known affectionately as the 'Flying Monk'.

Several Officers on No 8 Course went on to attain 'Air Rank', for example Wing Commander Harry Burton was destined to become Sir Harry Burton, Commander in Chief, Strike Command, and Wing

ANOTHER FLYING START

Commander Peter Horsley, who had been Squadron Adjutant of the OUAS when Sir Christopher Foxley-Norris was the CO, was later to become the Senior Air Staff Office Strike Command. Peter Horsley and I were in the same syndicate together, and frequently teamed up on exercises, taking it in turn to be either the pilot or the navigator.

On one occasion we had been flying over Norway on a night sortie, with Peter as the pilot. Returning to East Anglia, I nearly navigated us both into a watery grave while I was talking Peter down on our approach to Manby. I had only misread the altimeter by a mere ten thousand feet! Peter suddenly yelled out

"For Christ's sake, there are white horses ahead!"

"Impossible!" I cried "We're still above ten thousand feet."

With that I groped forward to see for myself. Sure enough, I saw foaming white crests flashing past beneath us, so close we could have reached down and wetted our hands. We crept into Manby keeping a low profile, saying not a word to anybody. Neither of us was a 'Navigator', we were used to flying monoposto, which means every man for himself.

Halfway through the course, we spent three days in Germany at the combined Services HQ in Munchen Gladbach. One evening, Peter and I decided to go 'Night Clubbing', ending up at about three am rather drunk and very hungry. Staggering out into the street, we managed to grab a taxi, shouting "Essen! Essen!" to a bewildered driver, indicating our needs by means of sign language. We collapsed into the taxi, and knew no more until rudely awakened by the driver who was likewise shouting "Essen! Essen!" It took a few seconds for the truth to dawn on us - there was no doubt about it, we really were in Essen! After a cup of coffee, we persuaded the driver to take us back to Munchen - a very expensive misadventure.

Towards the end of the Course we were asked for our preferences for posting. I took it for granted that I would get a flying appointment, so when I was told it was the Air Ministry again for me, I was shattered beyond belief. A second tour flying a desk would be a disaster, and I asked Gus Walker, the Commandant, to do his best to change it. He good humouredly told me to belt up, and accept my new post gracefully. Besides, he said, it was one of the plum jobs in the RAF, and an almost certain guarantee to further promotion. I knew Gus was talking sense, I had always had a lot of time for him, he was a great leader, so the Air Ministry it was to be. I was to take over a Branch called OR23, responsible for future RAF Fighter requirements.

CHAPTER SIXTEEN

LANDLORD IN ABSENTIA

I succeeded Wing Commander Tommy Balmforth DFC, an experienced Fighter Pilot, with effect from 15 December, 1956. Our accommodation problem was solved by being allocated a Married Quarter at RAF Hornchurch, thus committing me to a daily grind, on the Upminster Line between Elm Park and Charing Cross, involving twenty-one stops each way!

I was lucky to have two extremely clued-up Squadron Leaders working with me, Peter Thorne, who had been a Test Pilot at A & AEE Boscombe Down, and Duncan McIver, who inter alia had done an operational tour on Javelin Night Fighters. It turned out that I was still able to get in some jet-flying, including a fortnight's detachment at RAF Odiham, flying Javelins with 46 Squadron.

As Head of the Branch, I was responsible for several interesting projects. From example, I wrote the original OR for the Hawker, PV1127 later to become famous as the Harrier Jump-Jet. This necessitated my working closely with Sir Sydney Camm and his Design Team, including Hawkers' Chief Test Pilot, Bill Bedford. Another assignment was the NATO Lightweight Strike Fighter project, for which several EEC countries had submitted design studies, to be followed up by evaluation trials of prototypes. One of these was the Folland 'Gnat', later turned to good account by the world famous Red Arrows.

I made frequent trips to the Continent to attend NATO Meetings to decide the successful contender. Fiats of Turin won the contract with their 'G 91'. It was regarded as a political, rather than a practical expedience. I was also thrown in at the deep end with the new highly sophisticated long range, 2-seat 'All Weather' fighter-recce aircraft, labelled OR 329, but the project was scrubbed out by Duncan Sandys, the then Minister of Defence, in his 1957 White Paper. Later, however, the venture was resurrected as the TSR2, which was actually built and flown, but again, for economy reasons, was scrapped.

All in all I had very little to complain about, Gus Walker was right, it was a very good job indeed. Seldom a day went by without my phone ringing with invitations to lunch, from reps in the Aircraft Industry such as Hawkers, English Electric, Vickers, Follands and Deccas. I wined and dined at all the top West End restaurants at their expense. Two of these reps came to be among my closest friends, Wing Commander John Hyde (Decca Navigator), and Group Captain 'Mary' Tudor (Follands), sadly both deceased. With hindsight I know now that I was learning a new trade

Postprandial Group of past Commanding Officers of the Oxford University Air Squadron and other University dignitaries, on the occasion of a presentation to Miss Olive Round, MBE, to mark her retirement, after 45 years as the Squadron Secretary. Left to Right: Wg Cdr Hamish Harvey — Sqdn Ldr Margiotta, then CO of the OUAS — Wg Cdr Mike Constable-Maxwell — N.K. — ACM Sir Christopher Foxley-Norris — N.K. — MRAF Sir Michael Beetham — ACM Sir John Gingell, the then Black Rod — A University dignitary — Wg Cdr John Douch — the Author

RAF Flying College, Manby — visit to Bristol Aeroplane Company, Filton, 1956

On the lawn of the Officers' Mess, RAF Little Rissington at a CFS Reunion Dinner, Summer 1966.
GHNE, Paddy Dunn, U.K., U.K., Ivor Broom, U.K., U.K.

LANDLORD IN ABSENTIA

- that of gastronomy, and the ability to put it to good use.

I had a fortnight's leave at Easter (1957), which we spent in Pembrokeshire with Pan's Aunt from Cheltenham, who had a bungalow in a small hamlet called Newgale on the coast, near the RNAS Station at Brawdy.

After a few years in the Cotswolds we had developed a taste for antiques, so one morning we went to an auction sale of the contents of the Castle Hotel, Haverfordwest, a typical County Town Hotel, large rambling and old-fashioned, with a wealth of pictures, prints, antique furniture and artifacts of every kind. The sale was in the old Ball Room, where we wandered round looking for bargains. Suddenly there was a shout from across the room

"Hal! Hal!"

Looking round I spotted a familiar face, that of a German artist called Friedrich Könekamp, whom we knew ten years ago down in Sennen Cove. It turned out that he had moved from Cornwall to Pembrokeshire, and was living in a cottage he had bought from Richard Llewellyn, author of 'How Green is my Valley'. It was on the side of a volcano-like mountain called 'Carn Ingli' - Mountain of the Angels - overlooking the small coastal village of Newport, halfway between Fishguard and Cardigan. He asked us to tea the following day. Knowing we were keen on pubs, Friedrich suggested we should take a look at the 'Trewern Arms', a village pub near Newport, shortly coming up for auction. For some inexplicable reason we did just that, and fell for it.

The Trewern was a solid little pub, nestling alongside a small salmon river called the Nevern, which flowed into the estuary nearby. The structure was entirely of local stone of wondrous colours, softly reflecting a mixture of red, beige, green, yellow and blue. The road past the pub curved away to the right, over an old triple-arched bridge built of the same stone, beyond which could be seen the Church, Village School, and a few cottages sheltered in a delightful valley across the stream. It was a blissful setting.

Pan detested living in London, she saw this as a heaven-sent chance of 'doing her own thing'. With a week's leave to go, I agreed to find the owner and try to do a deal. I had no idea what the pub might fetch, nor where the money would come from. We found out that the Trewern had been on lease to a Miss Nesta Williams who, after discovering that her fiancée, an affluent and smooth-talking gent, was already married, slipped and fell down the stairs on her Wedding night and died.

We tracked down the owner, a local Squire named Edward Lloyd,

SPIT AND SAWDUST

who daily frequented the Private Bar of the Black Lion Hotel, Cardigan. Introducing ourselves to the Landlady, Mrs Moreton Smith, we found that the key to Edward's heart was several large gins in rapid succession. It wasn't long, perhaps a few days, before Edward Lloyd cancelled the auction, and agreed a purchase price of £3,500 for the pub, ten acres of land, some cow-sheds, and about half a mile of fishing. A wealthy Birmingham business man, Eric Tomkinson, an old family friend, guaranteed us for the money, and by 1 May we had the title deeds.

Before my leave was up, we returned several times to the Trewern, and made the acquaintance of the late Nesta Williams' two spinster sisters who, after a fashion, were running the pub until it was sold. One was Clara, the other Evelyn, both in their sixties. 'Crafty' Clara went out of her way to make matters difficult for us, but Evelyn displayed explicit symptoms of eroticism, by trying to sidle up next to me on the Bar settle, whenever she saw an opportunity to fondle my legs and thighs, which I found singularly repellent, although much to the amusement of the company.

We 'marched out' of our Hornchurch quarter in May and I rented a bedsitter at 111 Ebury Street, Victoria. Pan went back to Pembrokeshire and, helped by her Aunt and sister Paddy, took over the Trewern on 1 June. It was a nail-biting adventure.

Prior to 1 June, the handover day, Crafty Clara laid on an auction sale of all the pub furniture, which was put outside onto the road along the riverside. Buyers sat on the wall, while the auctioneer conducted the bidding from the porch. Luckily the weather was dry and sunny. Pan managed to buy most of the Bar furnishings, including two wooden settles for two and sixpence each, but she missed the double bed. A couple of days later I arrived on leave, to find we had to sleep on a mattress on the floor. There were no bedside tables or curtains. The only lighting was from candles, oil lamps, and some calor gas ceiling lights in the bar, with gas piped from bottles under the stairs.

The 'In-going' was minimal, a half-full kilderkin of draught Worthington, a mixed case of spirits, a few minerals, and a case of Seagers 'Green Goddess' cocktail, which evidently had been Nesta's favourite tipple. The whole lot didn't amount to more than twenty-five pounds. We never did sell any Green Goddess!

Electricity was our number one priority, so I drove into Fishguard to bribe the Manager of the local Electricity Board, Islwyn Harries, to send somebody to wire us up. He laid it on straightaway, and by sunset on our first day of business, we had the Bar all lit up, plus lights in our bedroom,

LANDLORD IN ABSENTIA

a thrilling moment. At this stage we had literally run out of money, exemplified by the grim realisation that we needed a cash float to give change, should any customers turn up. Pan emptied out the contents of her handbag, and I went through my pockets. Between us we scraped up several half-crowns, two shilling pieces, and some coppers. By the end of our first evening we had collected a few one pound notes!

In no time at all my leave was over. I 'borrowed' some money from the till, and bought myself a ticket from Fishguard to Paddington. For the next two and a half years I played the triple role of absentee landlord, weekday bachelor in Ebury Street, and weekend barman in Pembrokeshire. I used to catch one of the several Irish Boat Trains on a regular run from Paddington to Fishguard every Friday afternoon and evening between three and ten pm. Which one I managed to pick up would depend on how soon I could get away from the office. I seldom if ever caught the early one and occasionally, of course, I would miss a weekend, when my duty took me to the Continent for meetings on the NATO Lightweight Strike-Fighter. Things worked out pretty well, surprisingly enough; having a 'Spit and Sawdust' in the family didn't interfere with my RAF job, which I enjoyed to the full. Every Sunday evening I boarded the night-sleeper from Carmarthen which with luck would arrive at Paddington before six am, enabling me to get back to Ebury Street in time for a bath, breakfast, and a leisurely walk across the Park, to be in my office by nine am on Monday morning. If the weather was bad there were plenty of buses from Victoria. I used to reserve Sunday night sleepers for six months at a stretch.

In the early stages the idea of giving up my RAF career never entered my head, I merely thought that once my Tour at Air Ministry was over, we would sell the Trewern Arms, with luck at a profit. However, in the late 'fifties' a scheme known as 'The Golden Bowler' was introduced, offering early retirement with pension, plus a handsome gratuity, for Officers with little or no chance of promotion. By now Pan was settling down and enjoying herself at the pub. She had built the Trewern up into a thriving business. She talked me into applying for the 'GB', so I agreed to try my luck, and submitted an application in 1959, but it was turned down. I was told the reason was that I was a fairly senior Wing Commander with good career prospects, much Government money having been already spent on me when I took the Flying College Course. I wasn't upset about it, but Pan took a different view, she was determined to carry on at the Trewern, which was now a success story.

In the end, after lengthy and sometimes heated discussions, she persuaded me to tender my resignation. I went across to Adastral House to see my old friend Birdie Wilson, the Wing Commander 'Postings', and handed my cards in. Birdie quite rightly told me I was a fool, because a Group Captain's Post was in the pipeline for me, but it was too late, I had crossed the Rubicon, the Trewern Arms had won the day, and was to remain 'Spit and Sawdust' Mark 2.

"My problem now" said Birdie "is what to do with you? You can't be boss of OR23 any more, and you've still a year to go to qualify for a pension."

"Give me the easiest job you can find, Birdie, be a pal!"

So it was that I was assigned to HQ Eastern Command (Army), at Hounslow in Middlesex, as their 'Air Liaison Officer'. The job was a sinecure. Most of the time I was away down in West Wales, except when attending rehabilitation courses, which included studying for a Licensed Trade Diploma, and classes at the Cordon Bleu School of Cookery, Marylebone Lane, London, where I took general cookery, sauce making, and patisserie. In short, I was now into the 'up-market' cookery business. I needed to be, once my RAF salary stopped, I had to find a substitute fast!

One of our first visitors to the Trewern Arms, in the course of my three years' weekly 'to-ings' and 'fro-ings' between London and Pembrokeshire, was an old RAF colleague of mine, Hardy McHardy, and his wife 'Nobbie'. They were living near Llandeilo in Carmarthenshire. Hardy was on Hurricanes with 229 Squadron at Northolt during the Battle of Britain, and was shot down by Me190's over the French coast on Saturday, 26 October, 1940. He was captured and spent the rest of the war in Prisoner of War Camps in Germany. I first met him in 1953, when I took the Oldenburg Wing to RAF Sylt for a month's detachment on Weapons Training. Hardy was a pilot flying Tempests on the Target Towing Flight. It was February, and very very cold, the whole Island covered in snow most of the time, seriously limiting our flying programme. We were grounded for over a week, consequently parties brewed up in the Mess, mostly instigated by Hardy McHardy, who was a natural extrovert. He was tall, thin, with wispy dark hair and long angular features, set off by a pair of bushy eyebrows and a large handlebar moustache, reminiscent of Flying Officer Kyte, the celebrated wartime cartoon character.

In 1956 Hardy fell desperately ill, the diagnosis being cancer of the colon, possibly triggered off by his five years as a prisoner of war. He was still only in his early thirties when he was invalided out of the

LANDLORD IN ABSENTIA

Service. He was recommended to a Consultant in Bath, who had apparently begun some experiments with colostomy, which was the operation to connect up the intestines to an artificial alimentary canal, terminating in a bag attached to an outlet from the abdomen. Hardy insisted on knowing the truth, and was told he had only a few years to live. He agreed to undergo colostomy, on the understanding that if he survived the operation, he would write a report on his progress, together with suggestions and recommendations for improvements, especially with regard to the bag, and its connection to the outlet which Hardy called his 'bayonet clip'.

When Hardy and Nobbie turned up at the Trewern Arms in 1958, he had already had a second operation, and was fitted with what he described as his 'Ministry of Aircraft Production modifications'. He drank a great deal, who could blame him with perhaps only a couple of years to live? He would laughingly say that alcohol flowed freely through his new plastic guts, without the risk of getting ulcers, enabling him to become intoxicated with none of the usual ill-effects such as headaches, nausea and 'squitters' (diarrhoea). One day he arrived at the Trewern Arms, and coming up to the Bar to order a drink, I couldn't help but notice a strong fetid smell like the 'honeywagon' gives off on its daily round. I threw him a broad hint and the penny dropped, whereupon he vanished into the Gents to emerge a few minutes later with a broad grin on his face.

"Apologies, old boy" he cried "I completely forgot my cockpit drill. I was coming into land with undercarriage up, radiator gills shut and safety straps undone!"

Hardy was a passable artist, and used to make pocket money (or should I say beer money?) painting pub signs for various Hostelries around the West Country. The last two Christmases of his life he and Nobbie came to stay with us to help with the decorations. It became a feature of the district, attracting revellers to the Trewern Arms from as far apart as Aberystwyth and Swansea. Hardy turned the whole affair into a 'Yuletide Festival Week'.

Not long after I retired from the RAF, Nobbie phoned one day to say that Hardy was very sick in Carmarthen Hospital. I immediately downed tools, and motored the odd forty miles to see him. He was cheerful but resigned, he knew the end was near. I spoke to the Chief Medical Superintendent, who told me the only hope was to take him to Bath Hospital, where they would have to open him up again in a last ditch effort to prolong his life. For the second time I downed tools, and drove to Bath, where I found Hardy, having had another operation, full of cheer and optimism. His spirit was irrepressible, but I could see from the look of him that he was sinking fast. He told me that as soon as he was 'let out' he was going to book a long cruise in the Caribbean, and blow the expense. Sadly I started the long journey back to the Trewern, knowing it was the end of the road for him. Sure enough, within twenty-four hours, Nobbie phoned to say that he had peacefully passed away.

Hardy McHardy was remarkably brave and resolute, a credit to his fellow men. He cared very much about people, and desperately wanted the world to know whatever could be learnt from his traumatic experiences. He didn't live to know it, but colostomy today is as commonplace as shelling peas.

CHAPTER SEVENTEEN

LANDLORD IN SITU

The date for my voluntary retirement was set for September 1960. I still kept in flying practice, by making occasional trips in an old Meteor 8 from North Weald. About the middle of August I flew the Meteor 8 to Pembrokeshire for a final beat-up. News got around that I was coming, there were locals by the score lining the road and the bridge over the River Nevern. I gave the Trewern Arms a good working over, finally landing at RAF Aberporth, where I just scraped in on the fifteen hundred yards runway. Memories of Medjez-el-Bab! I stayed that night at the Trewern, returning to North Weald the next morning. That was my last solo flight on a jet aircraft; within days I was back as a civilian.

A welcome home party to celebrate my retirement from the RAF was laid on in the pub. A whole sheep was cooking on a spit in the enormous open fireplace in the 'Brewhouse Bar', supervised by Dominic Colella, our part-time gardener and handyman. Colella had been twice a Prisoner of War, once during Mussolini's Invasion of Abyssinia, and later in the Western Desert in World War Two. Afterwards he was interned in a Prisoner of War Camp in North Pembrokeshire, and on release settled down to live near Newport, working on the land, helping farmers at harvest-time, and generally making himself useful to the community. He was a fabulous worker, a 'one-off', gentle and generous to a fault.

About fifty guests were invited. It was a splendid evening, I wore my uniform for the last time. Several gate-crashers turned up after closing time whom we summarily dismissed, which later led to what might be described as a tricky situation, were it not for the fact that we were 'well in' with the police. At about four thirty am Sergeant Savage, the local police boss, an ex-Commando and judo expert, turned up unexpectedly; we were all more or less anaesthetised by now! Sergeant Savage confronted me, arms akimbo, when even in my inebrious state, I was startled to spot his pyjamas on under his uniform, as he started to speak.

"I have just received information, Sir, that 'after-hours' drinking is taking place on these premises."

"Ish jat sho, Scherjunt?" I replied with dignity. "Scho shorry to drag you out of bed scho early in the morning, but you schee itch my lasht day in the Schervish."

With a twinkle in his eye he accepted a large Scotch. Reaching unsteadily to my full height I threw him a meteoric salute.

SPIT AND SAWDUST

"Djoo reelije djish ish jer larsht time yew'll shee me in yoonie, hic, yoonieform?"

With that Sergeant Savage, standing up to his full height of six foot three inches, took three smart backward steps in military fashion, simultaneously bringing his right arm up in a fantastic salute.

"Indeed I do Sir, but it's not the last time you'll see me in uniform!"

Sergeant Savage was later promoted to Inspector at Milford Haven. He always had a soft spot for the Trewern. He never gave us any trouble provided we kept to the rules.

My ageing Mother, still at the Noel Arms, Chipping Campden, now decided to retire. Although I had taken the Cordon Bleu Cookery Courses, with the intention of creating a top-class restaurant at the Trewern, I had not so far had any practical experience, but as luck would have it my mother's chef, Francis Fane, asked me if he could come down to West Wales to join us in our new venture. Francis, born in Stockport, Lancs, of a well to do local family, helped us to open our new restaurant by Easter, 1961. It was converted from the old pub lounge. We added a small extension at the back to give more kitchen space. At a squash, we could seat sixteen by 'double-banking', and surprisingly enough it worked.

Within eighteen months we were in the 'Good Food Guide', signalised by a personal visit from the late Raymond Postgate himself. We were the first in Wales to be in the Guide, apart from the Crown Inn, Llwyndaffydd, Cardiganshire. I was gradually getting into cooking, but it took me a good two years slogging away in the kitchen, before I was competent to take over completely. Francis, now an Old Age Pensioner, was due to retire so, I knew the time had come to handle the catering side on my own, whilst Pan performed as 'front-of-the-house' director, at which she was exceptionally competent.

As the business grew, so the pressure built up, persuading us that we needed a refuge to which we could retreat when things got on top of us. Edward Lloyd, our erstwhile vendor, came into the pub one morning and said he was selling one of his properties to rake in a spot more gin money, so we pricked our ears up. It sounded just the place we were looking for, a three-bedroomed stone built cottage, nestling in a small valley at the foot of Carn Ingli, with five acres of land and a trout steam running past the front door. The way to it was across a shallow ford, seldom used by the public and, although within a mere two miles of Newport, it was known to but a few of the locals. We asked Edward how much he wanted for it.

LANDLORD IN SITU

"A thousand pounds" he replied. "No more, no less. It's occupied by tenants who haven't paid rent for over six years, so I've slapped an Eviction Order on them."

"Can we have first refusal?" Pan asked.

"It's a deal. Fetch me a half-crown out of the till!"

Wondering why, she handed the coin to him. Taking the half-crown in his hand Edward said

"I accept this as a Bond of Sale. The cottage is yours as soon as it becomes vacant."

About two years later Edward Lloyd came to the Trewern to tell us his tenants had at last departed, and the cottage was ours for the taking. In the interim, property prices had soared, of course, and by now the cottage must have been worth at least three to four thousand pounds. It so happened we were already in the middle of building an extension to the Trewern, which was going to cost us twenty-five thousand pounds minimum.

"Thanks a lot for telling us, Edward," We chorused, "We couldn't possibly afford it now!"

"Nonsense, it's yours for a thousand pounds, as promised two years ago. Surely to can afford that? Bedsides, you can pay me whenever you like, say over a year or two."

We looked at each other in disbelief. It was too good to be true. Edward was a man of his word, he insisted that the half-crown was a legal deposit. All we had do do was spend a little money to modernise the cottage and, thanks to Edward's generosity, the outstanding debt could wait. He had recently sold another property somewhere, so he wasn't short of gin money!

We finished the new extension in 1963, which more than doubled the size of the Trewern. We had a large purpose-built kitchen, servery, vegetable preparation room, staff toilet, boiler room and so on, not forgetting a wine cellar with racks for about a thousand bottles. At the rear, we added on a room for Dinner Dances and functions with a separate bar made from an ancient cheese press. Most of the furnishings were items with a history, such as tables from the old London Mint, pews from Lincoln Cathedral, and numerous artefacts including table lamps from St Donats Castle, Cardiff, which during the twenties was the Estate of Randolph Hearst, the American newspaper magnate, where he installed his mistress, the film actress Marion Davies.

One major problem remained, where was the music to come from? We remembered that when I was CO of the OUAS, the University Jazz

SPIT AND SAWDUST

Club used to play for our Squadron Dances. Ray Blazdell, the pianist, was a Member of the Squadron, so I telephoned the inimitable Miss Round to contact Ray, with the idea of forming a Jazz Group to play at the Trewern during the summer vacation. Response was immediate. By early July Ray, together with Peter Morgan the drummer, Dave Cooper the saxophonist, and Bob Hall on Double Bass, were installed in our cottage, and they played every night except Sundays throughout the summer until late September. It was for Diners only. The cost, including an à la carte menu and dancing, amounted to at least ten pounds each, a tidy sum for those days. We were fully booked throughout the season.

Our Jazz Group, now calling themselves the 'Dark Blues', played at the Trewern for four consecutive summer seasons. Their fame soon spread, and before long they were playing for Royalty. They played for Prince Charles' twenty-first Birthday Party and later for his Engagement Party, to mention but two events on the London Social Calendar.

Despite opposition from the Deacons and Ministers of the Welsh Chapel, the Court granted us a special Licence to serve drink with food and dancing until one o'clock in the morning, something unheard of in Wales at that time.

It was a long day for us, up at eight o'clock, and never in bed before two o'clock the following morning. As each autumn came around we were on our knees, so we would be looking forward to a break. We joined the RAF Ski Club and every January we combined a fortnight in Zermatt with a week in London staying at the RAF Club in Piccadilly. We took in Hotelympia at Earls Court, and the January Sales.

For my sins, I was persuaded one year to enter a competition at Hotelympia for the Beer and Sandwich Serving Championship, to be run off in six daily heats. I won my heat, and the Final was decided a few weeks later at the 'Horseshoe', next door to the Dominion Cinema, Tottenham Court Road. To my utter amazement I won the competition, and was presented with a handsome silver tankard. Later that night I collapsed into a sleeper bound, as I thought, for Carmarthen, but after a pretty bibulous evening I managed to board the wrong train, and ended up instead at Par in Cornwall in the early hours. It took a bit of explaining away!

It was on one of these jaunts to London to visit Hotelympia, that we nearly came to be arrested in the RAF Club. I used to buy all our steaks for the Trewern Restaurant from a firm called Peter Dumenil Limited, in Smithfield Market. The procedure was that they put our meat order on the Irish Night Mail from Paddington, which we picked up in Fishguard

LANDLORD IN SITU

Harbour Station the same morning. Just after Christmas, one whole consignment of fillets, despatched in the usual sewn-up sack, arrived badly contaminated, so I phoned Peter Dumenil, who immediately despatched a replacement order, with the suggestion that I should keep the offending fillets deep-frozen until I could return them at a later date. It happened that we were due in London within a week, having booked the Honeymoon Suite at the RAF Club. I decided to bring the frozen fillets up by car, and deliver them direct to Smithfield Market. We checked in at the Club, unloaded the car and took everything up to our suite. Without another thought I dumped the large sack of meat, still partially frozen, onto the marble floor of the bathroom, where we left it while we went out for a meal and a spot of shopping. Upon our return, the Club seemed to be in some sort of a turmoil. There were two Spanish chambermaids in hysterics in the hall, some other people aimlessly dashing hither and thither, and Reception was in an uproar, where two obvious plainclothes policemen were interrogating staff.

We were quickly spotted, the Manager pouncing on us with a wild look in his eyes, something between fright and horror.

"What on earth's the matter?" I protested.

"Matter? Would you kindly explain to these gentlemen from the police station what is in that sack?"

"What sack?" I almost shouted, I had momentarily forgotten about the fillets.

"The sack in your bathroom, the floor is swimming in blood." One of the Detectives interposed

"Suppose you tell us, Sir, what is in that sack"

I could see what they were getting at. The fillets, of course.

They must have thought the sack contained the cut-up remains of a human body. Memories of the gruesome Setty Murder case still doubtless lingered on in their minds.

"I think you had better come with us, Sir" he added, with a grisly glance at us.

"I'm sure there's no need for that, Officer. If you will bear with me I can explain everything."

Of course, I had overlooked the fact that central heating is highly conducive to rapid defrost. With that I gave them the full story. The panic subsided, whilst the Spanish ladies were hastily bundled away into the servants' quarters, still shrieking invectives. That a gruesome murder at the RAF Club had failed to unveil itself was, I am sure, a bitter disappointment!

SPIT AND SAWDUST

The crunch came in 1966 with the introduction of the Breathalyser. No one knew what the long-term consequences would be, but one thing was for sure, according to the 'Morning Advertiser', the daily paper for the Licensed Trade, country pubs relying almost solely on 'wheels for the wherewithal' were facing bankruptcy. Our overdraft, which we had raised to cover the extension costs, was paid off in part, so we paused to review the situation.

Thumbing through advertisements of 'Pubs for Sale', we noted with dismay a drastic drop in prices for Free Houses, indeed our already dwindling trade figures bore witness to this trend. It was obvious that we were in a bit of a jam. This new development, coupled with signs of physical exhaustion after nearly ten years of sweat and toil, plus a nagging yen for a change of scenery, and finally maybe a spot of panic, misled us into putting the Trewern Arms on the Market. There where plenty of vultures around looking for pickings, and one of them, a nameless 'foreign gentleman', persuaded us after prolonged and agonising negotiations, to part with our pub for a mere twenty-three thousand pounds, a fraction of its true value, as we were soon to find out. Within three years he sold the Trewern for eighty-five thousand pounds. Our self-reproach and mortification knew no bounds, but the deed was done, there was no going back.

From this wreckage we managed to salvage enough capital to invest in an old property in the centre of Newport village, just two miles up the road from the Trewern Arms. Until recently it had been a small but busy little clothing and haberdashery business. It was ideal for conversion into an up-market restaurant. We managed to complete it by doing much of the work ourselves, thereby saving sufficient funds to pay for furnishings, and a comprehensive range of modern catering equipment. We gave it the somewhat parochial name of 'The Pantry', after our cottage in the valley, but what's in a name so long as we were able to deliver the goods?

Within a year we were back in the 'Good Food Guide', and shortly after that we were awarded a 'Star' in the Egon Ronay Guide, which meant that we were on the map again.

The Pantry was small in comparison to the Trewern, small enough in fact to run the business ourselves with minimal staff, almost all of them part-timers. With several years catering experience behind us, we had come to realise that 'small is beautiful'. I did the cooking single-handed, Pan supervising the decor, table reservations, and dining-room layout, amongst many other chores. We looked to the village for our 'Mrs Mops', 'washer-uppers' and waitresses. It worked well, and soon we were seeing

LANDLORD IN SITU

a useful profit margin again.

It was during the 1968 Henley Royal Regatta that one morning I found myself talking to Maurice Buxton, a Cambridge rowing Blue, a Director of Barclays Bank, and Honorary Treasurer of the Leander Club. He knew that since retiring from the RAF I had become involved in the pub and restaurant business. He was telling me how Leander was going through a bad patch.

"George, Leander is deep in the red, would it interest you to know that the Committee is looking for someone new to regenerate it?"

"Hell, Maurice, what are you suggesting?" I countered. "Do you seriously expect me to ditch a successful restaurant business, to become a glorified Steward of my own Club?"

"Well, not exactly, George, but there could be many advantages. Your own self-contained rent free flat, for example, no rates, no housekeeping expenses, and three to four thousand a year pocket money, think about it."

It was undeniably food for thought.

Driving westwards back to Pembrokeshire the following day, the Regatta over for another year, I began to conjure up the all too familiar vision of deserted boat tents, the huge Marquees along the river bank Enclosures, now stripped of the glamour, gilt chairs and folding tables sprawling in drunken disorder across the trodden brown grass littered with strawberry stalks, fragmented lobster shells, Champagne bottles, broken glass, and countless Pimms No 1 goblets, empty, save for remains of sodden cloyed fruit for company to tell the tale. I had seen it all before. Yet Henley for me was, and always will be, something very special, recalling both joyous and sad memories, triumph and tragedy, thoughts of those once so close to me now wiped out by war. How was it I survived, and not they? I asked myself. Where was the logic, the reason behind it all? Was it destiny, fate or just pure luck of the draw? And now at that moment was I predestined to move in and take over Leander?

Leander Club was also something very special. I recalled with pleasure an occasion during the war, while I was stationed at Aston Down. I had been given a short leave, so we decided on three nights Bed and Breakfast at Henley-on-Thames with a Mrs O'Hara, whom I knew in my Oxford days. I popped into Leander, and to my surprise found that Potter the Steward, with his high wing collar and morning coat, was still there keeping the Club open for Members who, like myself, sought brief respite from the war front. He was delighted to see me, and agreed to lay on a dinner for us. It was a repast such as we had never seen since before

SPIT AND SAWDUST

the war. He must have broken all the food rationing regulations. We started with Sole Mennière and a half bottle of Chablis, then fillet steak with a bottle of Vosne-Romanée (vintage forgotten), crusty bread rolls, and real butter. We finished with crême brulée, Stilton, and a bottle of Quinta da Noval 1914 with coffee. It was a magic and unforgettable evening.

It now seemed as it I was about to become another 'Potter', ministering to the constant needs and often excessive demands of senior Members and young oarsmen alike. I couldn't deny that we needed extra money to build new clock rooms at the Pantry, so maybe this Leander venture would prove a godsend.

After I got home we discussed matters at great length. There was a young man whom I had taught to cook at the Trewern Arms, and who had shown exceptional talent. It so happened that he was available. We made the decision, he was just the man to run the Pantry for us in our absence. I phoned Maurice Buxton to say we would give it a go, on the understanding that it would be for a maximum of two years, which I figured would be long enough to get the Club back on its feet, to pay for our new cloak rooms at the Pantry, and to see the Club through to the 1972 Olympics. The British Olympic Squad was training from Leander, and most of them were Members of the Club anyway.

Maurice put it to the Committee, who straightaway agreed to my taking over before the end of the year.

By November 1969 we were installed, and spent two happy and memorable years in the driving seat. Running such an illustrious body as Leander was no walk-over, maybe being a Member myself was at times a disadvantage, but in general we had a smooth passage, and the Club finances began to stabilise. Within months of taking over, we organised a Champagne Luncheon for about one hundred and fifty members of the local branch of the Conservative Party, many of whom were also Leander Members. It was a great success. People were reluctant to leave, so in the end Pan put the Bar shutters up. I came through from the kitchen to see how things were going, when I overheard Pan tearing an almighty strip off two or three elderly Members, who were clamouring for more drinks. I recognised one of them, Sir Richard Turnbull, who until recently had been the Governor of Aden.

"For Christ's sake Pan, do you realise who you are talking to?" I whispered.

"No I don't, and what's more I don't care. They were saying it's about time the new Manager got down to it, and cleared up all the litter round the garden. I told them it's about time some of the Members pulled their fingers our and cleared it up themselves!"

"Oh Lord!" I groaned.

It happened that our bedroom overlooked the garden, which was away from the riverside. The next morning, at about seven am, we were woken by a systematic scraping noise beneath our window. I struggled out of bed to take a look. To my utter amazement I saw Sir Richard Turnbull, togged up in a navy blue boiler suit and wellies, with a rake, brush and wheel-barrow, doing a first-class tidying-up job!

Out of the blue one day we had an unsolicited offer for the Pantry Restaurant from Robin Evans, an Old Salopian like myself, who originated from Pembrokeshire. He had resigned his Commission in the Army, and had decided to go into the catering business, to which end he was working in the kitchens of a well-known restaurant in Bath. He made an offer we couldn't refuse. The take-over date coincided with the end of our two year stint at Henley.

We now had to figure out what to do next; clearly it must be related to catering in one form or another. We hit on the idea of a Village Post Office and Stores, its special appeal being the idea of shutting shop around six o'clock in the evening, to enjoy a few leisure hours such as going to the local pub, playing cricket on the village green, and so on. I can hear the cynics having a good laugh!

The summer of 1972 saw us installed in the Post Office and Stores in the small village of Barford St Martin, halfway between Wilton and Shaftesbury. It was a large house with six bedrooms and two bathrooms, combining two separate units each with its own staircase. This happened to suit us, well because an old friend, Charles Levi, had written from Nairobi to ask whether we would agree to take him on as a partner, if he put some capital into the business. Amongst other things he part-owned an establishment called 'The Dambusters', situated in a hangar on the old airfield at Eastleigh, but he was becoming disenchanted with Kenya. It was all agreed, and before long he moved in with us. The handy lay-out of the premises enabled us to remain independent of one another. Charles took over responsibility for the Post Office.

There were extensive out-buildings on the site, including an old-fashioned bakery, and enough room for a car park. The vendors were crafty; their accounts showed no figures for baking, their story being that quantity bread production had long since ceased, although the husband used to bake a few loaves to sell in the shop to keep his hand in. So imagine our disbelief when, after the hand-over was completed, we were coolly informed that there was a daily baker's round extending from Dinton to Salisbury. They had been afraid to disclose it to us lest we changed our minds and refused to sign the contract. A battered Ford Transit van was on the Inventory, which was used for deliveries. We had no choice but to keep the round going while we reviewed the situation. I was lucky to have had very considerable cooking experience, because commercial baking, though ostensibly painless, is in reality a complicated and lengthy process, enough to intimidate even the most enthusiastic amateur.

We had about a fortnight to spare before taking over the business, so we decided to spend a few days in Pembrokeshire, looking up some of our old friends and customers. One of them happened to be Dai Evans who ran the Grove Bakery in St Davids. He was a character, and had been known for years throughout the county as 'Dai Crust' until recently, when Prince Charles, following his Investiture at Caernarvon Castle, was invited by the Mayor and Corporation of the Borough of Haverfordwest to a special Luncheon, in honour of the occasion. Dai Crust, being the best known baker in the district, was asked to bake the bread rolls. From that day on Dai Evans was known as 'Dai Upper Crust'. This story has gone the rounds to such an extent that its origin is blurred by the telling of it, but I can personally vouch for Dai Evans as being the one and only 'Dai Upper Crust'.

I telephoned Dai to give him the news that we had bought a Bakery in Wiltshire, by default as it were, so would he give me a few tips?

"Deeowl Bach" he said "You'd better come over to St Davids for a couple of days."

So I went to the Grove Bakery, to spend many hilarious but instructive hours, while 'Dai Upper Crust' showed me the ropes. He was a true artist, in the sense that he derived total fulfilment from the creation of bread from yeast.

"Look here Bach", he said, waving his arms round and above his head like some Druid soothsayer "Yeast is a living thing, it is alive, it is God's Minister who gives life to the world!" I was impassioned and fascinated by his genuine emotion. I have no doubt that these few moments with Dai Upper Crust strengthened my resolve to cope with the task ahead.

Back at Barford once more, I found myself rising at three thirty am every morning, to go through the whole laborious process of first firing the oven to get it red hot, making the dough with an enormous ancient mixer, then heaving it out to transpose onto a wooden bench where it would slowly start to rise beneath a cover of old flour sacks. Meanwhile the many loaf tins were to be greased with a canvas rag, before laying them out on large metal baking sheets. Once the dough had risen, now looking like the hide of some enormous reptile pushing its way up to the surface, Pan and I would knock it down by cutting it into one pound and two pound lots, which had to be weighed individually to comply with strict Weights and Measures regulations. We then carefully tucked them into the loaf tins, and left them to rise again. Finally I heaved the loaded baking sheets into the oven, which consisted of two brick-lined furnaces, one above the other.

Thoughts of village cricket, and pleasant evenings in the pub, quickly evaporated. We found ourselves in an entirely new world, going to bed after an early supper, and getting up again while the whole village snored. The bread round itself I found especially distasteful - driving the ramshackle Transit in fits and starts through the streets of Salisbury, dismounting at intervals with the brimming bread basket, suspended by its handle on my forearm, as I knocked on doors or rang bells. Frequently I was waved at in an insolent manner to go round to the back door. I used to wonder what on earth someone like Maurice Buxton, or Members of the Leander Committee for that matter, would think on seeing me like this. They would perhaps rush unbelieving into the nearest pub for a stiff drink to steady the nerves!

In no time at all we realised the bread round must be deleted from the 'script'. It wasn't part of our original economic strategy anyway, at the time we bought the business. It didn't take us long to discover that it was a hard slog for a paltry profit. The Grocery Trade proved to be little better, because of the new threat posed by the Supermarkets. Villagers were losing the habit of doing their shopping on a day-to-day basis, instead they would take the bus into Salisbury once a week to buy in bulk. The only profitable bit was the Post Office because with it went a small GPO salary which helped the cash flow, but was hardly a living for the three of us.

The time had come for decision making. Charles began to hear the call of Africa again, and I felt an urge to go back to real cooking. We resolved to convert the whole concern into a Guest House, the shop and PO area to be changed into a 'Cordon Blue' restaurant, and the old Bakery into a modern kitchen. Within a short space of time this is exactly what happened. We gave our notice in to the Post Office, we paid off Charles' share, and he returned to his beloved Nairobi. Within a few months we quadrupled our cash flow. We called it the 'Corner Kitchen',

SPIT AND SAWDUST

and we were back in the Food Guides within a year.

A wealthy Southampton financier started to patronise the restaurant and, before long, he was pestering us to sell. He wasn't into catering, but for him it was fresh fields to conquer. He kept at us for several months until finally, rather like Robin Evans over the Pantry, he came up with an offer we couldn't refuse, so bang went another 'Spit and Sawdust' within the space of eighteen months.

For a brief moment we were up in the clouds, but soon we came down to earth with a bump. We were renting a delightful cottage in the village of East Knoyle, just outside Shaftesbury. It soon dawned on us that, apart from the money angle, we weren't of retiring age yet, we had to do something, but what? Fate then intervened in the person of an old customer and friend of ours called Grahame Barrett, an Auctioneer and Estate Agent in Haverfordwest. He telephoned so say that the Tenancy of the Swan Inn, Little Haven, was coming vacant. The Swan was one of our favourite pubs, we used to call there in the old days whenever we had some time off, but it was a Tied House, belonging to an old-fashioned Firm of Wine and Spirit Merchants in the old county town of Narberth. We did business with them when we had the Trewern Arms. The firm was known as James Williams (Narberth) Limited, the Managing Director being John Lee-Davies whom we had dealt with for years. Grahame said he was sure that John Lee-Davies would jump at the idea of giving us the Tenancy, because the Swan was spoiling for someone to develop the catering side.

A Tenancy wasn't exactly our cup of tea, because we had always been in the Free Trade, which meant we could buy anything we wanted from any wholesaler of our choice. There was no denying that this looked a good bet, and it meant that we could hang on to our capital. We signed the Tenancy Agreement and moved into the Swan on 1 May 1974.

GHNE in the wine cellar of the Pantry Restaurant, Newport, Pembrokeshire (circa 1970)

GHNE first from the left, together with the Joint Winner at the final of the Hotelympia 'Beer and Sandwich' serving competition, held at the Horseshoe, Tottenham Court Road (circa 1966)

THE FOUR HOSTELRIES RUN BY THE AUTHOR AND HIS WIFE
BETWEEN 1956 AND 1983

RAF officers take honours in Trade diploma exam

SUMMER COURSES HELD IN SEVEN CENTRES

ONE hundred and sixteen candidates passed the Trade diploma examination held last July. Nine gained honours and 34 credit passes.

The examination followed courses in London, Birmingham, Oxford, Manchester, Blackburn, Liverpool and Llandudno.

Top honours were secured by Flight-Lieut. T.H. Gates, with 261 marks out of a possible 300. Runner-up was Wing-Commander G. H. Nelson-Edwards with 258.

Of those who gained honours, five attended the course and took the examination in London. Manchester and Liverpool each provided two honours winners.

"A small course but a satisfying one." commented a National Trade Development Association official yesterday.

"Perhaps the most interesting thing about this summer examination—always the smallest from the entry point of view of the three held during the year—was the high percentage of Trade candidates. About 75 pc of those taking part were from the Trade, more than usual for the summer session."

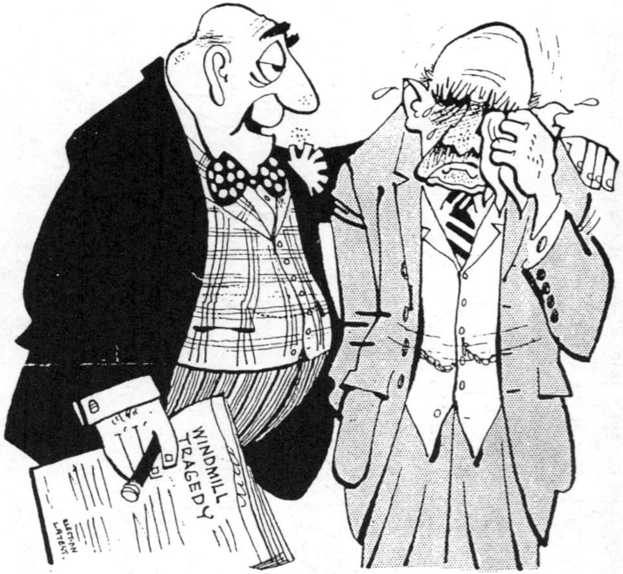

'CHEER UP, CHATTERLEY, THEY MIGHT HAVE A CLOSING DOWN SALE!'

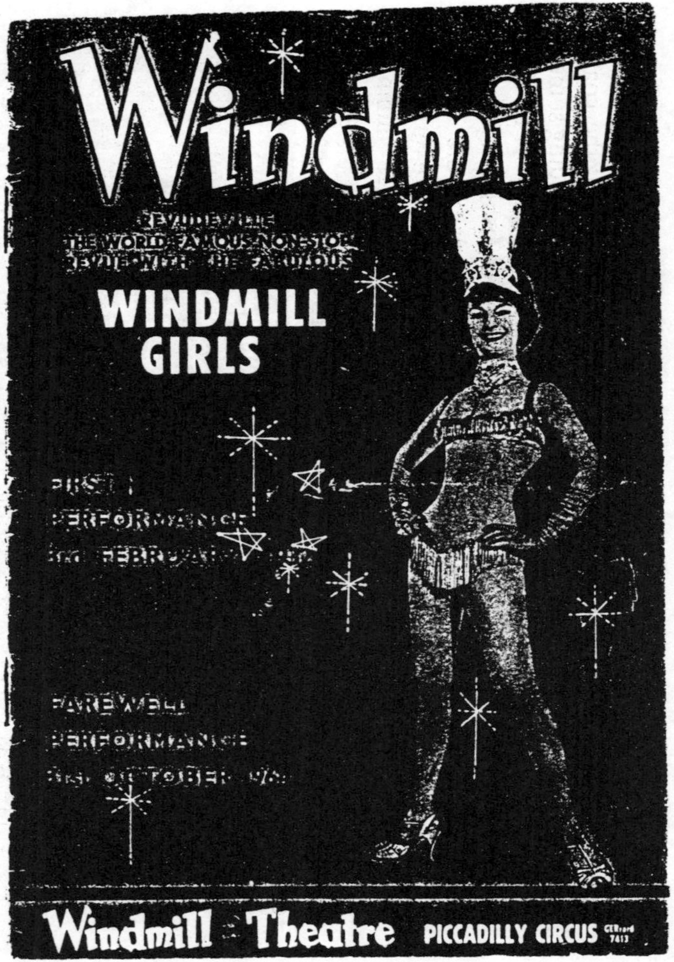

CHAPTER EIGHTEEN

ONE FOR THE ROAD

The Swan Inn was our last and final 'Spit and Sawdust'. The Swan had been a pub since the early nineteenth century, at the height of the coal boom. There were many open-cast mines in Pembrokeshire, yielding some of the best quality anthracite to be found in Wales. Road transport as we know it today was non-existent, so many of the small fishing villages dotted round the West Wales coast, such as St Dogmaels on the Tivy, Newport on the Nevern, Portgain and Solva near St Davids, were thriving little communities, involved with shipping coal and other mining materials, including chippings for road and track laying, eastwards to England. Little Haven was just one of these small coastal roadsteads, enjoying a modicum of prosperity, and the Swan was well known to the mariner as a friendly inviting hostelry.

It lay back on a ledge of rock some fifty yards from the beach, along a cliff path bounded on the sea side by a stone wall, which extended past the front door and continued on up to the 'Point', a high peninsular jutting out into the ocean where, standing on the rocky headland, one had the illusion of being on the bridge of some vessel, plunging its bows through the scudding rollers, which pounded the rugged crags below.

There was only one way to the pub, a short walk up the cliff path after finding somewhere to leave the car, perhaps back in the village where there is a car park and boat yard

The Swan is something after the style of the famous 'Spaniards' pub in Kinsale, maybe five times as many customers sitting out on the wall as could be accommodated inside. It is reputed to have the longest bar in West Wales, which is the Sea Wall, of course, reaching for more than five hundred yards from the slipway up to the 'Point'. Winter and summer, weather permitting, scores of people could be seen sitting on the wall, with their pints of beer and 'Trawlermens' mugs filled with steaming home-made soup, which I used to make daily by the gallon. In summer time they had a fine view of the sea and the people fishing, sailing and swimming. It was the perfect spot for parents to sit and enjoy a drink, while keeping an eye on the kids playing on the sands below. At the height of the season, we could expect to lose more than two dozen glasses a day, not so much due to breakage as escape into the unknown. We never ceased to wonder how so many glasses went missing without trace, the cost of replacements rising annually, in line with inflation, perhaps one might say 'index clinked', if I may be forgiven the metaphor.

The sheer rock face behind the pub precluded any extension

SPIT AND SAWDUST

rearwards, but we created an attractive patio on some waste ground on the cliff beyond, which, including chairs, tables and colourful umbrellas, could seat about forty people. Access was via stone steps with a wrought-iron balustrade. The view from there across the Bay was magic.

The interior of the pub badly need refurbishing, but without destroying the character. The first priorities were new loos and enlarged storage space. The 'Gents' was known as the grottiest in the county, the 'Ladies Loo' was little better, both had to be demolished. There was just enough room to build an extension at the 'down-stream' end, to house a smart new beer cellar, stores and modern cloak rooms, all of which our Landlord, John Lee-Davies, agreed to pay for. He was not prepared to install a new bar at his expense, so we designed and reconstructed one ourselves, from antique timbers and panelling out of an abandoned country mansion. This was a splendid opportunity to install two sets of old manual beer pumps with glorious porcelain, handles which I had retrieved from the Noel Arms, Chipping Campden, when my mother, at the instigation of Flowers Brewery, changed to a new 'top pressure' system. I had fortunately managed to hang on to them after all these years.

The new 'old bar' was the focus of attention, especially for Real Ale enthusiasts, dispensing Worthington Best Bitter and Bass Pale Ale on draught. In the middle of the room was the most expensive ash tray in the world. It was a three foot sawn-off section of the base of a ship's mast, allegedly from HMS 'Neptune', which had fought at Trafalgar. After the battle, the 'Neptune' towed the battered 'Victory', with Lord Nelson's body on board, into Gibraltar under the shadow of the great rock, on 28 October, 1805, the first lap of the immortal Admiral's last voyage to his final resting place in St Paul's. I paid £100 for it. It stood on a plinth, the top having been hollowed out to accommodate a large marble mortar, edged round with a five inch wooden rim on which people could rest pint pots. They gathered round it, and ashed into the sand-filled mortar as if at an Indian pow-wow.

Our dining-room was diminutive, seating fourteen in reasonable comfort, or sixteen inconsiderable discomfort. We were back in 'square one', just like the original Trewern Arms dining room, where we sat only sixteen. There was no call for a chef, I did all the cooking myself. As usual Pan was the front-of-the-house boss in charge of decor, reservations, etc. We gave silver service, table accoutrements being antique silverware, and linen napery. We specialised in private dinner parties which were much in demand, our customers coming mostly from the senior staff and Directors of the various Oil Refineries at Milford Haven such as Esso,

ONE FOR THE ROAD

BP, Amoco and Gulf, plus a few sub-contractors. We had an abundance of fresh fish and shell-fish right there on our doorstep, including oysters delivered daily from a bed in the Haven, which at long last had become productive. One again we found ourselves in the unsolicited Food Guides, we even had a write-up in the American Gourmet Magazine.

Early one summer evening, four decidedly sophisticated young men turned up at the Bar, who so intrigued Pan with the strangely familiar slapstick and banter, that she called me from the kitchen, where I was sweating over the proverbial stove, to take a break and talk to them. I soon realised that they where RAF types. The Royal Naval Air Station at Brawdy was being rehabilitated for RAF use, so it came as no surprise when they said they were 'Fighter Boys' flying Hunters, and had just moved from RAF Chivenor, North Devon, to form the new Tactical Weapons Unit at RAF Brawdy. I felt like a bloody idiot, standing there wearing my chef's apron with a red and white spotted scarf round my neck, as I admitted to once having been an RAF pilot myself. I could see the sideways signals they threw at each other that they could scarcely believe their ears.

"Well then indeed!" one of them exploded "And what did you fly, old boy, Sauce Boats?" They all joined in hearty guffaws.

"As a matter of fact", I replied, not to be put out, "Like you, I was once a Fighter Pilot."

"That's turn up for the books if ever there was one! What Squadron were you in?" Asked one of them, whose name I gathered by now was Mike Shaw.

"I was in 79 Squadron during the Battle of Britain", I replied.

"Well, stap me sideways," cried Mike "You'll never believe this but we are 79 Squadron, how about that? Fantastic! This calls for a celebration! George, meet me old helpmates, Al Mathie, Bob Partridge, Tony Chaplin and Puddy Catt."

With that I stripped off my apron, and we all got down to some serious drinking combined with reminising. This remarkable turn of events put me right back into the RAF galaxy, so that the Swan became a regular meeting place for Fighter Pilots.

The Tactical Weapons Unit's task was to run courses on current tactical Fighter Operations, for experienced pilots, prior to onward postings to frontline Squadrons. From time to time, some of those taking the Course were senior Officers selected to be future Squadron Commanders. 79, and 234, the other resident Squadron at Brawdy, ran the Weapons Training programmes, firstly with Hunters and latterly with

SPIT AND SAWDUST

Hawks. The ageing Meteor continued in use for instrument ratings, and target towing. Both Squadrons retained their Number Plates but were excluded from the peacetime 'Order of Battle.' I thus established a double connection. I did my first operational tour during the war with 79 Squadron, and 234 was one of my Squadrons in the Oldenburg Wing, during the fifties.

Before long I was elected an Honorary Member of 79. To mark the occasion, Pan and I were asked to a Dinner given by the Squadron in our honour. When it came to the speeches, the CO, Squadron Leader George Lee, stood up holding a small silver tankard which had been filled with beer, and he asked me to step forward to drink from it. Not realising what it was all about, I took the tankard and was about to drink, when I spotted an inscription on the side which read: 'Presented to 79 (F) Squadron by Flying Officer G H (Neddy) Nelson-Edwards, July 1941'.

I must admit I was amazed. For one thing I had completely forgotten I had presented a tankard to 79 almost forty years ago. For another thing I would never have thought it possible that I had enough money at the time to buy one! Yet there it was before my very eyes. It gave me quite a kick to know that it had survived the years. Soon after this I received a letter from the PMC, informing me that I had been elected to Honorary Membership of the Brawdy Officers Mess. I made a point of attending Mess functions whenever my work permitted.

A particularly memorable occasion was when I went to a Luncheon Party given for Neville Duke, to mark the twenty-fifth Anniversary of the Hunter as a front-line operational fighter aircraft. (1954--1979).

For the next few years both ,79 and 234 used to hold 'end of Course' parties at the Swan. It was always a help-yourself Buffet, with an eighteen gallon kilderkin of Worthington Best Bitter, tapped and spiled, ready for the boys to help themselves.

Flight Lieutenant Al Mathie was one of the leading lights of 79. He owned an Auster which he kept on the Station, and being a Real Ale fanatic, he flew it on two occasions to collect samples of his favourite draught beers. The first was to Norfolk to bring back five gallons of Theakston's Old Peculiar, the second to Culdrose, to fetch five gallons of home-brew called 'Spingo', from the Blue Anchor at Helston. Al laid on special beer tasting sessions at the Swan, and his wife Dot used to come with him, bringing their beautiful Irish Wolfhound bitch called Kanga. Kanga stood about three feet high. At one of the parties she scoffed most of the cold buffet, while the boys were drinking in the Lounge Bar. After that she was under strict surveillance at all times.

ONE FOR THE ROAD

Every year there was an Open Day and Air Show at Brawdy, which attracted huge crowds from all over West Wales. Throughout our nine years at the Swan, I don't think we were able to attend more than twice, chiefly because I was always tied up in the kitchen, preparing for a full Dining Room in the evening. The Battle of Britain Flight was a regular feature at the Show, sometimes the pilots staying overnight at Brawdy, when they would drop into the Swan for a few beers with some of the Brawdy boys, which gave me the chance to get to know them.

The 1982 Air Show, which was to be our last before our retirement, found me as usual busy with preparation work in the kitchen. Sometime that afternoon Pan answered a phone call, which turned out to be the Senior Air Traffic Controller yelling her to grab me from the kitchen, and rush me out onto the Wall, from where I would spot something very unique and exciting approaching from seaward. I just made it as I sighted the Battle of Britain Flight in a shallow dive, flying straight past at no more than three hundred feet, the Lancaster in the lead, with the Spitfire and Hurricane in close formation either side. We could almost see the pilots as they started gently to ease up over the shoreline. I am not ashamed to confess I was overcome with pride and nostalgia, a thrill running down my spine, my eyes filling with tears. It was a totally unexpected gesture to me personally, an honour all the more poignant because there are so many Battle of Britain Pilots far more deserving of this compliment than I, who was not even classed as an 'Ace'. So be it.

For quite some time the 79 Squadron boys, unbeknown to me, had been trying, with Pan's co-operation, to fix a date for me to attend a special Party in the Squadron Crew-room. Everyone knew by now that we were retiring at the end of the summer. As usual we were flat-out every lunch-time and evening, which meant there was hardly a moment left when I could snatch time off from cooking.

After several false starts, Pan phoned the Squadron one morning to say I was free to come up at lunchtime for a couple of hours. Not knowing what it was all about, I drove up to the airfield towards the Squadron HQ. I saw their Hawks parked on the tarmac in a neat line in front of the Crew-room, some of the pilots standing at the entrance looking suspiciously like a Reception Committee. I vaguely wondered what it all meant, I certainly didn't think it was anything to do with me. I was ushered inside where I saw a buffet laid out at one end, at the other end the Squadron Bar was covered with numerous tankards along the top, a Kilderkin of Worthington lying ready and waiting. Then each pilot moved forward to take his tankard from off the Bar, to fill it from the

SPIT AND SAWDUST

barrel. As I approached at the end of the queue the CO thrust a beautiful new silver pint tankard into my hand, simultaneously delivering a short speech. I saw an inscription on it which I immediately realised was exactly the reverse of the inscription on the tankard I had presented to 79, just over forty years ago, the only exception being the year 1982 in place of 1941.

I was overwhelmed, and much moved by this honour the boys had paid to me. I felt proud, yet deeply humbled, that an 'oldie' like myself could still make an impact on the new generation of Fighter Pilots.

The memory of those two tributes, first the compliment paid to me by the Battle of Britain Flight, second the 79 Squadron presentation, will remain with me until my last breath.

POSTSCRIPT

It is my humble hope that my story may be representative of that generic group of pilots who made up the major part of Fighter Command's front line Fighter Force in those solemn sunlit days of the 1940 high summer.

They came from many walks of life, from all corners of the Globe. They were modest men in the main, with no express desires or aspirations, except for stemming the tide of the Luftwaffe's onslaught, with an unquestioning readiness to die. Some were braver than others perhaps, and some had more luck and skill than others in notching up victories.

As to my victories, I failed to reach the score of five enemy aircraft destroyed to be rated an 'Ace', for which I make no apology.

In truth, I never knew what my official score was during the Battle of Britain period. The same applied later, when I commanded 93 Squadron (Spitfire 5C's) on Operation 'Torch', in Tunisia in 1942-43.

After extensive enquiries, I have discovered that numerous claims I recorded in my Log Book may never have been properly processed. For example, on 27 September, 1940, I shot down an HE 111 which I had followed down till it crashed into the sea. A few seconds before that, a Hurricane suddenly appeared and made a pass at it. Two crew had already baled out, the remainder probably wounded or dead, so there was no doubt that this was my Heinkel, yet the official report gives the credit to two other pilots as well as myself, which I never knew until recently. Clearly there must have been a mix-up, because I was also credited with a third share in another Heinkel 'probably destroyed', thus ending up with a 'third share' twice!

Likewise on the 29th September, I was the first to attack an HE 111 out of a formation of about nine enemy aircraft, near the Irish Coast just off Cork. I couldn't stake a claim because I was myself shot down, and went missing for a couple of days. Although I hit the Jerry from close range, setting both engines on fire, causing it to jettison its bomb load and one of the crew to bale out, I was credited with nothing, as I found out later on returning to the Squadron. The Combat Reports had already been submitted. It seems I was given a third share in one Heinkel 'probably destroyed', for which I hadn't written a report. At the time I truthfully believed that I had destroyed two He 111's in those two days.

Two years later, in North Africa I got one Ju88 'destroyed' and one 'probably destroyed'. I also got several Me109's 'damaged', which was never recorded, more than likely the Records were lost in the confusion,

SPIT AND SAWDUST

during the first months of the Campaign. My total confirmed 'kills' could have been at least five, and six, if I had dishonestly claimed the Me110 over the North Sea on 15 August. However, it wasn't to be that way, it was just the luck of the draw. Despite it all, to my amazement and gratification I was informed that I had been awarded the DFC. It had been submitted to King George on 19 February, 1943 and gazetted on the 26th.

Finally, on this 50th Anniversary of the Battle of Britain, it seems fitting to take a backward glance at the colourful and manifold experiences I lived through in those far off days.

My thoughts turn to those Sunday afternoons in our Study in Churchill's House, when the three of us, John Keitley, Dick Hillary and myself, would pore over the pictures of the Spitfire, Hurricane and Messeschmitt, John and I spellbound by their sinister portentous beauty, whilst Dick remained his usual phlegmatic cynical self. The idea of Dick ever flying one of these incredible machines, which he held in such contempt, seemed to us quite absurd. Yet how differently things turned out.

In another Study, a few doors further down the passage, were three boys destined to fly Fighters during the Battle, Christopher Andreae and Paul Davies-Cooke, both of whom gave their lives before October 1940, and Nigel Farmer who, like myself, survived.

Dick's story and tragic end are known world wide through his own writings, and need no further embellishment from me.

John, perhaps the keenest 'Flyer' of us all, fell in a rearguard action on the withdrawal to Dunkerque. Sadly he never lived to know the 'feel' of a Spitfire.

As for myself, I am reminded that it is almost 50 years to the day, 29th September, oddly enough the birthday of my Ancestor, Admiral Lord Nelson, when I was faced with certain death by drowning. Had some unseen hand, Nelson's maybe, guided the SS Dartford, the lone Merchantman, to the exact spot from where the crew saw and heard my stricken Hurricane blow up? I had no way of knowing I had been spotted, while I drifted slowly downward towards the grim grey wastes of the Irish Sea, momentarily gripped by a blind desire to get it all over with fast.

Perhaps Man, if he had the answer, would never have known the glory and the pain of combat and death, an abiding stranger to both Victory and Defeat.

BIBLIOGRAPHY

ACES HIGH Christopher Shores & Clive Williams - Neville Spearman.

THE BATTLE OF BRITAIN - THEN AND NOW Edited by Winston G Ramsey - Battle of Britain Prints International Ltd.

THE HURRICANE STOREY Paul Gallico - Michael Joseph.

THE LAST ENEMY Richard Hillary - Macmillan & Co Ltd.

THE NARROW MARGIN Derek Wood and Derek Dempster - Hutchinson & Co Ltd.

RICHARD HILLARY Lovat Dickson - Macmillan & Co Ltd.

SIGH FOR A MERLIN Alex Henshaw - John Murray (Publishers) Ltd.

THE PROSTITUTES' PADRE Tom Cullen - The Bodley Head Ltd.

BATTLE OF THE BULGE Charles B MacDonald - Guild Publishing.

THE RISE & FALL OF THE THIRD REICH William L Shirer - Book Club Associates.

THE LOST COMMAND Alastair Revie - Purnell Book Services Ltd.

Licensed Trade Diploma

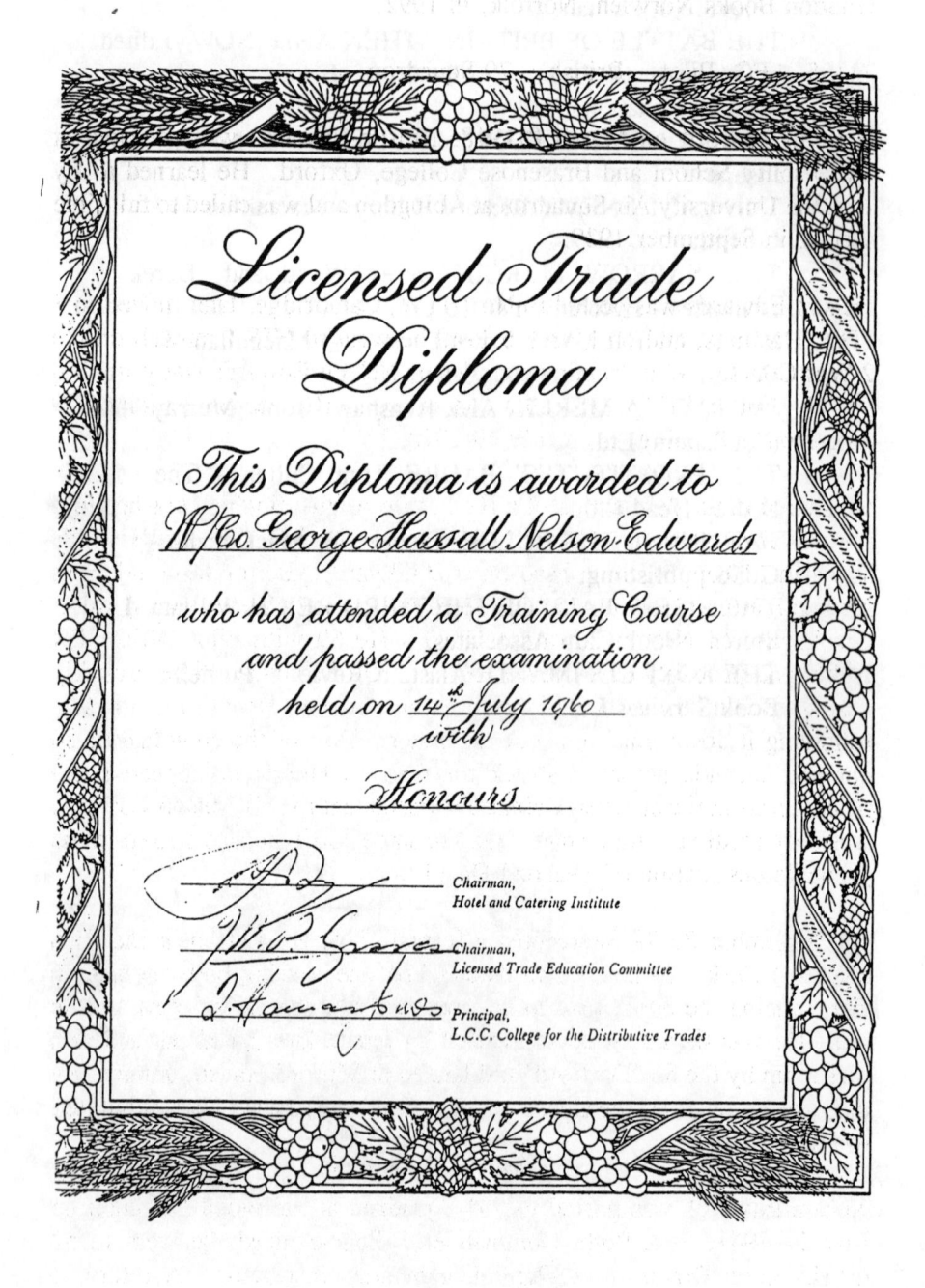

This Diploma is awarded to

W/Co. George Hassall Nelson-Edwards

who has attended a Training Course and passed the examination held on 14th July 1960 with

Honours

Chairman,
Hotel and Catering Institute

Chairman,
Licensed Trade Education Committee

Principal,
L.C.C. College for the Distributive Trades

Copy of entry in the SUPPLEMENTARY VOLUME of the 'MEN OF THE BATTLE OF BRITAIN' BY KENNETH G Wynn. Published by Gliddon Books Norwich, Norfolk, in 1992.

74355   FO Pilot   British   79 Squadron

Born in Stafford on March 8 1918, Nelson-Edwards was educated at Shrewsbury School and Brasenose College, Oxford. He learned to fly with the University Air Squadron at Abingdon and was called to full-time service in September 1939.

Nelson-Edwards was posted to No 1 ITW, Cambridge, later moved to 3 ITW, Hastings, and on March 6 1940 he went to FTS Cranwell on No 2 War Course. With training completed, Nelson-Edwards was posted to 6 OTU, Sutton Bridge, and after converting to Hurricanes, he joined 79 Squadron at Acklington on July 20 1940.

He shared in the destruction of a He 111 on August 9 which crashed into the sea off Sunderland. On the 15th over the North Sea Nelson-Edwards saw a Bf 110 approaching head-on at 2000 yards. Before he could press his gun button it blew up and was apparently never claimed by any pilot. On August 28 Nelson-Edwards shared a He 59 with Pilot Officer BR Noble and probably destroyed a He 111. On September 6 he probably destroyed a Ju 88, on the 27th he shot down another He 111 into the sea, following it down until it struck the water. Two of the crew had baled out and seconds before it struck the water a Hurricane appeared and made a pass at the stricken Heinkel. Consequent to this Nelson-Edwards was only credited with a share. On the same sortie he also shared in the probable destruction of a second He 111.

On September 29 79 intercepted a formation of He 111s near the Irish coast off Cork. Nelson-Edwards attacked one, setting both engines on fire, causing the bomb load to be jettisoned and one of the crew to bale out. He was then shot down himself by return fire, baled out and was picked up by the SS 'Dartford' and landed at Milford Haven, unhurt. By the time he rejoined the squadron all claims had already been submitted to HQ 10 Group.

Nelson-Edwards was posted to 504 Squadron at Fairwood Common on July 27 1941, as a flight Commander. Tour-expired, he went to 52 OTU, Aston Down, as a Flight Commander Instructor. A return to operations came on June 3 1942, when Nelson-Edwards was given command of 93 Squadron, then forming at Andreas. On October 20 it went overseas, to take part in the Anglo-American invasion of North Africa, and landed at Algiers on November 13 1942. Nelson-Edwards probably destroyed a Ju 88 on the 26th and had another confirmed on December 4. He was awarded the DFC (26.2.43).

He was posted away to Combined Operations HQ on March 12 1943, as an Air Planner. On June 2 Nelson-Edwards was sent on a course at the Army Staff College, Camberley. Afterwards he did a Mustang conversion course at 41 OTU, Hawarden and on December 20 1943 took command of 231 Squadron at Redhill. The Unit was disbanded on February 2 1944.

Nelson-Edwards was promoted to Acting Wing Commander and appointed RAF Fighter Operations Liaison Officer at HQ 9th USAAF North-West Europe and remained there until the end of the war. He retired from the RAF on September 30 1960, as a Wing Commander.

PO 16.9.39   FO 26.9.41   SL 7.6.44   SL 1.9.45   WC 1.7.45

AT NEWTON WE PUBLISH New Author's books and also SELL THEM... Recent releases:

"A WALK WITH GIANTS". Bill McEwan has an unusual story to tell from his time with the Army in France, the evacuation from Dunkirk, remustering to the RAF, shot down in the Channel and captured by the Wehrmacht. His three years experiences in POW Camps. Return to UK, difficult times, hard work and move to Africa. The problems of involvement in the countries with their change to Independance. It is a highly informative and enjoyable narrative. The Foreword is by **Bill Reid VC, BSc.** ISBN 1 872308 18 X, SB. Price £15.95

"AN ELECTRICIAN GOES TO WAR" Ken Whittles gripping descriptions of action flying in Blenheims, attacking shipping from 50 feet, operational flying 1940/41. Then on to B25 Mitchells, daylight operations in support of the invasion of Europe, 1944. It reads like a living diary. Foreword by Ivor Broom KCB, DSO, DFC**, AFC. ISBN 1872308 SB, Price £14.95

"AN AIRMAN'S LOT" Leonard Bridge's account of his thirty years RAF service as an airman, groundcrew are recorded with insight and humour. Service readers will readily relate to his description of life through his training, on numerous operational stations in UK, Malta, Egypt and Germany. The author brings out clearly the cameraderie & esprit de corps in the good and bad times common to all who served. Foreword by Air Commodore Ian C Atkinson CBE. ISBN 1 872308. SB price £12.95.

"ASPECTS OF ANXIETY" by Dr T V A Harry MB, Ch.B (Manc), DPM., This is an eminently readable book covering anxiety, a normal response to stress a psychiatric and physical illness. The book encompasses an enormous breadth of material including manifestations and treatment, giving a well balanced view of the dependency problem. There are also useful chapters on self-help and the techniques of relaxation. The literary style is delightful and scholarly. A work well worthy of a small space on the bookshelves of most doctors and anyone with an interest in problems associated with anxiety. ISBN 1 872308 27 9. SB. Price £6.95.

"BLACK SWAN" by Sid Finn A history of 103 Squadron. From formation prior to WW1, peacetime, WW2, operations in the Far East to the final disbandment, a worthy record. Foreword is by Air Chief Marshal Sir Hugh Constantine, KBE, CB, DSO, LLD. ISBN 1 872308 00 7. HB. Price £14.95

"BOMBER'S MOON" Victor Minot the author, an ex Bomber Command air gunner on Wellingtons and later a pilot writes from a position of strength. The tale is based on actual experiences of the author, and by fictionalising a romantic element which becomes part of the story, illustrating the considerable effect on morale of the women they left behind. "Bomber's Moon" reflects the fact that more than two out of every three aircrew lives in Bomber Command ended in death in action. Foreword by Air Vice Marshal F Hurrell CB, OBE, FRAeS. ISBN 1872308 67 8. SB.Price £14.95

"BEGINNING OF THE END" A true moving story of the Chindits in Burma by Ex-Staff Sgt. Des Chrage of the Royal Army Medical Corps. They followed the Long Range Penetration Group the "CHINDITS" into Burma behind the Japanese lines for the purpose of dealing with casualties and their evacuation. With no lines of communication they had to rely on the RAF to fly & drop in their supplies. ISBN 1872308 72 4. SB price £12.95

"COMBAT AND COMPETITION" by David Ince, DFC,Bsc. A fascinating story of a gunnery officer turned Typhoon pilot. Operating with 193 and 257 Squadrons through the summer of 1944 to the bitter end of Hitler's dying Reich. As a trained test pilot, the author marketed advanced flight control systems. He is a dedicated glider pilot, chief instructor, active in sailplane development testing and a past member of the British team squad. Foreword is by Air Chief Marshal Sir Christopher Foxley-Norris, GCB,DSO,OBE,MA,CBIM,FRAeS. ISBN 1 872308 23 6. HB price £15.95, SB £14.95.

"DEATH OR DECORATION" Ron Waite's fascinating story of a pilot from day one of his training, through to operational missions and beyond. His six years of war with No. 76 Squadron, 1658 and 1663 HCUs makes enthralling reading. Foreword by Wg Cdr P. Dobson, DSO, DFC, AFC, (CO No 158 Squadron). A jolt to the memory for those who were there...A seat in the cockpit for those who were not! ISBN 1 872308 08 2.
HB price £14.95, SB price £13.95.

"ESCAPE FROM ASCOLI" by Ken de Souza of 148 Squadron. This book is a fore runners of **"Una Bell Passaggiata"**. Ken's vivid and fascinating tale of survival in the desert, against the odds. His escape from PG70 Italian POW camp, operating with the SAS and final get-away from Occupied Italy. Foreword by Air Chief Marshal Sir Lewis Hodges, KCB,CBE,DSO,DFC. President of the RAF Escaping Society.
ISBN 1 872308 02 3. HB. Price £12.95

"FAITH, HOPE AND MALTA GC" The author is Tony Spooner, DSO, DFC. The foreword by Air Marshal Sir Ivor Broom, KCB,CBE,DFC**,AFC, himself an ace Malta pilot. It is the gripping story of the Ground and Air Heroes of Army, Air Force and Navy defenders of the George Cross Island.
ISBN 1 872308 50 3. Price £16.95.

"FEAR NOTHING" David Watkins accurate history of 501 (F) County of Gloucester Squadron, Auxiliary Air Force. The 'part-timers' were in action from May 1940 over France followed by the Battle of Britain. Later re-equipped with Spitfires, Tempests and the Vampires. Foreword by Wg Cdr K.MacKenzie, DFC,AFC,AE.ISBN 1 872308 07 4. HB. Price £14.95

"FROM PILLAR TO POST" by Norman Harris. An interesting and well written narrative of the author's journey through life. Commencing with an RAF Admin. career in 1939, posted to East Africa. On demob from the RAF, involved in local politics, Elected Mayor of Nairobi, then Minister for Information and Broadcasting in the Kenya Government. Move to Australia, the author writes with insight & clarity. There are excellent descriptive passages. A Serviceman's journey through life, full of humour in the reporting of everyday incidents that beset the wanderer. Foreword by Air Marshal Sir Maurice Heath KBE,CB. ISBN 1 872308 65 1 SB Price £14.95.

"GREEN MARKERS AHEAD SKIPPER" by Gilbert Grey. Aged 15 at the outbreak of WWII the author had completed a tour of 34 operations serving as a Flight Engineer with 106 Squadron before his 20th birthday. Foreword by Wg Cdr M J Stevens, DFC, RAF,(Ret'd) who comments: "What a wonderful book for passing on to posterity because it describes what it was really like being a member of the aircrew in a Lancaster bomber in 1944." ISBN 1 872308 11 2, SB. Price £15.95.

All available ex-stock: Newton Books
P O Box 236, Swindon Wilts SN3 6QZ. Tel: 01793-641796.